Yard Bull

Dean O'Shea

On the Mark!

Sequim, Washington

ISBN:
0-9797738-9-X (10 digit)
978-0-9797738-9-1 (13 digit)

On the Mark!
P.O. Box 4147
Sequim, WA 98382
www.theyardbull.com

Illustration by Dean Vavak, www.vavakstudio.com

Printed by Signature Book Printing
www.sbpbooks.com

To Mom & Dad

For childhood adventures and lots of advice -

you were right, after all.

And for introducing the love of Jesus by never giving up on me -

you were right again.

Preface

In 1862, President Abraham Lincoln signed the Pacific Railway Act, opening the way for the iron horse to transport mail, cargo and people across mid west prairie and California mountains. When the hammer's final blow struck a golden spike at Promontory Summit, Utah in 1869, a continent had been linked; life in the wild, isolated west would never be the same.

But while the railroad provided opportunities for settlers, fortune seekers and businesses, it also caught the attention of robbers like Deaf Charley, Butch Cassidy, and the Sundance Kid who were soon relieving trains and passengers of their wealth. America's first private eye, Allan Pinkerton, was called in and along with his agents, proved an effective force against outlaws.

Eventually, the railroad hired its own police to guard trains, some of them as rough in character as the thieves they arrested. By the turn of the century, they were called "detectives" in the eastern United States and "special agents" in the west, but to the hobos and derelicts riding the rails, they were "yard bulls."

Ruthless gangs and felons have long since replaced yesterday's hobos, and the railroad has incorporated computers into its system and cabooses out of it. But the age-old struggle between law-breaker and law-enforcer has never changed.

Contents

Chapter 1

"Adversity introduces a man to himself."

Anonymous

Sitting behind the steering wheel of my Mustang sports car, I stared hard into the night and then glanced impatiently at my watch. The green illuminated numbers showed 1:53 a.m., exactly three minutes since the last time I'd checked.

A stiff March wind had steadily increased to where I could now feel its force against my car, like invisible hands pushing to get inside. I nervously touched the grip of the .357 Smith & Wesson belted at my side and felt a little safer -- but only a little.

Three long, dreary hours passed, and my 5'8" frame began to feel cramped from sitting too long in the same position. The fierce wind had not let up, bending branches and limbs in a frenzied dance as if by a puppeteer gone mad. I felt like the haplessly doomed character in a low budget horror movie.

"What a way to make a living," I grumbled, "sitting in the middle of spooky nowhere, waiting for someone to do something illegal."

At 25, I'd been hired as a state-commissioned railroad police officer to find and arrest people committing crimes against the railroad, its property or personnel. The irony of it all was that I'd often been on the wrong side of the law as a teenager, with regular visits to our small, hometown jail. It didn't help that the arresting officer, Hiram Crook, happened to be an acquaintance of my distraught, pray-without-ceasing parents. So when the railroad's Divisional Special Agent offered me a job, I accepted, figuring it had to do with my military record or dad being one of their conductors. But I never bothered to ask. Besides, I liked the railroad's style – no formal training, just turning me loose with a gun and handcuffs to make arrests my way: a good fit for the heroic loner in me.

My first day on the job, though, did hold a few surprises. Unlike public police departments, we had to buy our own equipment. My patrol car was my 289 bright yellow Mustang convertible-- not exactly what I'd call 'low profile' for catching criminals unaware. For communication, we were to check in with a railroad operator every two hours from a payphone or railroad office phone; radios were deemed an "unnecessary expense." Our official job title was "Special Agent," but to the transients who lived illegally among the tracks we were "Yard Bulls."

I stretched my arms and drained the last of my cold coffee. Tonight's watch had started to worry me. I was supposed to catch whoever had been stealing wood from a remote lumberyard on the outskirts of Lincoln, Nebraska. I'd set up surveillance and rehearsed in my mind how the scene would play out -- like a hero in the movies I loved to watch, I'd pull out my gun, the bad guys would fold into a fearful, compliant state and I'd call it a night. Now if someone would just show up!

My head and shoulders slumped back against the seat as I thought about my life over the last few years. Though my blonde hair and round face gave me a boyish appearance, my blue eyes held a shadow that aged me. Four years had passed since my return from Vietnam as a grunt in the 4th Infantry Air Mobile Division. I'd seen and done things I wanted to forget but my brain kept dragging me back to those hot and humid days in the jungle, when I feared I'd never see my family again...

My platoon (typically 30 men) had spent a long day advancing single file through swamps and tangled vines, each of us hoping our point man's next step wouldn't be the one that triggered an explosion or trap. The enemy had developed ingenious ways to maim us, knowing we moved slower with wounded soldiers than dead ones.

From the green canopy above us, primitive shrieks and howls echoed back and forth, while on the ground, lines of fierce biting ants intersected our trails. Black leeches waited for us in every stream, able to wriggle beneath fatigues and start sucking our blood within seconds. We'd been sent to a land completely alien to our American upbringing, to kill a people we didn't know, and only our youth and training made us believe we could survive.

After several hours, the jungle's trees became sparser, allowing the late afternoon sun to beat down on us from a cloudless sky. The Lieutenant gave the order to set up camp. Sighs of relief accompanied heavy rucksacks falling to the ground and the smell of cigarettes lighting up. Except for Wally and I. Told to set up an observation post, we jogged in boots heavy with the day's mud to the edge of a clearing. This open area would create an ideal 'field of fire,' a term referring to a lack of cover for the enemy to approach us unawares. While the others built their hooches -- simple tents made by draping ponchos over branches -- Wally and I would wait until the end of the shift to build ours. Setting up security always took priority.

We concealed ourselves behind a clump of tall grass about 75 yards from the rest of our unit, passing the time speculating what life would be like when we got back home.

"Can't believe it's only been three weeks since we landed at Chu Lai. When I get back to the world, I'll never complain again."

Wally, our radio operator, set the boxy equipment on the ground beside his leg.

"I got me a dream car waitin' fer me --'57 Chevy, new wheels. What d'ya say you an' me go cruisin' an' pick up some *fine* ladies."

"Sounds good! And eat all the hamburgers and fries we..." Movement from the corner of my eye sent a chill through my body. I nudged Wally and whispered, "Someone's over there."

We strained our eyes at a point directly in front of us, not daring to breathe. Giant leaves sprang to the side as several Vietnamese stepped out of the jungle, wearing loose black pants and shirts, each carrying a rifle. The determination on their young faces shocked me; they looked just like us. But because of the war and our training, they were not like us -- they were an enemy named "Charlie."

I'd never shot a person before and everything I'd learned from my parents and church told me killing a human being was wrong. But Charlie wasn't supposed to be human. My mouth went dry. I sighted my M-16 rifle on the living targets moving toward our unsuspecting soldiers, my heart pounding in my ears. Sweat trickled down my neck as I applied pressure to the trigger. "Oh God, please let me do the right thing."

My rifle boomed and the instrument of death came alive in my hands. The soldier I'd aimed at screamed before crumpling to the ground. The rest of his company melted back into the foliage.

I heard Wally's frantic voice on the radio, "We got VC, we got VC! We're at observation post east of you – we need help!"

We sighted our rifles where we'd last seen the enemy soldiers and fired shot after shot until we'd emptied our ammo clips. Loading another clip, I realized I only knew Wally as a guy from Philly and one of the few colored people I'd ever met. But at this moment, when our lives depended on each other, he felt closer than a brother.

The Vietnamese were now returning fire with a steady stream of bullets flying over and around us. Each volley had two sounds: the initial "crack!" when the trigger was pulled, followed by a sharp "snap!" as each bullet passed close by our heads. I suddenly felt vulnerable hiding in the weeds.

"Can you tell how many there are?" I shouted above the noise.

"I'd say there's enough!" Wally shouted back.

After what seemed an eternity, the rest of our platoon joined us and as one unit, we shot at the figures now sprinting across the clearing. I noticed one crawling low through the grass. I set my sights, took aim and fired. He stopped, looked around and began to crawl faster. Again I locked him in my sights and pulled the trigger once, twice, three times. The man fell onto his stomach, twitched a few times and then ceased to move.

With adrenaline pumping through my veins, I looked for another Charlie but those who could still run had made it across the field. The shots ended as abruptly as they'd started.

"Hey Wally, you alright?" My voice sounded raspy.

"Yeah, but ya' think they gone for good?"

"I don't know," I answered, "but I'm sure we're gonna find out."

The Lieutenant barked orders to advance across the clearing. We spread out, putting distance between each soldier to create a fan-like formation across the field. One step at a time, in a hyper-vigilant state, my heightened senses seemed to register everything. Despite my ringing ears, I could hear the softest breeze blowing through the grass as each step brought me closer to the enemy's last position. I fervently hoped they'd continued fleeing because our situation had been reversed: we now stood without cover in a field of fire.

A low moan arose from somewhere close. Our entire platoon crouched in the grass as one; all eyes fixed on where the sound originated. We held our positions and our breaths, but nothing moved. The Lieutenant motioned with his hand; we straightened up and resumed our advance.

Suddenly, anxiety gripped my heart like an icy hand, squeezing tightly until it felt like it would burst from my chest. I could actually feel someone looking down his sights at me. With each step, I braced for a bullet to rip through me but the silence remained unbroken.

We continued until we reached rows of earthen berms where we'd last seen enemy fire and split up to do a search. Edging alongside one of the mounds, I saw the back of a VC soldier and dropped to my stomach, leveling my rifle in his direction. But he showed no awareness of my presence.

I crawled closer and punched the side of his leg - no reaction. I slowly stood up behind him, expecting him to turn at any moment. When he didn't, I moved to his side keeping my rifle aimed at his head, and peered closely at his face. His eyes were open in a fixed, glassy stare. Upon his left shoulder, in firing position, an RPG rocket launcher pointed directly where I'd been walking across the field. With his hand covering the trigger housing and finger poised on the trigger, he'd taken his last breath with me in his sights. In less than a second, he would have completed his mission by ending mine.

Wally came up next to me and nodded toward the corpse. "Dang, that was close."

"Must've got lucky," I muttered, still hyped from the battle and not wanting to think about how--or even if--luck had played a role in my being alive. I needed to focus on this ultimate game of survival.

The Lieutenant called out, "Everything's clear. Let's do a body count."

I returned to the place in the field where I'd shot the crawling soldier, marked by a patch of matted grass. He'd died face down, hands tightly fisted against each side of his head. Fighting a queasy feeling in my gut, I reached into his back pocket and pulled out a photograph. There, smiling at me, was a nice looking Vietnamese man with his arm around a pretty, dark haired girl. My stomach lurched as I realized the smiling girl would never feel his arms around her again.

Using my foot, I flipped the body over onto its back and cringed at the gaping hole above his belt. But it was his face that would haunt me. The eyes were wide open with a permanent expression of pain and terror etched into his features. I stood there, frozen, staring into those vacant eyes....

My mind jolted back to the present. A strange sensation welled up from my feet, paralyzing my entire body. My breathing became shallow as I sensed someone close. I turned my head; a pair of yellow eyes stared out of the darkness just inches from my window. I stared back, trying in vain to swallow the lump in my throat. Forcing my limbs to move, I sprang from the car, the interior light exposing the monster - an Irish Setter with a panting tongue hanging out of a wide, grinning mouth, its feathered tail wagging gracefully side to side. He sized me up for a moment, then turned and ran, leaving me clutching my chest. I'd have no trouble staying awake now.

Shakily, I climbed back into the car, slumped down in the seat, then sat abruptly forward against the steering wheel. Right in front of me were two -- no, three people inside the area I was supposed to be watching. They were throwing lumber over the fence to an accomplice. Since I didn't have a radio or railroad phone nearby, this was my chance to prove myself. Fortunately for me, the gusting wind and rumbles of thunder had covered the sound of my door opening and closing.

I stepped outside again, holding my flashlight in one hand, my gun in the other. Using brush and piles of debris for concealment, I advanced on the unsuspecting thieves. But when I was close enough to hear them, I realized these weren't teens getting into mischief on a boring night. They were rough talking adult men. I'd have to use my most intimidating voice when shouting the phrase I'd practiced since being hired.

Shielded behind a wheelbarrow tipped forward, I lowered my chin and yelled,

"Police! Stop where you are and put your hands up!"

The effect on the outlaws was like a film put on fast-forward. Without a sound, the three men inside the fence cleared the top in one fluid motion, picked up the stolen lumber and simply disappeared. Just like that, they were gone; leaving me still poised with gun and flashlight. And right on cue, the clouds opened up and the rain poured down in wind-driven sheets.

I spent the rest of my shift driving through the dark railroad yard in wet clothes, disgusted with my failed attempt to arrest the thieves. What had gone wrong? What should I have done differently? Clearly, Hollywood villains were far more predictable.

Half an hour after my shift ended and the sun rose, I parked in front of a small, two-bedroom house on Kingsley Street in Air Park, a suburb west of Lincoln. I swung open the wooden gate and crossed the yard, knowing everything in my home would be exactly as I'd left it the previous evening.

When my feet scraped the porch steps, the scurrying of dog paws could be heard on the other side of the door. I turned the key and out bounded my roommate of three years, a black Cockapoo with the cutest overbite. He jumped up and down with sheer delight at my return.

"Hey, Snoopy, did ya' miss me?"

He trotted behind me to the closet and watched me remove my gun and handcuffs. A quick change of shoes and I opened the back door. Snoopy shot across a common grassy area behind the houses, nose to the ground for any new smells since yesterday's stroll.

Once we'd walked from one end to the other, we played fetch with his favorite ball and then lined up at the backyard's boundary. I'd count "1-2-3-Go!" and we'd race back to the house, Snoop keeping just a few feet ahead of me. He always crossed the finish line first. After making a big fuss over him, we ate breakfast together.

My duties now officially over, I could finally relax. For me, that meant kicking off my shoes and drinking beer in a creaky recliner, one of two pieces of furniture in the living room, thanks to the local St. Vincent's.

The cold liquid felt good going down my throat. I took a long drink, then another, the tension melting away as I escaped memories of explosions, helicopters, and screams. The screams were the worst. I continued drinking until the people I watched die--some quickly, some slowly--blurred into a collage of disembodied faces and voices. Once my brain found its sanctuary, I fell into a fitful sleep...

The dream begins softly with an old woman shuffling across a dirt floor. She's tiny and frail, wearing black baggy pants and a shirt that hangs loosely on her thin frame. Tears stream from her slanted dark eyes, following weathered lines furrowed into her cheeks. I'm standing in the doorway of her hut as she walks toward me, holding a small piece of paper. Her eyes are unblinking as her lips move in a silent chant. She extends her arm and I take the piece of paper. Instantly, horror grips me as I recognize the photograph of the young man I killed. When I throw the picture back at the woman, she disappears and the doorway closes behind me. The walls change into four enormous photographs moving steadily toward me, closing me in between them. I push and pound against them but where my fist connects, blood streams out. I open my mouth to scream for help but there's no sound. I've become as mute as the boy in the photograph.

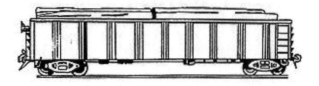

Gondola

Chapter 2

My fellow Special Agents and I shared an office in the Lincoln Station on 7th, between 'P' and 'Q' Streets. Behind the stately three-story, red brick building ran several lines of tracks used by freight and passenger trains. Built in 1910, the station was now part of Haymarket Square in the capital's historic downtown, where Victorian warehouses had been renovated into trendy gift shops, restaurants, and art galleries.

Frequented by locals and visitors, the Haymarket really came alive between September and June. Thousands of fresh-faced students from the nearby University of Nebraska thronged its taverns and café's, celebrating Cornhusker football, new friends, and life without parents.

Driving to work one April afternoon, I realized nature had awakened from its winter sleep with a shout of color and song: crimson furls of new leaves sprouted from every branch, fluttering songbirds chirped anxiously for mates, and rainbows of crocus blooms peeked out from window boxes. Even the youth had emerged wearing trendy clothes and carefree postures.

Parking my Mustang in front of the Lincoln Station, I slid across the black leather seat and locked the door. Like I did most days, I paused to admire my car's sleek lines, its yellow paint glowing from the wax I'd carefully buffed into every inch of its surface; even the silver mags shone spotless and bright. I especially loved it when strangers approached me for a ride in my "Tang," and when they were female and pretty, I happily obliged.

Stepping through the depot's double doors, the rumble of train engines could be heard moving on the tracks out back. I smiled as each 'whoosh' and 'clang' evoked warm childhood memories of train rides with my dad when he was a conductor for the CB&Q Railroad. (CB&Q would later merge with Great Northern and Northern Pacific to become the Burlington Northern Railroad in 1970).

On those special days, I'd be up early, dressed and sitting at the table with Dad, eating the same cereal as he did and with the same sized spoon. When the last drop of milk had been slurped and Mom's final kiss had been planted, we'd be on our way.

Our family lived in a small, white house in McCook, a tidy little town in southwestern Nebraska's rolling hill country, bordered by the Republican River. My older sisters, Sharon and Carrol, had been born in the front bedroom facing Fifth Street. But by the time I came along, my mother had joined other modern-thinking parents who were having their babies in the newly built hospital on West 4th Street.

Right next to the house, dad had built a carport toward which my skinny 10-year old legs now carried me. Pulling open the heavy door of our red '55 Ford Station Wagon, I climbed into the front seat normally reserved for Mom. Dad and I drove the short mile to the depot, parked in the employee parking lot and walked to where a four-man crew (engineer, fireman, brakeman and flagman) waited for their conductor.

The tall, smiling men always shook my hand and patted me on the back, treating me like an important member of the team. I'd follow them up the stairs and into the small crew room to await "our" train while they talked of corn and cattle prices.

Dad would go to the dispatcher's office to get his train orders; a piece of paper detailing number of cars, instructions for specific areas and warnings about any hazards. He'd then hand a copy of the orders to the engineer who would read it aloud. If Dad had anything to add, he'd let the engineer know.

Just before the train we'd be taking to Hastings entered the yard, we'd all head back downstairs and wait on the platform. As it passed at barely a crawl, Dad and his crew did a "roll-by inspection," looking for signs of damaged cars or shifted freight.

Once the train came to a stop, the engineer, brakeman and fireman would be driven to the front engine in a "crew hauler" (usually a van) while Dad, the flagman and I walked across the rocky ballast to the caboose. I'd grab onto the railing and Dad would boost me up the high metal steps.

An avid fan of cowboy stories, the "old west" came alive for me every time I stepped into the narrow interior of the caboose or "crummie," as the living quarters for railroaders were once called. I could picture the rough and tough train crews of yesteryear warming themselves beside the black oil stove that still stood in the corner, and at night, sleeping on one of the narrow, hard bunks bolted into the caboose's wood-planked walls. Their tools, replacement knuckles and air hoses for emergency repairs on an Indian-patrolled prairie would have been kept in the storage rooms on either side of the aisle.

With Dad behind me, I climbed a metal ladder fastened onto the side of one of the storage rooms to reach my favorite place; the cupola, a small space spanning the top of the caboose, enabling its occupants a birds-eye view of the entire length of the train. Dad looked out over the right side of the train, the flagman checked the left, and I squinted into the distant horizon for any signs of outlaws.

When satisfied all was well, Dad would pick up a phone-like radio and hold it to his ear. "Set the brakes," he'd instruct the engineer, his eyes on a gauge in front of him. The needle would move until it stopped somewhere between 70 and 80 pounds. He'd push a button on the radio and inform the engineer, "Release the brakes. We're okay to go."

My heart would burst with pride knowing my dad was the boss! And then the train would begin to move, each car lurching forward with a loud "bang" as its steel knuckle tautened from the pull of the car preceding it. Dad would warn me to hold on as the train's slack action made its way back to the caboose. I'd grip the chair arms tightly and hold my breath as the domino sounds of metal against metal grew closer and closer until our car jumped forward. We were underway at last.

Once the train pulled out of the yard and picked up speed, Dad and I would climb down from the cupola and step outside onto the rear platform. Sometimes we'd stand quietly, watching the endless rows of corn, towering concrete silos and white-faced Herefords looking back at us through barbed wire fences. But most of the time he'd regale me with stories of derailments, lost freight, and human tragedies, pointing to the places along the tracks where they'd occurred. And when we'd get to within a few miles of a depot or town, he'd warn me to be on the lookout for "them Special Agents" who'd send me home if they caught me. Of course, the risk of being apprehended only added to my adventure with Dad.

The memory faded as my hard-soled shoes echoed through the Lincoln Station's Great Hall where people purchased tickets to ride Amtrak passenger trains at awning-topped windows. The room's 19-foot high ceiling, embellished with large-scale woodwork and brass chandeliers, gave the hall a timeless dignity.

Through a glass door marked *Burlington Northern Special Agents*, I could see my boss, Tom Schaefer, hunched over a desk with a phone cradled under his chin, both hands gesturing. Surrounding him, an assortment of filing cabinets, desks, and old leather chairs filled our entire department's office space.

I'd just eased into a squeaky chair with a ripped seat when Tom hung up the phone and crooked his finger in my direction. "Dean, that was dispatch. There's a guy acting weird on the tracks over at the Grain Yard. An eastbound train just missed him. Find him before he gets flattened."

I nodded, groaning inwardly. The Grain Yard's access road was a pot-holed, muddy mess from the recent spring rains. Holstering my loaded .357 Magnum, I looped my handcuffs over the back of my pants and walked to my car. Turning the key to start my Mustang, I wished for the hundredth time that we had company cars.

Having a hunch where the man might be hiding, I headed to the outskirts of Lincoln on 'O' Street, turning left when I reached SW 40th. Once I'd crossed the multiple lines of tracks entering the main Cushman Yard, I turned left onto a dirt access road that paralleled the long, narrow Grain Yard in Cushman's southeast section. I downshifted into second gear in an attempt to keep my car clean for at least one more day.

The sunlit rows of tracks created silver ribbons traversing the flat Nebraska terrain, connecting sellers with buyers from across the Midwest. When passing trains slowed to enter or leave the isolated Grain Yard, opportunistic derelicts could easily board freight cars unobserved.

Painstakingly maneuvering my car around each muddy hole, I searched the tracks on my left and a ragged border of tumbleweeds to my right, hoping my hunch would pay off. And it did. A man sat alone in a clearing, about 75 feet from the road.

I carefully parked on a narrow dry strip of ground and walked toward him, cautiously scanning the area for anyone else who might be there. When the man showed no fear or curiosity at my approach, I became suspicious and felt for my holster.

Moving closer, I could see a thick, black layer of grime covered his hands and face as if he'd been dipped in oil. His graying hair lay matted against his head. I stopped about 10 feet from him and opened my mouth to identify myself as a railroad police officer. But the words never made it out. A foul, hideous smell shot up my nose, sending me staggering backwards.

"Man, that's awful!" I gasped, frantically pulling my shirtsleeve over my nose, but to no avail. The hideous stench had seeped into my taste buds. Blinking back tears, I managed to ask, "What *is* that *smell?!*"

The filthy man casually waved his hand. "Got cancer in ma gut an' they gimme a drain bag but don't wear it when ridin' the rails. I travel alone an' ma best pertection from bein' hassled's ma smell. Been doin' this fer years an' ain't had no problems from no one, not even dem bulls."

His reasoning had logic: I wouldn't let him near my car, even if I could put him in the trunk. At this time in my career, Special Agents didn't collect information from contacts made in the field, for which I now felt grateful. I truly believed my senses would have suffered permanent damage if I'd had to get close enough to check his ID and clothing.

Pulling my sleeve tighter over my nose and mouth, I yelled out muffled instructions. "I'm one of 'dem bulls.' Now pick up your stuff and get off this property and if you *ever* come back, I'll run you through a car wash before taking you to jail."

"Car wash?" He scratched his greasy hair. "What'd ya throw me in jail fer—ain't done nothin'."

"Assault with a deadly odor! Now move it."

Shrugging his thin shoulders, he gathered up his pack and sleeping bag before trudging off. But a few yards shy of the road, he stopped and peered back at me, his blackened owlish face revealing a glimmer in his eyes. Tapping his nose, he said,

"Vicks--covers the smell."

Driving back to town with all the windows down, the strange man's preference for filth reminded me of when we'd be in the jungle for weeks without washing. My socks would be so stiff from the muck and sweat, I could tell the left from the right when I slid them off each night. On the rare occasions our unit returned to base-camp, we'd receive mixed reactions from the "base-camp warriors." Some openly admired us for fighting in the jungle while they slept on clean sheets, but others would knock over chairs in their hasty evacuation of Mess Hall at the first whiff of our collective body odor. Since we were more interested in hot food than showers, we'd head straight for the chow, eating with bloodied, mud-stained hands. I'd learned a person can be desensitized to anything if they're around it long enough.

Returning to the present, I decided to patrol Havelock Yard, a two square mile fenced compound east of Lincoln, owned by Burlington Northern. The enclosure held several railroad administrative offices along with specialized buildings for remaking damaged cars, welding and grinding steel wheels that were out of round, and painting over graffiti. Alongside these structures, miles of tracks were lined up side by side for storing and moving cars around the compound. In order to thoroughly check in and around each building and train car, I'd have to patrol on foot, and since it was after 5:00, I should be the only one around.

Parking my car in the late afternoon shadows, I walked across the enclosure. I could hear pigeons cooing from the roofs above me…and footsteps running behind a line of rail cars. I moved toward the sound. The steps slowed. I held my breath and waited. We'd had complaints of recent break-ins -- could this be the thief?

I tried to tiptoe alongside the car but the gravel-covered ground crunched under my shoes. I winced, sure the other person now knew of my presence. Every few feet, I'd stop and scan beneath the cars, trying to spot a pair of legs. I could hear the trespasser doing the same: walk, pause for a few seconds, move behind another car and pause again. Was he trying to avoid being caught -- or looking for me?

Finally, I caught a glimpse of jean-clad legs wearing black boots, one car length ahead of me and on the opposite side. I shadowed him, stopping when he stopped, moving when he moved, until there were three cars left on the line- his hiding places were about to run out. Positioning myself between the last two cars, I un-holstered my gun and waited.

Time ticked by. Footsteps moved haltingly. A gangly man with rumpled blond hair stepped out from behind the last train car, moving toward one of the office buildings, away from me. He held a pistol above his head. Remaining hidden, I locked my hands around the grip of my weapon and steadied my self.

With the middle of his torso in my sights, I took a deep breath and shouted, "Stay where you are and drop your gun -- now!"

The man turned in my direction.

"Stop moving and drop your gun!"

He continued to turn until he faced me. Knowing he could aim and shoot in less than a second, I began to apply pressure on the trigger. "For the last time, drop your gun NOW!"

The rage in my voice and the realization he was looking down the serious end of a .357 Magnum must have registered; he unclenched his fingers and let the weapon clatter to the ground.

"Keep both hands in the air."

He acted confused. "Wha, what's the matter? I wasn't doin'... who are *you*?"

Ignoring his question, I lowered my voice. "Turn around, keep your back to me." When he complied, I continued. "Now kneel down and cross your ankles."

He became annoyed. "What's your problem, man?

Breathing a little easier, I reached for my handcuffs in the back of my pants. "I'll tell you what the prob..."

A scuffling sound behind me. I wheeled around to face a second man casually carrying a gun in his hand. With no time to think, I pointed my pistol at him. "Drop your gun and get your hands up!"

His reaction was the complete opposite of the first suspect's. His eyes bulged, his mouth flew open and he threw the gun away as if it were on fire. With shaking hands held above his head, he pleaded, "Please don't kill me, please don't kill me, I don't wanna die, I'll do whatever you say, man, whatever you say."

I hadn't identified myself as a police officer, and since we didn't have uniforms, he must have feared an armed robber or worse. Repeating the same instructions as with the first suspect, I waited for him to comply before asking, "Are there any more of you out here?"

"No, we're the only ones."

"I'm with the railroad police. Now, what are you two doing out here?"

The first man answered, "Just messin' around."

With my pistol still trained on them, I went over to examine their weapons. Nudging them with my foot, I noticed they felt light. "What the...?" Picking them up, I realized they were plastic models of real handguns.

"Are you telling me you two were in a fenced area, on private property, with toy guns for no reason? I'd say you've got more explaining to do. Now, do you want to answer my questions here or in jail?"

The spokesman for the two spoke in a low voice. "We were playing cops and robbers."

"Cops and ro...how old *are* you guys?"

"Uh, he's 23, I'm 25 and we live over there."

They nodded toward a cluster of houses a few blocks from the tracks. After searching them and asking more questions, I believed they were telling the truth.

"Do you realize how close you came to being killed today?" I shouted. "I could've blown both of you away!" At the thought of just how close, my knees went weak.

Driving home from work later that evening, I couldn't stop replaying what almost happened; my finger squeezing the trigger and sending bullets slamming into those overgrown boys. When I arrived, my anguish diminished somewhat when I saw Snoopy, front paws on the sill, curly-haired face peeking out the window. We did our usual run in the park and returned home, but the earlier feelings of anxiety began to overwhelm me. I immediately opened each bottle in a six-pack of beer and began downing them as fast as I could but this time, the liquid tranquilizer didn't work the way I needed. Images of mangled bodies marched into my conscious mind, taking me to a place I didn't want to go.

I could feel the weight of the M-16 in my hands, the unrelenting sun beating down on my face. My limbs were covered with raw, open sores -- a condition known as jungle rot -- from cuts that wouldn't heal in the filthy, humid environment. When I walked point, the razor sharp, chest-high, elephant grass sliced my arms, leaving long, thin cuts that burned and bled. But even those were bearable compared to the miserable itching from a severe case of ringworm covering my torso.

Our company's footsteps rustled through the grass of the central highlands surrounding AnKhe, the base camp we'd recently been assigned after Pleiku. With no signs of threat, I'd begun to breathe normally as we continued advancing. But without warning, explosions erupted from a low ridge to the left of us, followed by a roaring avalanche of bullets.

We ducked and ran into a stand of trees to escape the terrifying assault. A panicked scream came from Rick, our M-60 machine gunner, who'd fallen to the ground beside me.

"Oh God I've been hit! Mom! Mom!"

With shock and horror, I watched a fist-sized bloody stain in the middle of his back spread into a pool of red dripping down his sides. It had taken only minutes. When Barry, our field medic appeared, I took Rick's hand and shouted, "Rick, you're gonna make it. Doc's here, you'll be okay."

But in Barry's eyes, I saw a reflection of what I felt.

Time stood still as the attack continued unabated. We knew we were in trouble but no one wanted to actually say the words. Sweat drenched my body as I struggled to swallow each gulp of sticky spit. The ringing in my ears and smell of gunpowder turned my stomach. We were pinned down at the base of a hill, concealed by a thin stand of trees with dead and wounded; our only option to fire back until we ran out of ammo. For the first time in my life, I could literally taste fear.

And then we heard them, so faintly at first we couldn't be sure they were real or the collective force of our desperate wishes before we died. But then the beautiful sound of helicopter blades above us came in loud and clear - the cavalry had arrived! Looking up through the leafy canopy, I thrilled at the sight of three choppers coming in high with door gunners firing machine guns. With renewed energy, we blasted away at the enemy's stronghold.

I watched one of the helicopters launch an attack from the east, paralleling the enemy's location on the ridge. As the pilot flew his craft, he dropped low -- too low. I could see the gunner framed by the door when the chopper began to tilt in slow motion. The sounds around me dimmed as the surreal scene played out in front of me. The pilot sat still, looking rigid behind the chopper's windows, not moving his arms or head while his machine continued its forward arc. Suddenly the nose pointed downward as if sniffing the ground.

The powerful helicopter plunged to the earth, throwing the gunner through the air and into a crumpled heap on the field. The front glass shattered when the whirling blades struck the ground, creating a high pitched shriek of crushing metal and grinding gears. My mind couldn't grasp what my eyes saw. The chopper collapsed in on itself, entombing its occupants in broken steel, flames and billows of black smoke. And then it was over. Those incredibly brave soldiers who'd swooped from the sky to save us just moments ago, now lay burning in the middle of a dispirited war.

The shock sent a wave of nausea through my gut but grieving would have to wait until I got back to the world…to the world…Snoopy's warm tongue licking my hand brought me back.

Still trembling from the nightmare, I stroked his curly ears. "I know little buddy, I've got to stop dredging up those ugly scenes."

Quickly downing another two beers, it occurred to me that drinking might become a problem. But the thought of facing the demons with a clear mind and raw nerves seemed far more intimidating than becoming an alcoholic. Throwing the empty bottles into the trashcan, I snapped the top off another beer and sank deeper into the sofa. Snoop's soft brown eyes showed complete trust in his master. I drifted off thinking it must be nice being a dog.

Chapter 3

In the first months of my career, it became painfully obvious the majority of the people I arrested were both taller and heavier. I blamed my slight stature on a smoking habit begun at the tender age of 11 as a way to impress the brown haired girl who lived across the street. By 21, it had turned into two packs a day – and I never did get the girl.

Fortunately for me, the Special Agent position didn't have a minimal height requirement, just minimal common sense about which end of the gun to point. But when criminals continued to challenge me more often than my peers, I had to find a way to look more intimidating. I decided to enroll in a martial arts class.

After a few phone calls, I learned the Lincoln Health Club offered Tae Kwon Do. I signed up and purchased an all-white gee, the loose fitting, two-piece uniform of the self-defense practitioner.

Early on a Monday morning, I walked into the club, feeling as confident as May's promise to turn into summer. Inside the entry, a small store's advertising for vitamins and protein supplements caught my eye. Glossy pictures of tanned men flexing vein-popping muscles in front of swooning bikini-clad women convinced me I needed to give those ingredients a try.

Straight ahead, stairs led down to a room from where clangs and grunts could be heard. Must be the weight room, I guessed, as I continued to the rear of the building and into a large room with mats spread across the floor. I found a dressing room to change in preparation for becoming what I hoped would be a fearless fighting machine.

When I emerged, several others had arrived, all wearing their white gees. In the center of the room, a dignified Asian man in black pants and a white top watched in silence. The black belt around his waist identified him as our teacher or "sensei."

Instructed about protocol when signing up, I remembered to bow before stepping onto the mats and joining the others in a crooked circle around the sensei. Our attempt at a second bow to him ended up out of sync, resulting in a burst of nervous laughter. The teacher didn't crack a smile.

Introducing himself as Mr. Lee, he explained Tae Kwon Do's three principles: honor, fighting spirit and integrity. He summarized what we'd be learning, the format for each lesson and how classes would begin and end with bows of respect to him and the room.

With the initial formalities out of the way, Mr. Lee led us in some basic bending and stretching exercises but after ten minutes, I'd worked up a sweat and a strong craving for a cigarette. Mercifully, the warm-up came to an end so I could catch my breath and wipe my face while Sensei Lee demonstrated a series of fast, high kicks. Talk about impressive – and impossible. No way were my short legs going to reach that far off the ground without pulling a ligament or muscle out of its natural position. Now I really needed a cigarette.

Sensei Lee repeated the sequence or "kata," instructing us to follow his moves. To my dismay, every other student gracefully bent sideways and raised one leg while I tipped backward and hopped, my arms flailing like windmills.

As soon as class ended, I hurried out to my car without stopping to change clothes or put on shoes, and lit up. Leaning against the open door, I inhaled deeply, relishing the familiar sense of wellbeing. My mind and body began to relax and the feelings of embarrassment at being the least coordinated in the class fueled a resolve to practice faithfully between lessons.

May's warm days and cool nights kept their promise, transitioning into the hotter, longer days of summer. Air conditioning and thermostats became a part of my daily routine as the humidity rose with the temperatures. Work continued to be sporadic as I juggled different shifts to fill in for vacations and sick days, wreaking havoc on my sleep patterns. But I never missed a lesson with Sensei Lee and practiced every evening for an hour in front of a plastic-framed mirror hung on my closet door. To finish each workout, I did 100 push-ups.

By July, even Sensei Lee could see the difference in my attitude and moves. My arms now had definition and tone, and my newfound strength made me believe I could quit smoking – which I did – several times.

Standing outside the club one morning, I took a last drag from my cigarette before snuffing it out in a sand-filled canister. A man with bulging biceps, wearing a sleeveless T-shirt, approached me. He smirked at the gee slung over my shoulder and asked, "Why don't you come to the weight room and work out like a *real* man?"

He swaggered away, not waiting for an answer, which intrigued me. I followed him down the stairs to a gym whose mirrored walls reflected strained expressions of sweating men lifting enormous weights. The air reeked of sweat. Colored illustrations on how to build specific muscle groups were taped to the limited wall space. I gulped, knowing my chest and arms, in comparison with theirs, were a dead giveaway to my beginner status. But the "muscle heads" as they called themselves, welcomed me without condescension, so I gave it a try. By the end of summer, I'd found weight lifting to be the perfect fit for my personality; hard driving and self-directed. I quit Tae Kwon Do.

My workouts were soon two hours long, five days a week, as I strove for the ultimate endorphin rush. At first I left Snoopy in the car, surrounded by bowls of food and water and a cushy doggie bed. But after being introduced to the manager, he became Lincoln Fitness Club's mascot, shadowing me as I worked out at each station.

When done with my routine, showered and feeling high, Snoop and I would head to the park to play. As the weeks passed, my routine of lifting and running began to pay off. I'd replaced cigarettes with sunflower seeds and swizzle sticks – bags of them. I looked and felt stronger, which improved my ability in handling criminals. But it didn't improve my loneliness. I hated to admit it, but I longed for someone with a soft voice, and even softer skin, to snuggle with and love.

Prior to Vietnam, the girls I dated were immature and clueless, like me. We'd meet at parties where throbbing music and alcohol made it easy to pretend we knew who we were and what we wanted. Lewd jokes and secret dares broke down barriers and our desperate hearts willingly paid the price to fill aching voids.

But in Vietnam, the game of lust proved even more base. For just "figh dollahs," a girl would pretend to be mine -- no strings, no talk, not even a name. She would hang onto my arm as we strolled through Sin City, smile and laugh as if she cared, giving me anything except what was real. And for the duration of our charade, I could forget about the war and what might be waiting for me in the jungle. Instead, I was just a regular guy hanging out with his girl in a noisy, smoke-filled bar.

In pensive moments, I'd wonder if true love even existed. And if so, did someone wait for me? My parents' solid, unquestioning marriage seemed so easy for them but when coworkers and friends complained about their spouses, marital bliss sounded as elusive as luck and fortune.

I began a shift at Havelock Yard one cool fall evening. Several employees had recently been laid off and, according to the railroad grapevine, a few had threatened revenge.

Driving through one of the yard's four gates, I re-locked it and parked the car. After checking in and around the buildings for over an hour, I found no evidence of foul play. Returning to my car, I opened the door and paused; somewhere in the compound, tires were rolling on gravel. A white Ford Galaxy came into view, cruising toward the administration offices.

"Hmm, who could this be?"

I jumped into my Mustang and followed from a distance, headlights off. I could make out two silhouettes in the front seat, a driver and passenger, each wearing ball caps. When they were within a few feet of the main entrance, they stopped their car but left the engine running. Their heads huddled close around a light that flickered -- a flame.

Flooring the accelerator, I steered straight for them just as the passenger threw a bottle out the window, a lit rag protruding from its top. The Molotov cocktail made a direct hit on the Plexiglass doors but failed to break. Instead, the flaming container bounced back and hit their car, shattering on impact. The burning fuel coated the rear side of the Ford like an orange wave. In that same moment, the driver saw me.

He sped away, adding new life to the fire engulfing the back of his car. As they wildly careened across the dark compound, I followed each twist and turn, courtesy of the bright flames. When they reached the fence, the driver spun the car around and took off again but I kept my distance, not wanting to damage my Mustang in case of flying debris from an exploding gas tank. The driver finally found the gate they'd broken through and escaped into the night.

I decided not to pursue -- the repairs needed for their burnt car would be a fair exchange for one broken lock. Returning to the building,

I inspected the doors, relieved there were no dents or signs of the arson attempt. Good, this report would be brief. After notifying city police to watch for a smoldering Ford Galaxy, I cleaned up the broken bottle and replaced the cut cable on the gate. Taking a final drive around the remainder of Havelock Yard's perimeter, I noticed a locomotive with its diesel engine idling, a common practice.

Dad and Grandpa (also a conductor) had once explained the complicated process of starting a train engine during one of our "men only" evenings on Grandpa's front porch. I recalled sitting on the old wooden chair that had always been there, my feet swinging freely above the porch's faded planks. Between my knees, lightning bugs flashed off and on in a canning jar from Grandma's pantry.

In the humid night air beneath the porch light, I watched with wide-eyed fascination as Dad and Grandpa re-enacted the opening of the relief valves for each cylinder. Grandpa's weathered hands worked in sync with Dad's large, strong hands as they'd crank the pretend engine to blow out the cylinders, shut off the valves and prime the fuel before turning on the switch to start the motor. Since it usually didn't catch the first time, the entire process had to be repeated over and over until it did.

So an idling engine in Havelock Yard didn't surprise me, but the Honda Civic parked next to it, did. Pulling up beside the metallic blue hatchback, I noticed a BN hard hat on the front seat. Now why would an employee be working on a train this late and on an isolated track way out here?

I climbed the lighted steps, glad I didn't need my flashlight so I could keep my presence a secret. At the top, I crept along a catwalk that hugged the length of the engine until I reached a glass door, one of two entrances into the front cab. Peering in, I could see the small compartment where the engineer and one or more crewmembers would sit while driving the train. Rows of gauges covered one wall with more located on a panel beneath the front windows. No one appeared to be inside and everything seemed in order.

On the back wall, another door led to the interior workings of the diesel motor, an area that could accommodate one or two people. I decided to check this rear compartment.

Entering the cab, I knew the idling engine would cover any sounds I made. Movement caught my eye and I stopped, the dim glow from the gauges casting an eerie light in the cramped space. Directly below me, on the engineer's seat, a writhing mass moved against the vinyl upholstery.

Narrowing my eyes to see better, I immediately regretted it. Two faces pressing against each other atop bare bodies, one male, the other female, came into sharp focus. Fortunately, they were too distracted to see me standing over them or hear my hasty retreat. Back on the ground, I shined my flashlight into the side window. "Railroad police! Come out of there!"

A man stuck his head out the side window. "I'm a machinist oiling the engine."

"I know what you're oiling, and it's not the engine! Now get your clothes on and get down here."

In short order, a man fumbling with his shirt buttons and a smiling woman adjusting a dress came down the stairs. When they reached me, the man looked understandably worried but the woman had clearly moved on, twirling her hair and giving me winks and smiles.

"Would you two explain to me why, with all the places to have sex, you chose here?"

The woman spoke up. "We was havin' a coupla drinks when I found out Jimmy here worked for the railroad so I said, hey, I ain't never done it in a train before."

The smeared makeup around her eyes gave her a ghoulish appearance. She leaned in close and lowered her voice. "Don' cha think this here's a great place for romance?"

"Not for him, it isn't. This could cost him his job."

After checking ID's, I sent them on their way, reminding the employee he'd be contacted by our department once I notified his supervisor.

When I drove back to the depot to write my end-of-shift report, two transients were sitting at the base of a security light in the parking lot. They each held a bottle and were shouting so loudly, I could hear them through my closed windows. Swearing under my breath, I drove within inches of their feet, high beams directed into their faces.

Cracking my window, I yelled, "Get your things and get out of here or you're going to jail."

They sat blinking into the glaring headlights, obviously confused, so I leaned on the horn and inched the tires even closer. "Move it or you're going to jail!"

Eventually, the blinding lights and continuous horn had the desired effect. Each held onto the other while they staggered to their feet and zigzagged off the property, calling out obscenities over their shoulders.

An overwhelming rage urged me to run them over but the dilemma of what to do with the bodies forced me to stop and reason with myself. After several deep breaths to decompress, I leaned back, clenching and unclenching sweaty palms around the steering wheel. My reaction frightened me. Why had I come so close to losing control over something so trivial? How could I be calm one moment and escalate to thoughts of murder the next?

A frightening possibility came to mind: perhaps the war had returned home with me, seeking targets like a missile without an off switch. And its radar had found a new enemy in homeless drunks. I decided to be more careful with these impulses – besides, what else could I do? Admitting I had a problem transitioning from soldier to civilian would cost me my job. No, any weakness would have to be squelched, ignored or dismissed from this point forward.

Fortunately, I had the next day off. Snoop and I started the morning with a run in the park beneath trees wearing crowns of red and yellow. September's dropping temperatures had triggered an itch to migrate in the noisy formations of Canada geese flying overhead and the dull colored robins fluttering restlessly from ground to branches. I knew one day I'd find them all gone, as if a telepathic message went out announcing, "It's time."

Since the cooler weather made our runs more enjoyable, we took an extra lap around the park. Once home and showered, I cleaned the house in eager anticipation of my first date with a girl named Sandra. She worked as a railroad telephone operator, a job that attracted young, single females, much to my delight. Once I'd detected her interest during my required call-ins every two hours, I convinced Sandra the finest dining in Lincoln just happened to be "Dean's Place."

After a final glance in the mirror, I patted some cologne on my neck and returned to the kitchen. "Now Snoop," I spoke into his long, soft ear. "A lady friend is coming over and we need to make a good impression." He responded with a rapid thumping of his tail against the floor.

Being a fairly good cook, I enjoyed the opportunity to prepare meals for special occasions. By the time the doorbell rang, the mixed aroma of Cornish game hens, rice pilaf and honey-glazed carrots filled the house. A Chardonnay chilled in a bucket of ice while a Barbra Streisand album turned on the record player.

I held my breath and opened the door, hoping Sandra looked as good as her sultry voice sounded. Jackpot! A willowy brunette wearing a gorgeous smile, hot pink sweater and short black skirt stood in my doorway.

"Hi, Sandra, come on in."

I reached out to shake her hand but she gave me a limp, left hand instead. Something fruity wafted from her skin and hair, like strawberries. I didn't realize perfumes were made from strawberries but at this point, she could have smelled like blue cheese.

"It's nice to meet you...secret *agent* man." Her left eye winked provocatively, giving me a glimpse of unnaturally long, spiked lashes.

"Uh, just call me, Dean. And this here's my roommate, Snoopy."

She studied him for a moment and scowled. "He's kinda shaggy. Does he have fleas? I knew a girl who got lice once and she said it was from her neighbor's mutt and they had to cut off *all* her hair and it was even longer than mine."

"Oh you don't have to worry..."

She gathered her hair up with both hands, stepped carefully around Snoop, and flopped into a chair in my living room. Clearly Sandra was not a dog person but since the evening had just begun, I chose to overlook what I considered to be a serious character flaw.

I offered her a glass of wine, which she accepted and drained in one gulp. Deciding we better eat before the wine ran out, I pulled a chair out from the table and invited her to join me.

"Well, aren't you a perfect gentleman," she cooed, and seductively lowered herself into the seat, letting her skirt ride high on her legs. Things were certainly going better than I expected.

Throughout the meal, the conversation remained lively but one-sided, with me doing all the listening. When I began clearing the dishes, Sandra didn't miss a beat in her talking, following me from the table to the sink. When she paused to take a breath, she pulled a tiny bottle out of her purse and sprayed a sweeping wave of fruity perfume all around her, causing Snoopy to sneeze several times and rub his face on the carpet.

"Omigosh, is your dog epileptic?" She hurried over to the couch and sat down, curling her legs beneath her.

"Uh, no, he's really a great dog. You should get to know him."

Making an excuse to leave the room, I sneaked back to see if there were any breakthroughs. Snoopy lay on the floor, head on his paws, facing Sandra. She leaned forward and waved her hand. "Go away, mutt. Shoo!"

He jerked his head up, clearly understanding her tone. With drooping tail, he rose to his feet and padded out of the room. Well, that settled it. I rejoined Sandra, allowing her to snuggle close, but knowing this first date would be our last. Her fingers began tracing a pattern on my sweater. "Have you ever felt your destiny, Dean? I mean really felt it deep inside you?"

"Um, well, not sure if I've actually *felt*..."

"Me too! See, my natal chart showed Uranus was in Leo..."

"Uhhhh, my what was where?"

"Ya' know, Leo, in the horoscope...anyway, it means my job as a railroad operator is not big enough for me and my manicurist knows this lady whose brother works in West Hollywood -- which is where all the stars go to parties, ya' know -- and she's gonna get me his number so I can send my portfolio -- all the real stars have portfolios, ya' know – and once I get enough money saved up, I'm gonna..."

My mind went numb. I needed to end this, and quickly.

Snoopy trotted back into the room, jumped up and managed to squeeze his body between us. Sandra stopped mid-sentence, folded her arms and pouted. When I didn't react, she nudged Snoop off the couch. He ran to the front door and whined, clearly wanting to go outside.

Sandra stood up. "I'll let him out." But when she opened the front door, Snoopy slyly turned back and returned to me. Leaning against my arm, he gazed defiantly at Sandra.

She struck a dramatic pose in the doorway, one hand on her hip, breasts pushed outward. "Fine! You can have your stupid mutt but you can't have me." With a toss of her hair, she left, slamming the door behind her.

Snoop and I sat together for some time, my hand scratching his ears as he dozed on my lap. I'd never really considered what my future might hold before Sandra mentioned it. Did people really have specific destinies or did we make do with whatever life sent our way? And did these destinies include a special love or could we have a future with any one of thousands, depending on who we met first?

"Well, Snoop, there's one thing I do know – our future lady will have to love dogs because you and I are a package deal."

I leaned back and closed my eyes, silently urging destiny, wherever it happened to be in the universe, to hurry up and find me.

Chapter 4

By October, nature's slip into dormancy could also be seen in the lives of the community. Only a few hardy joggers and bicyclists still used Lincoln's trail system, swing sets hung empty in the parks, and tractors and combines were no longer a common sight along the highways, having been retired after long weeks of harvest.

And since I too now spent more time indoors, I no longer had an excuse for putting off housecleaning, something Snoopy dreaded. So when I dragged the Hoover from the hall closet one Saturday morning, I let Snoop out on the porch to lessen the stress.

Over the vacuum's drone, I heard something hit the front door. I turned off the machine and two more raps followed in quick succession.

"What's going on out there?"

Opening the door, I found Snoopy trembling against the house while two boys re-loaded wrist rockets with stones. Outraged at their cruelty, I flew across the yard, leaped over the fence and grabbed each boy by an arm, squeezing them hard through their jackets. With revenge seething inside, an image of Mrs. Monroe, my childhood Sunday school teacher, popped into my mind. Her round body, thick-framed glasses and beehive hairstyle had been a constant source of jokes for us unruly boys. I could still hear her say with all earnestness, "Love is stronger than hate."

But why had I thought of that? And why now? This unexpected distraction gave me a chance to calm down and rationally think of a better solution than threatening these kids. My hands relaxed their grip.

"Why would you kids try to hurt an animal who'd love to play with you?"

They shrugged their shoulders and looked at the ground.

"Come on, I want you to meet Snoopy."

The boys wiped their noses with their sleeves and followed me into the yard. Snoopy, with a dog's ability to forgive, trotted across the yard to where his favorite tennis ball lay. Picking it up, he ran to the boys, dropped it at their feet and backed up in anticipation. Tentatively at first, they threw the ball and Snoopy retrieved it, even when they pretended to throw it another direction. Soon, their play evolved into a wild game of chase, the boys laughing as they slipped and rolled on the brown, muddied lawn in their attempts to catch a darting, dodging Snoopy. When they'd exhausted their energy levels, they sprawled on the ground, the prized ball safely between Snoop's furry paws.

"Can we come over and play with him again?"

"You sure can, just knock on my door to let me know you're here."

We shook hands as they passed through the gate and I returned to my cleaning. If Mrs. Monroe could have seen me today, she'd be thrilled – and shocked – to find her worst student had actually been paying attention.

Raised by God-fearing parents who read Bible stories to me each night, I'd gone to church every Sunday and learned songs about Jesus. As a child, I believed because I trusted my parents. If they said it, it must be true. But when I left home at 17, I also left behind any and all principles they'd tried to instill in me, especially their belief in God. From my superior teenage perspective, my parents' faith looked more like a suppressive guilt trip than relevant information.

Once my stint in Vietnam ended, however, I'd returned home to a life with no close friends and a society that had progressed without me. The possibility of God now entered my mind almost daily.

I'd recall times during the war when I should've been killed but instead, survived. A buddy casually tugged on a tree branch as we walked a trail, an insignificant action that caused a huge explosion. Shrapnel struck him and several others, killing them instantly. A burning piece of jagged metal landed mere inches from where I stood in shock, untouched, while bleeding bodies lay around me -- why?

In Vietnam, my division was an air-mobile unit. Helicopters would fly us to a "hot zone" where we'd fight to regain or hold a piece of land. If it ended with us still alive, we'd be flown to fight for a different hill or field. En route between battles, I'd sit on the floor of the chopper, legs dangling over the edge for a quick exit during these "insertions." As the landscape passed beneath, I'd imagine myself no longer a part of the conflict down there. I could relax and revel in the strong wind on my face, the powerful roar of the engine, the rotor blades beating the air above me. But a bullet piercing our chopper would bring me back to reality – I'd been sent to fight, and most likely die, in the war below the clouds.

Whenever these anxieties surfaced, I found refuge in alcohol, work, and the gym. But one night, the drinks weren't numbing me fast enough. Fearing the nightmares, I desperately flipped through the Yellow Pages for anything to do with God, only to discover God didn't have his own listing. I went to the "Church" section and punched a number that promised to answer life's questions. A recording asked me to leave my name and number, which I did, and then slammed the phone down. I knew I'd never hear from anyone.

Grabbing a final beer for the night and turning on the TV, I tucked Snoopy under one arm and settled on the couch. "Looks like we're going to have to sort this one out ourselves."

Eventually, the TV shows' dialogues lulled me into a restless sleep where I dreamed of flying high with the guys from 4ᵗʰ infantry.

The next day, Sunday, I awoke feeling hung over. Cutting my morning routine short, I checked in at the office without saying the usual niceties to coworkers, and headed straight to our problem area -- Havelock Yard. Tension from former employees still existed so we were to check the administrative buildings every shift.

When I arrived, I spotted a hole in the fence big enough for a person to squeeze through. And three young boys, about nine or ten years old, were inside the compound near some empty railroad cars.

"Hey guys, hold up a minute." They stopped and faced me. "Come over here. We need to talk."

They complied without hesitation or fear. Lining them up in front of me, I cleared my throat for the standard lecture I reserved for kids who just didn't know better. As a way of introduction, I flipped open my wallet. "This, gentlemen, is..."

My badge flew from its holder. We watched the five-pointed silver star, respected symbol of authority, bounce off one of the boys and land unceremoniously in the dirt.

"Ow!" He rubbed his chest while I hastily retrieved my badge and dusted it off.

The other two shifted their feet, which I took to be nervousness--until I heard their giggles. I tried to recoup. "I'm a police officer and you gentlemen, are breaking..."

More giggles and squirming – their attention span had clearly reached its limit. Giving an abridged version of the dangers of playing near trains, I escorted them off the property. "Now am I going to see any of you around here again?"

"No way, Mister cop. You might hit me again with your badge." They scurried off amid loud guffaws, punching each other in the sides.

I repaired the fence and did a thorough check of the yard. Afterward, I positioned my car at an angle so I could watch the buildings while close to the highway paralleling the train yard.

Surveillance is 90 percent boredom so I passed the time singing with the radio and guessing where passing drivers might be headed this crisp fall Sunday afternoon. Drumming my fingers on the steering wheel to a Rolling Stones song, I watched as a motorcycle carrying two people without helmets, headed east. For no apparent reason, the car in front of them braked. The motorcycle crashed into the fender, sending both riders flying over the top and into oncoming traffic. To my horror, a westbound car slammed into their bodies, spun out of control, and came to rest on the shoulder in front of me. Incredibly, the driver of the car who'd caused the accident drove off.

Grabbing my CB radio, I called out to anyone who might be listening. "This is an emergency. Can someone call the police for me?"

A female voice responded. "I'm here, what's your emergency?"

I hurriedly described the accident, making sure she had the correct location. Then I ran to the scene. The driver who'd hit the riders, a youth who looked to be in his teens, slumped against a road sign, sobbing, "Oh my God!" I immediately felt sorry for him, knowing the nightmares that lay ahead.

Traffic had stopped in both lanes. People milled around, hands over their mouths, mesmerized by the grisly scene. My legs shakily carried me to the closest body, a girl with long black hair, a light jacket and tan colored pants. Her vacant brown eyes told me she'd already passed on.

Twenty feet from her, the other rider lay with his legs contorted beneath him. He looked a few years older, perhaps in his early 20's. The side of his scalp and both legs bled profusely, creating a dark red outline.

I knelt beside him, surprised when he lifted his head. His eyes were dilated and pleading so I put an assuring hand on his shoulder.

"Just stay still. Help is on the way." He made a feeble attempt to say something. I leaned closer.

"My sister….how's she…"

"Don't worry about her, she's going to be alright."

His cracked lips formed the words "Thanks." His eyes closed. A light shudder went through his body and his breathing became shallow and quickened.

"It's….cold." Moments later, he joined his sister in death.

When the ambulances and police arrived, I gave them my account and then spent the rest of my shift numb from what I'd witnessed.

Arriving home that evening, a morbid, dark mood settled over me. Even Snoopy couldn't lift my spirits so he resigned himself, with an audible doggy sigh, to sitting beside me. The accident had been my first experience with death since Vietnam, resurrecting the faces of fallen comrades. Loss, grief, and helplessness flooded over me.

A knock on the front door jolted me out of my trance. Through the peephole, I could see two men in suits and ties standing on my porch, their breaths visible in the cold night air.

Cracking the door wide enough for them to hear me, I asked, "What can I do for you?"

"Are you Dean O'Shea?"

"Who's asking?"

"I'm Bob Conrad and this is my associate, Wayne Goebel."

He gestured toward a smaller man with brown eyes and a gray mustache. Both men appeared in their early 50's and carried themselves with a strong, quiet confidence.

"Dean, we're here to talk about the questions that have been troubling you. Do you have time for some answers?"

Realizing they must be from the Bible information service I'd called the night before, I shook my head in amazement at their timing. "Come on in."

As soon as we were seated, I skipped formalities and blurted, "Why does God allow so much suffering in this world?"

Bob looked at me with a kindness not usually seen in people I knew, let alone strangers. He opened a Bible on his lap and told an amazing story of a love older than time, a jealous hatred born in heaven, the subsequent battle for our souls, and the freedom we now have to choose between the two; love can't be love if it's forced. But with that freedom came the risk people would choose to hurt others and themselves. And yet God still preferred love to defeat the enemy instead of control--completely opposite the methods of man. Mrs. Monroe had been right, after all.

"Some of this sounds familiar to me from when I was young. But isn't the Bible more for people who lived a long time ago?"

Wayne sounded excited as he rattled off some facts. "The books of the Bible were written on three continents, in three languages, by many different people over a period of about 1,500 years. Most of them never met and their education and backgrounds varied greatly. But their writings held a common thread about a God who never gave up on His wayward children."

A tiny glimmer of hope began to take root as I listened to their words of encouragement, assurance, and unconditional love. Rather than a lightning bolt, it felt more like a gentle tugging at my heart, an intuitive awareness that healing had begun in my soul. By the time they were ready to leave, I knew I'd never look at life's events the same.

Walking them to the front door, I handed them their coats. "I'm surprised how quickly you guys responded to my phone message last night."

Exchanging glances, Bob spoke in a quiet tone. "We don't have an answering machine and we're not listed in your phone book. We work for an organization in Canada and were given your name and address as a contact for the next time we were in Lincoln."

Wayne smiled. "We're not sure who you called but we *are* sure who called us." With a handshake, they were gone.

For a long time, I lay in bed pondering how often life's events are not as they appear. My time in Vietnam had been labeled a "tour" as if changing the name changed the reality. We saw ourselves as heroes for our country but the hostile reception back home told us we were no one's heroes.

I recalled a time when our platoon hiked Vietnam's Central Highlands. After several hours, the sticky heat and stress of being on "tour" began to take its toll, even though we'd only covered a few miles. Each step had to be cut through tree limbs, brush and wait-a-minute vines, so called because the plant's strong tendrils would grab our clothes as if to say, "Wait a minute!"

We finally stopped for the night. After placing guards on watch, we assembled our hooches and dug shallow foxholes around the perimeter of camp. About 20 feet in front of the foxholes we positioned claymore mines; what the military called "antipersonnel" mines. About 12 inches long and 6 inches high, plastic dynamite covered the back while each mine's slightly curved front held a mass of steel ball bearings imbedded in putty-like dynamite. Fiberglass encased the entire mine. Two sets of folding steel legs allowed us to stick them upright into the ground, curved side faced outward. A blasting cap went into one of two top holes, connected to a long wire that attached to a hand detonator held by each guard. If they believed we were under attack, they were to detonate the mines, sending the steel bearings forward in an explosive swath of destruction.

We settled into our foxholes just as the jungle's nocturnal creatures began their chorus of howls, grunts and whistles. The darkness seemed impenetrable, like being entombed in a coffin, without the slightest shade of gray.

Within the first hour, one of the guards crawled to me, fear in his voice. "Sarge, someone's pullin' my claymore wire!"

We knew this to be a trick of the enemy. They'd quietly turn our claymore mines so the deadly steel bearings faced us, and then pretend to attack, hoping we'd detonate the mines on ourselves.

I whispered to the guard, "Do *not* blow your mine! The VC must've turned them." I radioed another guard to see if anything unusual was happening at his side of the perimeter. A cold chill went through me when he replied, "Affirmative! Someone's throwing rocks." I repeated my orders, "Do *not* blow your claymore. They've been turned."

The word passed down to everyone in our company: VC are outside the camp and will be attacking any moment...be ready. Firing our weapons first would create muzzle flashes, giving away our positions, so we'd have to wait for the enemy to make the first move.

The ground felt damp against my legs as I stretched out, straining my eyes for any signs of faces or guns. I had to remind myself to breathe. Why were they hesitating? I didn't know which was worse-- the actual battle or waiting for the first bullet.

Suddenly, a small figure leapt out of the veil of darkness and landed right between our radioman and me. Before we could react, it launched back into the air and disappeared. I hissed at Wally, "What the hell was that?"

Wally's voice had a catch, "I...don't...know."

The night dragged on. Minutes became hours as each man feared what this battle might bring to him or to the platoon. Who would be shot? Who would lose a leg or an arm? Or the worst possibility — would any of us be taken prisoner?

Our claymore wires were tugged and pulled throughout the night. Rocks tumbled into our circle at random, catching our collective breaths. Just when we thought the nightmare would never end, the dark shroud rose in increments with the sun. Each man quietly lay on the hard ground, raised his weapon and prepared to look into the eyes of the enemy. But as wisps of mist swirled and dissipated like the ending of some ghostly convention, the jungle revealed no soldiers looking down their sights at us. Instead, the canopy of leaves and branches stretching over us like a green dome was alive with monkeys; dozens of leaping, grooming, scratching, monkeys. Our sleepless night of terror had been mere amusement for a troop of primates: things had not been what they appeared.

Three birthdays marked three years of change in my life; faith became my sanctuary instead of alcohol, dating several girls at once didn't feel right anymore and health became a priority. But to keep these commitments, I realized I'd have to find a place where no one knew the old Dean, where I could start over with a different circle of friends who'd support my choices and direction.

I'd have to leave home.

Chapter 5

Spreading a map of the United States across my gray formica kitchen table, my finger zigzagged over the western states like a dowser seeking for water. It came to rest on a black dot representing a city near the ocean -- Seattle. Tapping the name lightly, I studied its proximity to the sea.

"With all this water, there'll be views from every direction and lots of beaches to walk on...hey Snoop, how does moving to Seattle sound?"

I called the railroad's office and found a patrolman's job had just opened there. What timing! After faxing my application, it took only days to receive confirmation I'd been hired. I packed my belongings, left the sale of my house in the hands of a realtor, loaded Snoopy into the Mustang, and headed west on Interstate 80.

For five hours, the freeway followed the wide, sandy North Platte River as it stretched east to west through Nebraska's farmland and towns. Believing I'd never miss the miles of cornfields and open prairie, I muttered, "Goodbye, Nebraska!"

The Midwest's summer heat shimmered over the road's surface, as if transparent flames leapt from the asphalt. I tried keeping the air conditioner on low to improve gas mileage but it didn't take long before I resigned to leaving the setting on high. When Snoopy and I needed a break at rest stops, we'd take a quick stroll around the parking lot and then beat a hasty retreat back to the car.

After crossing into Wyoming and driving through its capital city, Cheyenne, I headed north on I-25, noticing a dramatic change in topography. Rounded, treeless hills rose up from sage-filled valleys, undulating across the land like solid waves. Giant shadows gliding ominously up and down their slopes warned of thunderheads on the move. Herds of wild Pronghorn grazing close to the freeway hinted of a west before settlers filled its borders.

When we reached Casper hours later, I was surprised to find the North Platte still flowed beside us -- a living landmark from home. We spent the night at a cheap hotel on the edge of town, the kind that wouldn't mind having a dog. After sharing a McDonald's hamburger, Snoop and I fell asleep on a thin, sagging mattress to the sound of idling 18-wheelers and a dripping air conditioner propped in the room's only window.

Early the next morning, we were back on the road before the sun rose too high. The temperature already read 91 degrees.

In Buffalo, I-25 transitioned into I-90, bringing us to eastern Montana's spacious Custer country. Seeing signs I'd entered Crow territory revived stories from my youth about Indians and gunslingers and trading posts. Eventually, the open grassland surrendered to western Montana's breathtaking mountain ranges and passes. We spent our second night in Butte, a city known for its colorful mining history.

By the third morning, we had our routine. Rise early for a pre-dawn walk, find the nearest McDonald's and get underway. The stretch of road from Butte to Missoula proved to be the most challenging – the looming peaks of the Continental Divide and Rockies begged me to take a detour and explore this wild, remote corner of our country. But reality -- and a job -- kept me between the white lines, heading west.

When we reached the top of Fourth of July Pass, we entered North Idaho's narrow panhandle, a scenic feast of hues more brilliant than the muted palette of the Midwest. I made a mental note to vacation here someday.

Lake Coeur d'Alene's photogenic bays and forested shores made it difficult to keep my eyes on the road, but once we passed Post Falls, the terrain became more open. Finally, a sign welcomed us to Washington State – we were almost there!

As we sped through the cities of Spokane, Ritzville and Moses Lake, I began to question Washington's nickname, *The Evergreen State*. The scenery looked so dry, with miles of sage-covered hills, an occasional small lake and swirling dust devils rising over empty plots of land. The only signs of life between towns were prowling coyotes and small bands of cattle walking single file along barbed wire fences.

Another hour and the Columbia Gorge abruptly appeared -- a jagged blue slash in a brown-toned landscape. Not until we crossed the bridge could the Columbia River's size and power be fully appreciated, its waters contained by sheer cliffs.

We stopped in Ellensburg for lunch. The air felt hot here but the lower humidity level made it tolerable. A continuous warm wind rippled the surrounding crop fields, evoking a surprising touch of homesickness, which I quickly squelched.

Back on the road, the town of Cle Elum appeared to offer the last gas and food before the highway began its ascent into the Cascade Mountains. When the car crested Elk Heights, I caught my breath. A solid line of blue peaks, each wearing a snowy mantle about its shoulders, stretched north and south like massive sentinels guarding the Promised Land. Above them, an expanse of sky and clouds matched the mountains' colors, as if one spilled over into the other. In the foreground, right below us, hung emerald valleys and slopes.

"Wow, Snoop, look at our future home!"

I put more pressure on the gas pedal, ignoring my body's aching numbness from days of driving. Another long stretch through a mountain pass and we were finally on Interstate 5 outside Seattle. I craned my neck for glimpses of the ocean.

"Look at all these cars. There must be a problem up ahead." I leaned out my window but couldn't see any ambulances or flashing lights.

An hour later, we were still bumper to bumper, with no sign of an accident or disabled vehicle. Impatient drivers cut in and out of traffic, setting off horns and hand gestures from offended drivers. What had I gotten us into? And where was the ocean?

Finally, traffic began to move and we pulled up to our new home; a nice apartment on a small lake with lots of trees for Snoopy.

Eager to stretch our legs, we bounded up two levels of stairs to the third floor. Opening the door, we checked out each room -- me looking, Snoopy sniffing. The recently built complex still had that new smell but it was the balcony that made it all worthwhile. Sliding open the glass door from the living room, scenic Angle Lake lay beneath us like a picture postcard. And better yet, a grassy park surrounded the lake where ducks and geese rested, heads neatly tucked beneath wings.

"What do you think of that, huh, boy?"

Unpacking a few basic necessities from the car, we ate a dinner of crackers and cheese, then set out to explore our neighborhood. Anticipating stricter laws in the city, I snapped a collar around Snoop's neck and tucked a leash into my pocket.

Within a block, we found a gas station and restaurant along a very busy Highway 99. For some time I stood on that corner, the faces of friends and family appearing against a backdrop of wind-blown prairie and small-town friendliness.

Home suddenly felt very far away, maybe too far. A quiet mood settled over me. For our first night in Seattle, we lay on the floor but neither of us slept well.

Early the next morning, I dressed quickly and took Snoop outside. The highest tips of the surrounding evergreens glowed where the dawn's rays touched them. Round webs hung from shrubs like grandma's lace doilies, their strands made visible by the dew.

Snoop and I walked, played ball and raced each other across imaginary finish lines, just like back home. But when it came to breakfast, I didn't have much of an appetite. I left the slider open so he could enjoy the fresh air on the balcony, and headed for my new job in Seattle.

With a city map, I figured out how to get to King Street and the Amtrak Depot, but not why I couldn't see the ocean. Parking my Mustang in the depot's lot, I stopped to purvey my new place of employment; a two-story, brick building surrounding an elegant clock tower soaring high above the roof. I liked its solid, quiet confidence and hoped the people inside would be as inviting.

Taking a deep breath, I stepped into the lobby and onto its impressive white and green marble floors, a beautiful use of Burlington-Northern's colors. Spacious white walls loomed two stories above me.

I entered the boss' office and Jerry Holmes, a large man with brown hair and a strong handshake, welcomed me. I instantly liked him.

"Good to have you here, Dean. You're officially the newest member of Seattle's railroad police team."

"Thanks. Can't wait to get started."

"I thought we'd have you be our main fill-in for officers who are sick or on vacation. Otherwise, you choose your hours. How does that sound?"

"Okay by me, boss."

I liked the idea of working different shifts so I could learn the problems and people associated with each. And I especially liked that Seattle Special Agents had company cars with communication radios. It finally felt like a real police department.

Jerry introduced me to four of the officers who covered the cities of Tacoma, Everett and Seattle. One of them, Henry Stone, made an impression on me. Standing a few inches taller and about 20 pounds heavier, his guarded demeanor and intense blue eyes told me he didn't trust easily. I knew how he felt.

I spent the rest of the morning completing forms and leafing through a thick, dog-eared manual containing hundreds of rules I'd be expected to follow for the duration of my employment. When I returned to the apartment, I felt both excited and exhausted.

Shortly after my arrival, five members of our team, including myself, boarded a plane at SeaTac Airport for a flight to Overland, Kansas. Once there, we joined police teams from around the country for training at the railroad's police academy.

Each day, we were given eight hours of hands-on demonstrations, class work and firing practice with both handguns and shotguns. Our teachers were Special Agents who'd once worked as city, county, or state police officers, ensuring a curriculum that not only covered the standard rules of law enforcement agencies, but the situations unique to railroad yards and property. At the end of six weeks, we were given a certificate and sent home to practice what we'd learned. From this point on, we'd be required to have 64 hours of continuing education each year to retain our commissions. The railroad had finally decided if they were going to have police officers, they'd be well trained.

For uniforms, we were to wear sports jackets and ties with badges clipped to our belts. Our company cars were unmarked, without lights or cages, because we shared them with other departments. For this reason, we couldn't transport suspects to the local jail but had to rely on our city and county peers for pick up and delivery. I imagined they weren't too crazy about that arrangement.

We were taught how to blend into the busy workings of a yard without giving away our presence until necessary. When we made an arrest or confronted someone, we were to fill out a contact card for each person, noting the subject's physical characteristics and visible tattoos, as well as his/her name, social security number, birth date and criminal history. Given the homeless population we dealt with, I knew getting any accurate information would be a challenge.

The sprawling area I now patrolled contained several train yards and hundreds of miles of tracks. At the South Seattle Intermodal Hub Center, receiving and shipping between truck trailers and trains went on 24 hours a day within an eight-foot high fence, two miles long and one-third of a mile wide.

Trucks would first stop at the main gate so their loads and trailers could be checked for dents, damage or flat tires. Following the inspection, trucks would enter the yard and park in "load lines" where drivers would unhook their trailers and leave them beside other trailers.

When a train pulling empty flatcars arrived, a truck hostler, (a modified small truck cab) would pull a trailer from the load line to its assigned flatcar. An enormous Piggy-Packer whose driver would be guided by a groundsman, would lift the trailer -- some weighed several tons -- onto its corresponding flatcar with giant steel arms, while the hostler pulled another trailer into position. This process would be reversed when trains arrived already loaded with trailers.

Everything from televisions to cars to sports equipment were transported this way, making them easy targets for train thieves who only had to break a thin metal seal, open the unlocked doors and carry the goods to a get-away vehicle. For this reason, a Special Agent manned the Hub Center 24 hours a day. It's where I began my first night on duty.

To inspect a train ready for departure, I drove alongside it, checking each loaded flatcar for movement or silhouettes. When a man stepped out of the shadows at the other end of the train, I stopped the car to watch. He casually faced each trailer's door without touching the seals and then moved on to the next car to repeat his actions. But when he saw me, he turned sharply and headed back toward the fence. I punched the accelerator and slid to a stop in front of him, my headlights illuminating a thin, middle aged man with long brown hair framing an unshaven, angular face.

Stepping out of the car, I called out, "Hey, Mister, stay right where you are."

He put his hands on his hips and glared at me from dark, hooded eyes. "Whaddya want?" His voice dripped with contempt.

Pushing my coat back to reveal my badge, I answered, "First, I want to know what you're doing out here and second, your attitude's going to get you in trouble so change it."

"Ain't none of yur business what I'm doin' out here."

I studied him closely; this guy didn't bluff. "Right now, you're illegally trespassing on private property and that's enough to get you a night in jail, plus a fine. It's up to you what happens from here on in, but I can promise you this: I'm going to win, no matter what course you choose. So let's try this again -- what are you doing out here?"

I knew he wouldn't tell the truth no matter what I asked but I needed to write something on the contact card.

He sneered, "I was lookin' for my lost kitty Puff an' didn't know this here was private land."

"The fence didn't give you a clue? Let's see some identification."

"What if I don't wanna show you ID?"

I again pulled my coat open, giving me better access to the gun strapped to my side. Keeping an even tone in my voice, I replied, "Then you're going to jail."

He swore and reached for his backpack. Taking a step forward, he handed me his driver's license without taking his eyes off me. He then pulled a cigarette and lighter from his front pocket, his moves too casual for the situation.

Suspicious, I commanded, "No smoking 'til I'm done with you."

He held the cigarette and lighter in his hands, glaring hard. If there were laws for being a jerk, I could've arrested him right then and there. I returned to the car to record the information from his license, sitting in the front seat with the door open. The man remained standing in the headlights.

I heard a step and looked up. His dark form now stood directly in front of me, a lighter in his hand, a lit cigarette in his mouth. He curled his lips back in a menacing leer, struck the wheel and flint, igniting a four-inch flame from the open nozzle. Thrusting the torch at me, he seared my face and hair. Without time to choose a defensive move, I pushed the lighter away. With the palm of my other hand, I smashed the cigarette into his face which made him stumble backward, giving me a chance to get out of the car. But as soon as I stood up, he dealt a blow to my left cheek, jerking my head back. Regaining my balance, I saw him coming around with his other fist but managed to deflect it. Grabbing his arm from behind, we scuffled for a few frantic minutes as I pushed him toward my vehicle. Once we were close enough, I slammed his face hard onto the hood. And then a miracle happened.

"I'm sorry fer trespassin', I'll never do it agin, officer, I promise." Remorse had entered his cold heart.

Between breaths, I told him, "You've just turned a warning…for trespassing… into an arrest for assaulting…a police officer."

I cuffed him and reached for the radio mike. "Yardmaster, this is the Special Agent. Call Seattle police and let them know I've got a suspect needing a ride to jail for assaulting an officer."

"I'll call right now, Special Agent."

When I resumed filling out the card, his new attitude proved to be temporary and he reverted back to cursing and threats. I'd soon learn to tune this part of the job out.

A city officer pulled up and together, we pushed the ranting man into the back seat. "Good job finding this guy. We'll book him but we need a copy of your report to go with it."

"No problem. I'll drop it off tomorrow morning. And thanks for getting here so fast."

I wiped the smears of blood and saliva off the hood of my car, realizing my singed hair had taught me a valuable lesson – I'd never take my eyes off a suspect again.

Knowing a train would soon be arriving at the Hub with several loads of truck trailers, I repositioned the car to face the tracks. Within minutes, an engine chugged into the yard, enabling me to study each flatcar for signs of tampering or illegal riders.

To my relief, the first 29 were "without exception," a term meaning nothing wrong or unusual. But when the last one rolled by, I saw a lone figure on the deck, leaning against a container (the deck is the floor of the flatcar, which is wider than the container it carries, creating a space of about 2 feet on each side). By his slumped posture, he must've been unconscious or asleep.

But he couldn't have picked a worse car to ride--its stench told me this container held cow hides. And in warm weather, these hides oozed foul, sticky goo that would seep through the cracks of the doors and onto the deck.

As soon as the train stopped, the engines were disconnected and driven away. Holding my nose, I peered over the edge of the flatcar, surprised to find a very young man sitting in a puddle of the smelly mess. His shirt and pants hung loosely and his jutting cheekbones and jaw gave his face a gaunt appearance. His closed eyes looked as if they'd sunk into holes.

I smacked the metal flatcar with my nightstick. "Hey, wake up!"

He opened bleary eyes but didn't see me.

"Hey, buddy, get up from there."

His face showed no comprehension.

Great – now I'd have to climb onto the flatcar and wallow through the muck to physically remove him. Holding my breath, I pulled myself over the edge and gingerly stepped across the slime until I stood over the rider. Rancid pieces of raw fish and what looked like potato chips lay spilled across his soiled pants.

When I nudged his leg with my foot, he turned to look up at me, revealing pinpoint pupils. His arms began to jerk as he mumbled incoherently. Must be a druggie, I thought with disgust.

Leaning against the container to keep from slipping, I tried to reason with him. "You've got to stand up so I can help you off the train." My eyes were burning from the stench and my lungs screamed for clean air.

Eventually, my coaxing reached some cognizant part of his brain. He pushed against the container's side and managed to get his feet beneath him in a limp, rag doll kind of way.

"That's good. Now we're going to take a step together and you'll sit back down, okay?" My plan was to hang his legs over the edge so he could slide down to the pavement without getting hurt.

Steadying myself on the slippery deck, I reached for his hand but he turned and lost his balance. He stumbled backward over the edge of the train car and fell headfirst onto the concrete. It sounded like a ripe melon being split open.

Jumping to the ground, I was shocked to see him moving despite a pool of blood spreading beneath his head. I radioed for assistance while the man babbled and flailed his arms about. Suddenly, his eyes rolled back exposing the whites, and his body went still.

I don't know how much time elapsed before two ambulances arrived. The paramedics from one checked the man's vital signs and strapped him onto a gurney. They loaded him into their vehicle and closed the doors. Within seconds, the doors flew open, the young man was taken out and loaded into the second ambulance.

When a medic noticed the question on my face, he said simply, "He died." And then both vehicles drove away.

I watched until the taillights disappeared. Looking down at my feet, I saw the circle of blood touched the tips of my shoes, triggering a realization that terrified me. This is what it would be like to die alone, without someone to hold my hand or whisper final words of love. How empty, how utterly meaningless…as if the life mattered so little, no one bothered to show up for the death. This man's final moments had been with strangers who saw him as another problem to check off in their busy day.

Looking up at the starless sky, I whispered "Oh God, please don't let me die alone."

Chapter 6

Spring in the Pacific Northwest meant perfect weather as far as Snoop and I were concerned. The muggy humidity we'd suffered back home didn't seem to exist on this side of the world. Now, instead of tossing and turning on damp sheets, I fell asleep to deliciously cool breezes tempered by the mountains and sea.

The flora also seemed to thrive here; from riotous patchworks of color in people's yards to blooming hedges and groundcover spilling across freeway medians and overpasses. My first winter had been mild enough for leafy clumps of primroses to bloom in January in my new front yard.

As soon as my house had sold in Lincoln, I'd used the profit to purchase a cozy split-level in a quiet neighborhood south of Seattle. And to my delight, the sellers had put a lot of care into the landscaping -- each month new flowers emerged somewhere in the yard. But nothing compared with what happened between March and May. Our official state flower, the Rhododendron – or what the locals called "Rhodies" -- made their appearance in a spectacular display of hues and sizes, some as tall as 10 feet. Domesticated hybrids ranged from deep purple to snowy white while their wild pink cousins mobbed the green forests and fields. Mom would be so envious.

"Well, Snoop, looks like it's time for you to get a haircut," I told my buddy after one particularly long run. His curly ears drooped; he knew what "haircut" meant.

Donning a ball cap and my favorite pair of ratty sweatpants with holes in the knees, I drove to a grooming shop I'd discovered in my own neighborhood. Snoopy sat dejected on the seat, not even tempted by the open windows.

Rubbing his back to console him, I tried to imagine what it would be like to have a stranger dunk me into a tub of water, vigorously scrub me with soap, rinse, and then blow-dry my hair into a giant puffball. After an hour of enduring scissors snipping away at individual strands, a frilly bow would be tied around each of my ears followed by a spritz of girly perfume in front of my peers. By the time we'd arrived, I was actually feeling sorry for the little guy.

Parking the car, I dragged a stiff-legged Snoopy at the end of his leash through a front door with bells on the knob. In the empty waiting room, two white chairs were positioned on either side of a white lamp stand. On the lamp stand stood a framed photo of a canine face, its eyes red from the camera's flash. The pink painted walls displayed smaller photos of bejeweled and clothed poodles with names like "Carmen" and "Farrah" scrawled across the bottom edges. On the lone windowsill, delicate blown-glass figurines of dogs pranced and posed.

I rang a silver bell that sat beside a fuchsia ashtray on a dark green reception counter. High-pitched barking immediately erupted from the other side.

"I'll be right there!" a husky voice called out above the din. An enormous woman in a bright floral dress appeared, looking like she'd just come from a luau. She waved a fleshy arm at me and then sharply clapped at the two toy poodles barking furiously at our feet. "Shut up you two! Get back here right now!"

Neither paid any attention to her. The smaller of the two wore a cast on her right rear leg, but it didn't seem to slow her down. Despite her tiny stature, she clearly felt capable of taking on Snoop and I. But when we failed to back away she snorted and trotted off in a huff.

"Name's Lucy. You must be Dean with our 11:00." She reached for my hand, causing her massive bosom to spread across the countertop, which resulted in a cavernous cleavage. Feeling embarrassed, I focused my eyes on her frizzy orange hair worn in the popular curly perm style, except her kinky strands didn't move like real hair. They didn't move at all.

She slapped a legal pad down and began asking me for general information. Each time she blinked, blue powder flashed from her eyelids and when she looked up, strange clumps coated her lashes like tar. Her jowls and neck were fleshy and loose, with an obvious demarcation line at her jaw between natural and unnatural skin tones.

She paused to size me up and gave me a knowing wink, as if we shared a secret.

"Been in the groomin' business 20 years, youngest daughter works fer me, other daughter's the pretty one. She wraps meat down at the grocery. Both are single an' free."

Up to that point, I'd been distracted by fluorescent pink smears across her teeth but the image of two younger versions of Lucy snapped me out of it. My eyes settled on my watch. "Uh, hey, look at the time... gotta get to work." I passed the end of the leash to Lucy and backed up, giving hurried instructions. "Give him an all over cut, leave his tail and ears long. I'll be back in a..."

The bells on the door jingled behind me, generating another round of barking from the poodles but this time, Snoopy joined them. I turned -- and had to stifle my own yelp. A slender blonde vision stood in the doorway.

"This here's Cassie," Lucy said from somewhere behind me.

I gazed into beautiful green eyes, searching for something to say but my brain waves had gone flat.

Lucy clapped again. "Shut up and get back here!"

This startled the dogs into silence and me into some level of coherence. "I'm Snoop, I mean, he's Snoopy and we're here--he's here for a hair bathcut...." My words trailed off and I could feel my face redden.

Lucy's voice boomed, "Name's Dean. Ain't he cute?"

"Hi Dean." She held out her hand, which I eagerly took, only to be caught off guard by her strength. She bent over to scratch Snoop's head. "And aren't you a handsome boy."

I no longer felt an ounce of sympathy for him. In fact, I fervently wished we could trade places. "You can pick him up in 2 hours. It's nice meeting you, Dean."

I left with weak knees and racing heart – poor Snoopy was in for a lot of haircuts. When I returned to the shop, showered, shaved, and wearing nice clothes, Lucy brought a fluffy Snoopy out from the back room, silky blue ribbons around each ear. Sliding my credit card across the counter, I rose on my toes to see over Lucy's hair for a glimpse of Cassie. "Uh, your daughter sure, uh, did a great job."

Lucy nodded toward the back room. "She's just gettin' started on a Teacup. Won't be done for another 30 minutes so you're stuck with me, handsome."

Signing the receipt, I mumbled my thanks and left, disappointed I couldn't thank Cassie in person. Stopping at a park on the way home, I let Snoop run and roll in the grass until he smelled like a dog again. When we returned home, I cut off the ribbons, filled his dog dish, and left for work, watching him in the rearview mirror, watching me from the bedroom window.

Images of Cassie floated across my preoccupied mind. Everything about her seemed pure and sweet and beautiful – she must have been adopted. Absent mindedly, I turned up the radio and began singing along with the lyrics

"Please change your mind,

and take the time,

Baby, I'm single and free,

So take a chance on me..."

And then the words struck me – they must be a sign! I slapped the steering wheel, believing God wanted me to ask Cassie for a date. I drove the last few miles, singing at the top of my voice,

"Since we're each alone,

I'm waitin' by the phone,

Baby, I'm single and free,

So take a chance on me..."

I entered the office and found Special Agent Tony Penna sitting on a desk, talking in low tones to a young woman who happened to be a clerk for the railroad. She lightly tapped a pen between her lips as she listened intently, her chair swiveling back and forth in a steady rhythm.

No matter what kind of women we met -- those who legally worked for the railroad or those who illegally used railroad property to sell sex—they all liked Tony. I grabbed the patrol car keys and jingled them between my fingers. "Come on Penna, time to make society a safer place."

"Be right there, Dean."

He turned back to his newest conquest. Taking the pen out of her hand, he wrote something on her palm. With blushing face, she leaned forward to watch, teetering on the very edge of her chair. When he joined me at the door, she sat dreamily studying her hand.

I elbowed his side. "I can't believe how women fall for your moves. Someday, you'll have to teach the rest of us."

He returned my good-natured jab. "Why would I do that? You guys are the reason I look so good."

For several hours, Tony and I patrolled the most likely places for transients; Stacy Yard, King Street Station, beneath the Alaska Way Viaduct and Fourth Street Bridge, but no luck. With an hour left in the shift, we decided to check the tracks running outside Bellevue, one of Seattle's bedroom communities.

As we neared the city's eastern boundary, we passed a line of warehouses. "Hey, slow down, Dean. Somebody's up there." Tony pointed to a stairway on the side of one of the darkened buildings, where a man stood alone. "Wonder what he's up to?" Tony mused.

"It *is* late and there's no car around..."

The idea struck us at the same time. "Let's check him out."

Parking a block from the warehouse, we sneaked up on the suspect. Technically, we weren't on railroad property and should have called city police but it had been an awfully slow night.

We paused at the bottom of some concrete steps, listening to the unmistakable sound of a door being jimmied. With a nod to each other, we bolted up the stairs and tackled the suspect, scraping his face against the brick facade.

Once the man recovered from his initial shock, he fought back -- to our delight. Three pairs of fists swung, hit and missed in the dark as we jostled in the limited space at the top of the steps. When we began to tire, Tony jumped the man from behind and knocked him down. I swiftly cuffed him.

No one said anything as we each caught our breath. And then the man spoke, clearly angry. "Who the *hell* are you guys?"

"Railroad police."

The man's voice raised in pitch. "This isn't railroad property!"

Tony and I feigned surprise. "Are you sure?"

We walked him down the steps, sputtering threats about calling his lawyer. After making a call for Bellevue police to transport him to jail, we discussed our options for the arrest, settling on attempted burglary and prowling. Once that was done, Tony moved on to his passion – sports.

"So, do ya' think Bochte (all-star first basemen for Seattle Mariners) will have another good year?"

"Hope so…what do you think, Mister? You or your lawyer a Mariners fan? Whoops, never mind, your ride's here."

A car pulled up, two officers emerged and we shook hands. While one helped the suspect into the backseat, the other told us some good news. "We called the building's owner. He confirmed no one should've been on the property at this hour."

Tony and I gave each other high fives, thanked the officers for their quick response time and returned to the office to make a report. "Hey, Dean, why don't you go home and let me do the report."

"You sure, Tony?"

"Yeah, I've got a date in an hour so I've got some time to kill."

"A little late for a date, isn't it?"

Tony winked. "Not for this girl." With a slap on his shoulder, I said goodbye and headed home.

The next morning, the phone rang early – too early to be a random caller. I'd only been asleep a few hours but managed to drag the receiver to my ear. "Yeah, hello, this is…" My groggy mind couldn't think of any more words.

"Dean, I want to see you, now!"

Recognizing the boss's voice, my mind snapped to full alert. "Uh, hi, Jerry, what's goin' on?" I squinted to read the clock near my bed, the room still dark from the early morning hour.

"Get down to my office, ASAP!"

He slammed the phone down hard. I dragged myself out of bed around a still sleeping Snoopy, pulled on a pair of jeans and left without brushing my teeth or hair. What could be so important? And had he forgotten I'd just worked a night shift?

Parking my Mustang beside Tony's Camaro, an uneasy feeling came over me. When I saw him in the hallway, I asked, "Do you know what this is about?"

"Nope, but I'm sure we can explain our way out of it."

"Explain our way….Penna!"

When we presented ourselves in the boss' doorway, Jerry waved us in, a paper held tightly in his beefy hands. I noticed his large blocky body matched the massive oak desk he sat behind. We stood awkwardly in the middle of the room, waiting for him to say something -- anything. His deep scowl didn't help.

"Looks like you boys had quite a night."

I glanced at Tony who gave me a thumbs-up. "Yeah, Jerry, we busted a guy breaking into a warehouse."

"And which one of you wrote the report?" His voice sounded strained.

Tony puffed out his chest. "That would be me."

Jerry slammed the report down, rising from behind the desk like an enraged grizzly about to charge. "Apparently you two are a little *confused* about your commissions so I'm going to make it *perfectly* clear. You're paid by the *railroad* to patrol *railroad* property and protect *railroad* personnel. And if that isn't exciting enough for you, we've got plenty of *railroad* office work for you to do. Am I CLEAR?!"

Jerry crumpled Tony's report and threw it into a trashcan. His eyes glared at us from a very angry, flushed face. He definitely had our full attention.

"And you sure as hell don't state in your report you were patrolling non-railroad property because you were *bored*!"

I looked incredulously at Tony. "You *wrote* that?"

Tony shrugged his shoulders.

"Now re-write this report and have it back on my desk in 15 minutes. Think you can handle that boys, or is that not *exciting* enough?"

"No problem, boss, we'll take care of it right away." We left the room in unison, nearly getting stuck in the doorway on the way out. Once out of earshot, I jabbed Tony's side. "She'd better have been worth it." The smile on Tony's face confirmed it.

We found a vacant desk and while I pecked out the words on an electric typewriter, Tony hovered behind me to catch my many spelling errors, fixing them with a tiny bottle of liquid paper. We returned to Jerry's office with the revised report, which he grudgingly approved and I headed home.

Since my next shift began that afternoon, I took Snoopy for a quick run around the lake and headed back to the office. To my relief, I'd be patrolling alone. I quickly scanned the roll call -- daily notices from the city police department, describing suspects who needed to be captured. I checked my gear: .357 Magnum, portable radio, metal flashlight, cuffs, 12 extra rounds of ammo, and a nightstick.

Next, I went to the Chief Clerk's office where I signed in and received keys for the pool car I'd be driving. Once settled in, I buckled my seatbelt and tuned the FM radio to a Christian music station. Its melodic harmonies competed with the company radio's discordant voices and continuous static.

"Amtrak Agent to Burlington Northern Special Agent."

I turned down the music and picked up the mike. "This is the Special Agent. Go ahead."

"Amtrak train crew in depot reports a deranged man needs to be removed from train."

"I'm on my way."

Since Amtrak didn't have its own police force, Burlington Northern's Special Agents covered their calls. And since the depot's downtown location attracted "unique" characters, we received these kinds of calls on a regular basis.

I re-parked the car, mentally preparing myself for what the dispatcher might have meant by "deranged." Was he a giant hulk threatening passengers with a weapon or a wild maniac tearing the train apart with muscles bigger than my waist? I threw open the depot's front doors and rushed inside. A ticket agent recognized me and waved me over. "This guy's crazy. We can't get him down from the upper deck because he thinks he's a chicken ... on a nest. Follow me."

"Uhhh, *nest?*"

The agent nodded. "Here we are."

Entering the train car, I climbed the narrow, spiral staircase to the upper level, taking note of the passengers' nervous glances and low tones. I found the conductor standing beside a neatly dressed man in a seat, legs tucked beneath him. He looked to be in his early 20's, wore his hair combed, had a clean-shaven face and trim build. Nothing unusual, except for the continuous soft "baaa, buck, buck, buck" coming from his half-opened mouth. He sounded like the plump red hens that scratched for bugs in my sister's garden.

I gently shook the man's shoulder. "Hey there, buddy, you okay?" He didn't react; his face maintaining a fixed expression of surprise.

The conductor spoke. "Somebody saw him drinking at the bar a little while ago and then we found him like this."

Assuming he'd mixed drugs and alcohol, I radioed for paramedics. Within minutes, two appeared at the top of the stairs, carrying medical equipment. They pulled gloves on, did an exam and told us, "We'll need to take him to the hospital for further tests."

One medic then addressed the man. "Sir, we're going to stand you up and help you down the stairs to the ambulance. Do you understand?"

He showed no comprehension.

The paramedics awkwardly lifted his unbending body and managed to get him down the aisle but the circular staircase to the lower level presented a dilemma. When we tried to carry him horizontally, his rigid body couldn't get past the first curve. If we held him between two of us, the stairs weren't wide enough for three people. Out of desperation, I heaved him onto my shoulders and took a few shaky steps before his dead weight sent me sprawling onto the floor.

And throughout all of this, the other passengers' attitude underwent a dramatic change. With each new idea, they'd cheer us on, wildly applauding until it failed, and then burst into laughter. Clearly, they'd embraced the challenge of removing our "fowl" friend from the train.

And then an idea struck me, or perhaps it was the only one left to try. Bending chicken man's knees, I sat him on the top step. With a paramedic behind him to keep him seated, I pulled his legs toward me, which slid his butt to the next step with a "thump." He stretched his neck as high as he could and squawked "CLUCK!" And that's how we descended to the lower deck -- Thump...CLUCK! Thump...CLUCK! Thump...CLUCK!

Once the paramedics securely strapped him onto a gurney and loaded him into the ambulance, I ran back upstairs to retrieve my radio. To my surprise, the Amtrak passengers jumped to their feet and gave a rousing ovation, the kind of appreciation we in law enforcement only dream about. I made several deep bows of gratitude and thanked them for their support.

When I reached my car, I heard a voice behind me. "You the Special Agent?"

I turned to find an Amtrak employee wearing the standard coveralls of the maintenance staff. I nodded and he continued in a frantic voice. "We're cleanin' a sleeper car an' found a dead guy in one of the beds."

I followed him across three sets of tracks to where a car had been uncoupled from the main train. Stepping through the metal door, we walked down the carpeted aisle, a row of windows to our right letting in shafts of light that fell on the walls of bedrooms to our left. Today's private sleepers had come a long way from the old-style berths of yesteryear.

The employee led me to where two coworkers waited in a doorway with solemn expressions. I squeezed past them and stopped. A mountain of a man lay on his back on top of the bed coverings, arms to his sides. His brown and yellow checked sports jacket hung open, revealing a blue and white striped shirt whose buttons were close to popping from his enormous girth. At least his polyester pants matched his shiny black dress shoes. Surrounding his slack open jaw, a moustache merged with a full beard, and together, they spilled across his chest like black strands of frayed rope. He lay as still as a corpse.

I stepped closer to watch for his chest to expand but it didn't move. I vigorously shook one of the man's shoulders but his mass jiggled like Jell-O. I pressed two fingers against his fleshy neck and held his wrist but there was no pulse at either site. I studied his face for a long time.

"Can I borrow that?" I asked one of the employees, pointing to a metal flashlight in his hand. Puzzled, the janitor handed it to me. I turned back to the man on the bed and slammed the flashlight across the bottom of his shoes with a resounding "whack!"

All three employees gasped and swore. "What're you doin'? He's dead!"

Putting a finger over my lips, I held the light over my head. "You're about to see a miracle." Pivoting around to the prone figure, I took another hard swing at the giant's soles and then another.

The voices behind me took on a higher pitch as they asked incredulously, "Are you crazy? What the…"

The man's legs began to move. "Whasssshhh goin' on…"

"It's check-out time and this is your wake up call." I shouted into the man's ear.

With great effort, we helped him to a sitting position, slid him off the bed and with two of us in front, and two in back, guided him off the car and in the direction of a cheap hotel. Catching our breaths, we watched him falter across the parking lot on spindly – but well dressed – legs wobbling beneath his orb-shaped body.

The employees still watched in disbelief. "How'd you know he wasn't really dead?"

"Gentlemen, we are trained observers with a *nose* for details as fine as *hairs*, and I simply *moved* on the evidence presented me."

Flat Car

Chapter 7

Facing Elliott Bay, I inhaled deeply of the salt-soaked air, trying to calm my nerves. I'd come to Alki Beach in west Seattle for my open-water dive test after four classes in an indoor, heated pool. If I passed, I'd be a *real* scuba diver with an official diving license.

As a young boy, I never missed an episode of the TV show, *Sea Hunt.* My vivid imagination would take me on undersea adventures with sunken ships, marauding sharks and pirates. When I climbed the tree in our front yard, I was really in a crow's nest atop a tall mast, searching for an island with buried treasure...

"Time to get our gear on so we can get started."

Nine students and I lined up behind individual piles of gear under the watchful eyes of Mike, our instructor. First step – put on a rubber wetsuit to keep me warm in the 52-degree water. Inch by agonizing inch, I stretched the thick material over one limb, and then the other, trying to ignore the burning sensation of pulled hairs. Curious onlookers gathered on the beach behind us, making me self-conscious.

Next, I picked up an inflatable life jacket called a buoyancy compensator, placed its straps beneath my arms and blew into its rubber tube to fill it. This would keep me afloat until I needed to submerge. If I wanted to hover at a specific depth level beneath the surface, I could adjust the amount of deflation.

I hoisted a heavy metal air tank onto my back and wrapped a 15-pound belt of lead weights around my waist. Pulling a rubber hood over my head and neck, thick rubber gloves on my hands and cumbersome flippers on my feet, I finally felt ready to enter the sea. Or did I? Adjusting the bright yellow bug-eyed goggles across my face, the once friendly waves took on an ominous appearance from within the suffocating confines of my wetsuit and equipment. Flutters of panic welled up inside me as my heels sank into the sand.

Mike stepped into my goggles' field of vision, his muscular arm pointing to something in the ocean behind him, something tiny and bobbing among the gray swells. Squinting to see, I swallowed hard. Surely we weren't expected to swim all the way out there—didn't he believe in using boats? His shouted instructions sounded slightly muffled through my hood.

"…that buoy…dive to bottom…our class…wait 'til…me."

We stumbled into formation behind him like an awkward troop of ducklings tripping on over-sized webbed feet. When the waves splashed above our ankles, we turned to enter the water backwards, only to face our audience who now resembled waving mimes, their voices drowned out by the sounds of our own breathing.

I carefully lifted and placed one foot behind the other, concentrating on keeping my balance against the push and pull of the undertow. Once the water reached my waist, I relaxed my knees and let my body sink – and then heaved myself back up. The shock of icy water flooding in through my wetsuit's neckline caused involuntary gasping as muscles tightened and blood retreated. Blowing air out in short bursts like a woman in labor, I tried again, but this time in one-inch increments.

By the time my shoulders were beneath the surface, the others were ahead of me. I willed each limb to do its part; right arm up and over, kick legs, left arm up and over, kick legs. Like a wounded seal, I haltingly paddled toward a buoy that didn't get any closer, wondering why I'd signed up for this.

When I finally reached the buoy, the rest of the class had descended. I peered beneath the surface for a glimpse of them but the water's visibility ended just inches from the surface. "De-De-Dean, yo-yo-you're not ba-ba-acking out na-na-ow!"

Shoving the respirator firmly between my chattering teeth, I made sure air flowed freely. I took hold of the chain beneath the buoy. Slowly venting air from the buoyancy compensator, I began my descent, using the chain as a guide. When I reached a depth where I could no longer see light above, I stopped to hover in the blackness. Did I *really* want to do this? Maybe reruns of *Sea Hunt* would be enough.

Forcing a resolve I didn't feel, I continued pulling myself downward, headfirst, hand over hand, into the murky depth. When my fingers touched the soggy bottom, I carefully righted myself, keeping a death grip on the buoy's chain. I expected to see the others but instead, only thick sediment swirled around me. Had I descended the wrong buoy? Did the Twilight Zone really exist? I'd wait two more seconds before scaling the chain back to light, life and a land hobby.

A goggle-framed face suddenly loomed close to mine. Recognizing Mike's blue eyes, I feebly waved, thankful he couldn't hear my pounding heart. He motioned for me to remove the respirator from my mouth, which I did, and then return the rubber mouthpiece between my teeth, clearing it of water. Next, he pointed to my goggles, which I pulled off and then put back on, tipping my head while blowing air out of my nose to remove the water. Satisfied I could accomplish the basics, he motioned for me to follow.

At first, Mike's flippers and bubbles were all I could see in front of me, cutting a swath through the silt and debris. And then, as if we swam through a magical wall, we entered clear water and a world unlike any I'd ever seen.

Long blades of emerald surf grass and wrinkled kelp bent back and forth to the rhythm of the waves above, revealing synchronized schools of green and brown fish. Bump-fleshed sea stars, resplendently colored orange and purple, hugged dark rocks bristling with giant green anemones and spiny sea urchins. Red crabs grazed all around us, alternating claws to mouth as they moved steadily across the rocky bottom. Several of their smaller cousins clung to the brown kelp fronds like ruby brooches on wind-swept scarves.

Under Mike's supervision, we moved reverently among the swaying plants and surreal creatures. Even if we'd been able to speak, I believe we would have remained silent, floating awestruck above the sea floor as if afforded a glimpse of heaven.

Too soon, the air gages reminded us of our visitor status, forcing us to leave the world that supported our thin crust of land. One by one we rose, bobbing to the surface like the wild ducks that fed off these shores.

The return swim seemed shorter, the excitement of the dive fueling adrenaline to my limbs. Emerging from the water, my once more gravity-bound back felt relief as I shed the tank and weighted belt.

Our class lined up dripping wet with happy, goggle-indented faces for a final count. Mike shook each of our hands with his usual enthusiasm. "Congratulations, fellow divers. You can pick up your certificate at the shop tomorrow."

We dispersed amid calls of thanks and promises to keep in touch. Excited from the experience of achieving a boyhood dream, I strode quickly to Mike's pick-up and set the borrowed tank and regulator into the back seat. Keeping the wetsuit on, I jumped into my car and headed for the groomer's. I'd scheduled a bath for Snoopy to coincide with this dive in yet another attempt to impress Cassie. I hoped once she saw me in my gear, she wouldn't be able to resist a date with a *real* scuba diver.

Within half an hour I pulled up to the now familiar address. I ran my fingers through my damp hair, wiped the sweat off my forehead and flushed cheeks and got out of the car, ignoring a strange weakening sensation in my body.

My entrance through the front door generated the standard yelps but this time I made a big fuss over the poodle with the broken leg; I'd learned she belonged to Cassie. When I heard her voice, I sucked in my stomach, pushed out my chest and struck a casual pose, as if I always did errands in a wetsuit. Her eyes met mine, her mouth opened in surprise and I leaned forward to hear the words I'd been dreaming of.

"Aren't you *hot* in that suit? I've only been diving a couple of years but after a few minutes out of the water, mine just gets too hot."

My shoulders sagged as low as my hopes. "So you're a diver too, huh? Uh, yeah, these things do get hot but I didn't want to miss picking up Snoop, after his, uh, hair thing...so you've been diving for, uh, *years*?"

I felt like an idiot. Sweat streamed down my face and my body had turned into a clammy mush. Cassie tilted her head and smiled. "Why don't we go diving together someday?"

I looked up sharply, my senses rallying. "That'd be great! I'm off the day after tomorrow, how about then?" I didn't want to sound too eager but at this point, I had nothing more to lose.

She nodded. "You can pick the place since you've probably done more dives."

I made a mental note to purchase a book on dive locations since my entire experience consisted of a swimming pool and one buoy.

On the drive home, Snoop dragged his front paws over the bows in his ears, moaning in frustration. I gently tugged at them until they slipped off. "Look at it this way, Snoop. Now that I've got a date with her, you won't need as many haircuts."

After a quick run and shower, I left Snoopy at home and picked up the patrol car to begin an evening shift. Within minutes of leaving the depot, I received a call.

"Special Agent, this is dispatch."

His voice had the usual urgency but I couldn't blame him. Dispatchers were responsible for all trains arriving and leaving the train yards in a specific area, from a specific direction. For Seattle dispatchers, this meant three yards and four directions. Once a train pulled into a yard, the Yardmaster took over, but up to each yard's boundary, dispatchers were in charge.

Their office was a large room in one of the administration buildings. A board covered an entire wall with rows of blinking lights representing tracks and all standing and moving trains in any given area. Dispatchers had to know when to switch trains from a main line to a "siding" or sidetrack, turn on color-coded lights known as "signals" to control train traffic and be available by radio to all railroad personnel, while keeping each train's schedule a priority. Delays were costly.

"Special Agent, we've got a derailment northeast of Seattle, near Marysville."

"Dispatch, this is Special Agent. I'm on my way, ETA 60 minutes."

Any number of obstructions can cause derailments: from a broken rail to large rocks. When 10,000-ton trains traveling 60 miles per hour come off a track, the speed and weight of the cars are capable of pushing, flipping or crushing the cars in front, along with anyone riding inside. And depending on what the train carried, the scenario could include explosions and fires, spilled hazardous material or unidentifiable bodies.

Once a Special Agent has assessed the initial damage and delegated its containment to proper departments or companies, our primary challenge would be to stop the pilfering of spilled merchandise that still belonged to shippers. The railroad, as the carrier, held the legal responsibility for safely transporting goods from start to destination; Special Agents were part of that promised security.

"Special Agent, I've also notified the Mechanical Foreman. He's on his way."

"That's good news, dispatch."

The Mechanical Foreman will organize a team of workers and machinery to get derailed cars either back onto the tracks or cut up for scrap metal. Once damaged cars are removed, tracks can be quickly repaired. An out-of-service track means stopping and/or re-routing trains. And when train movement is affected across the country, delayed shipments to cities can result in huge monetary losses.

Along with the Mechanical Foreman, our Freight Damage Prevention Department would be sending a crew to re-load any merchandise scattered at the derailment site. And however long that took, Special Agents would be there to protect the employees and property while investigating the cause.

After driving north on I-5 for almost 40 minutes, I turned east onto Highway 528 just south of Marysville. The darkening sky looked gray where it met the deep black silhouettes of pine forests and not-too-distant Cascade Mountains. House lights stretched further apart in the increasingly rural landscape. I envisioned families settling in for the night: stories being read to pajama-clad children, pets curling up in favorite places, parents thankful for another day. At least those were my childhood memories of bedtime and I wanted to believe it held the same for others.

When my headlights illuminated a sign for Highway 9, I turned left, heading north once again. After a few miles, where the road intersected the tracks, I pulled over. I'd found the derailment.

A tangle of boxcars lay strewn for three-quarters of a mile, looking more like toys left by a giant toddler than cars weighing several tons each. A few had been reduced to compacted blocks of metal while others had slammed into each other so tightly they seemed melded into one, making it difficult to get an accurate count. Miraculously, the derailment had involved only the last section of the train, with the front cars and engines escaping unharmed. I picked up the radio mike. "Special Agent calling train 166"

"Conductor on train 166, go ahead Special Agent."

"Just letting you know I'm on the scene. The Trainmaster should be arriving shortly. Is everyone alright?"

"We're all okay."

"Glad to hear it, Conductor. I'll be here if you need anything."

Replacing the mike with feelings of relief for the crew, I hiked across the uneven brushy ground to get a closer look at the damage. I knew the train crew would wait in the engine until the Trainmaster arrived to question them and retrieve the speed recorder for analysis. Once done, and dispatch gave the go-ahead, they'd uncouple their engine along with any intact cars and be on their way. Since trains were beginning to run with computers, cabooses carrying the conductor and rear brakemen were becoming a thing of the past. And fortunately for this particular train, a computer had recently been fitted so the entire crew had been riding in the front engine.

Reaching what I guessed to be the halfway point of the mile-long train, I stopped in amazement. In either direction, the soft moonlight shone on twisted cars, train wheels and giant sections of railroad tracks angled sharply towards the sky. And covering the misshapen metal were countless rolls of toilet paper, their pastel colors gently waving like so many tattered banners.

An oddly shaped hill rising up from the derailed cars caught my attention. With my flashlight, I could make out the structure's base -- two boxcars slammed into each other to form an inverted "V." Two more cars had crashed into them and been thrust higher, creating a giant teepee. A tank car with the words PROPANE GAS across its side balanced precariously on top. Not good, I thought, as I caught a whiff of something familiar. My flashlight's beam revealed cans of salmon at my feet, many of them crushed and oozing.

A rumble from the steel above startled me but before I could react, hundreds more cans of salmon rained down, hitting me as I tripped and stumbled my way out of the growing pile. The sound attracted the Mechanical Foreman, who'd just arrived to do his preliminary evaluation. Noticing me rubbing my head and shoulders, he asked,

"You alright? I'm Frank Quinn…what have we got here?"

"Dean O'Shea, and yeah, I'll be fine. This seems to be the worst part of the damage. What does your manifest say about that propane tank?"

Illuminating his list with my light, he compared the number on the car's side with a line of tiny typed words. Fortunately for us, the propane car had been traveling empty.

"I'll continue looking around but since this is the weekend and we're on a branch line here (as opposed to a main line) with no emergencies, we probably won't get a team up here 'til Monday."

"Sounds good, Frank. I'll let my boss know so we can schedule our department."

We shook hands and I returned to the car to drive to Marysville where I found a payphone to call the boss. At this late hour, Jerry would be at home.

After one ring, he picked up. I gave him my initial assessment about toilet paper, canned salmon and one balancing propane gas car. Since the site would need surveillance 24 hours a day until repaired and cleared of cars, Jerry immediately set up a schedule for the Special Agents. I, of course, had the first shift.

Returning to the derailment, I spent the next few hours looking over, under and behind cars for further signs of damage or spilled material, as well as for any bodies of transients who chose the wrong train to ride this evening.

The temperature had continued to drop, feeling colder despite my jacket. I wished my replacement would hurry and get here. Up on the road, headlights pulled in behind my car. Jogging stiffly toward the approaching figure, my breath looked like the puffs of a steam engine getting started. When the figure didn't return my greeting, I guessed his identity before his scowling face stepped into my flashlight's beam -- Henry Stone.

To minimize my time in his presence, I recited the briefest of summaries, letting him know the Mechanical Foreman had already been here and the clean-up crews would arrive on Monday.

"That means we're the only ones here tonight and tomorrow." Henry muttered with disgust.

"But we're miles from town so the looters and media won't even know we're here."

Henry clicked on his flashlight, zipped up his jacket and stormed off in silence. Watching his retreating back, I mused, "He's either a brilliant eccentric or an anti-social jerk." I hoped one day to figure out why he showed so much hostility toward me...and everyone else, for that matter.

I made the long drive home despite bleary eyes and a numb brain, thankful for the minimal pre-dawn traffic. I fell asleep before my head hit the pillow.

That same afternoon I was back on I-5 north, passing miles of Seattle suburbs nestled beneath brooding skies, for my next shift at the derailment site. When I arrived, and with the advantage of daylight, I counted twenty-two train cars either knocked onto their sides, shoved into another car, flipped over or partially buried in the ground. In the center of it all, like an official monument to the event, rose the metal teepee with the propane car on top, prettily striped with bathroom tissue.

The special agent on duty, Gary Landers, approached me. "Bad news, Dean – a few people have shown up and taken some of the toilet paper. Otherwise, it's been quiet."

"I wish we could just let them have it," I muttered. "It'd sure be easier for us."

"But if someone gets hurt picking it up, you know we'll be blamed. Plus the railroad might want to recover their loss by re-selling it. Anyway, see 'ya tomorrow."

With a sigh, I trudged off toward the derailment, trying to convince myself there really was honor in guarding toilet paper. After an hour of checking around the site, I returned to my car and settled in for the long hours of boredom remaining in my shift.

Tuning the radio to a local station, I rested my head against the seat and closed my eyes. The DJ commented about storms moving into the area and then made an announcement.

"Hey folks, we've got some good news for our listeners in Marysville. There's been a train derailment on Highway 9 with lots of spilled stuff, free for the taking. Let's help the railroad out."

Sitting bolt upright, I envisioned mobs trampling me in their desperate rush for toilet paper and canned salmon. "Get a hold of yourself, Dean. How many people were even listening, and out of those, how many would actually drive all the way up here?"

Convinced by my logic, I leaned back, listening to the peaceful sounds of birds, crickets -- and slamming doors. A shiny Oldsmobile had stopped on the road a few hundred feet from where I'd parked. An elderly, gray-haired couple strolled across the field and began scooping up rolls of toilet paper. When their arms couldn't hold any more, they headed back to where I waited, holding out my badge.

"Good afternoon, folks. I'm with the railroad police and what you're doing is illegal."

The man looked at me suspiciously. "Well, that's not what they said on the radio."

Keeping a stern tone, I replied, "I'm sorry sir, you've been misinformed. Please drop the bathroom tissue and return to your car."

The couple let the rolls fall to the ground but the man had to have the last word.

"You better tell that guy on the radio he don't know what he's talking about."

"Sir, that's a good..." He slammed the door and drove off. Well, that wasn't too bad but my relief proved short-lived when the sound of more voices reached my ears. While I'd been confronting the couple, several vehicles had lined up at the opposite end of the derailment. A large group now swarmed the site.

I drove the short distance to the other end, parked and ran to the nearest looters. Holding out my badge while catching my breath, I called out, "Railroad police. Drop the toilet paper and return to your vehicles."

The crowd politely listened, some even smiled, and then they eagerly resumed their scavenging. Since I was in plain clothes and most people weren't aware of railroad law enforcement, I could understand their not believing me.

A young man in faded jeans and a plaid shirt defiantly strode toward me with an armload. "If it's on the ground, it don't belong to nobody so it's free."

The others paused to watch. I cleared my throat. "That's where you're wrong. The railroad is still responsible for this merchandise and if you take it, you're stealing."

He sized me up and then passed me, tightly clutching the stolen goods. I ran up and pulled his arm, causing the rolls to fall. "Let me ask you," I said, hoping a different logic would change his mind. "Do you really want to go to jail over toilet paper? Imagine what your cellmates will think when you tell them why you're doing time."

The image must've weakened his confidence because he hesitated. Just then, a female voice broke in, "Billy, let's get outta here."

Saluting me with his middle finger, he joined a young girl in a pickup and sped off down the road. A few others had overheard our conversation and were returning to their vehicles, empty handed and grumbling about the unfairness of it all. But as quickly as they left, new looters replaced them at both ends of the site. I needed a different angle.

"People, please, I've got to warn you. This toilet paper has been treated with a special chemical called dye-oxy-snoop. It causes a burning rash that lasts for weeks. I'm with the railroad and I wouldn't be able to sleep tonight knowing you didn't know what we know so I, uh, wanted you to know."

"How do they get the chemical out before selling it to the public?" A woman's skeptical voice rose from somewhere in the crowd.

Thinking quickly, I answered. "Well, I'm not supposed to let you in on company secrets but once the paper reaches the warehouse, special ultraviolet lights neutralize the chemicals before going to the stores. But when transported, it has to be treated to prevent the bugs and rats from eating it."

A heavy silence. People exchanged glances. Rolls were tossed down and the disappointed returned to their cars only to be replaced with another wave of hopeful bargain hunters. I must have run ten miles that shift.

When the setting sun's last flush of color still tinged the horizon, the roiling billows of clouds released a heavy rain, sending people scurrying to their vehicles. The pretty pastel tissue dissolved into gray fibrous clumps dotting the brush and running down the sides of train cars.

The railroad, being self-insured, wrote off the 925 cases of 74,000 rolls of toilet paper as a loss.

Chapter 8

With the Marysville accident requiring additional hours from our department, my day off had been cancelled in order to fill a downtown night shift for a fellow officer. Normally, I'd be sleeping in preparation for the shift but Cassie had agreed to spend the day with me and no amount of sleep deprivation could deter me.

While Snoop stretched out in a square of morning sunshine on the living room floor, I pored over the book *Best Puget Sound Diving.* After considering our options, I decided on Underwater Park in the picturesque community of Edmonds. True to its name, the park lay beneath the waters of the Puget Sound and featured several man-made reefs, a guiding rope and buoy system. But my primary reason were the small floating docks for divers to haul out and rest on – I didn't want to expose my beginner status by drowning on our first date.

With rented diving equipment and filled air tanks in the backseat of my Mustang, I nervously pulled up to an older, two-story waterfront residence on Redondo Beach, where Cassie lived with her mom. I took my time locking the doors to give my thumping heart a chance to settle down. The front door swung open and out stepped Cassie wearing a blue swimsuit, white shorts and a dazzling smile. The sunlit halo around her blonde hair confirmed to my awestruck mind that she really was an angel. I leaned against my car for support.

She waved and said, "Hi."

My voice caught and what came out sounded like a squeak. Cassie laughed as if I'd done it on purpose, and winked. "Looks like we're ready to go diving."

We packed her gear into the trunk and headed north on I-5. As it turned out, her inquisitive, open personality made conversation easy.

"I've always lived in the northwest so I can't imagine living anywhere else. It has everything I love – ocean, mountains and cool weather. During a college break in my freshman year, some friends and I hiked the Chilkoot Pass in Alaska. It took us five days but it was so *beautiful* being so high up in the mountains."

Her expression grew reflective, her voice softer. "Being in nature brings out a feeling in me that I don't get anywhere else, like my spiritual side is more free somehow." She paused. "Does this make any sense? Am I boring you?"

"Yes…no, I mean, yes, it makes sense and please don't stop talking…I'd love to know *every*thing about you."

Peripherally, I could see her studying my face while I watched the road. Had I come across too crazy about her too soon? Seconds ticked by. A jazz tune played on the radio, its alto sax' sensual, smooth melody weaving effortlessly around the deep timbre notes of a steel guitar. The one light and playful, the other focused and constant.

Stealing a glance, I saw her bite her lower lip. I understood her hesitation -- each step toward trust was a leap into risk. "Okay, but only if you tell me about you. Deal?"

Somewhere between doggie baths and today's drive, her voice had forged a secret line of communication with my heart. Whenever she spoke, giggled or sighed, this betrayer of feelings would tremble or race. "Deal. So go on about your wild spirit."

She gazed out the window, allowing me a glimpse of her profile: gently curved forehead, a straight nose and high cheekbones that framed her full mouth, like two halves of a pear. Sprinkled across the widest part of her cheeks were a smattering of freckles, the color of light gold.

"When I was little, I imagined rainbows were the stained glass ceiling in God's church, birds were the choir and mountain peaks the steeples. Whenever Mom decided we needed church -- which happened whenever she and dad didn't get along -- we'd go to Calvary Chapel. And it was so hard for me to sit through those long services so I'd beg Mom to take me to God's church where I knew I could run and climb trees. Of course she'd ignore me."

She giggled at the memory; my heart raced accordingly. "Mom would get so frustrated with me at times…but I think children have an intuition that's more true, less cluttered." She sighed; my heart skipped a few beats.

I took the exit for Edmonds and followed signs to the ferry terminal, the easiest landmark for finding Underwater Park

"Anyway, that's why I'm passionate about nature. And since my parents divorced many years ago and I'm not a kid anymore, going to Calvary Chapel with Mom is actually something I enjoy." She looked directly at me. "Okay, Dean, your turn to talk."

Being a guy, I preferred the abbreviated version to reduce the chance I'd flub my words. I nervously tapped my finger on the steering wheel and took a deep breath.

"Raised in Nebraska, two sisters, both married with kids, they and my parents still live back there. As far as God's concerned, my parents took me to church every week but I didn't take to church until after Vietnam, and even then, I wasn't sure what I believed. For years after the war, nightmares and flashbacks kept me drinking and smoking."

I stole a quick look to see her reaction but to my relief, sadness without judgment shone from her eyes. My finger slowed its tapping.

"When I finally decided to put in the time to learn about *who* Jesus is, life became more clear and my crutches less necessary. Just before I moved here, I quit smoking and drinking so my mom would have less to worry about."

Cassie sighed, "That's so wonderful." She clasped her hands tightly. "Nightmares *are* awful. There were times I was afraid to close my eyes at night…" Her voice trailed off.

"Because why?" The protective male in me began to stir.

She pointed ahead. "Hey, we're here already."

We'd turned onto Main Street and were crossing a set of tracks when I saw where she pointed: a small parking lot fronting a stretch of sand called Bracketts Landing Beach. This natural boundary would be our entrance into the protected acres of Underwater Park. South of the beach, the Washington State ferry's dock extended over the water, where vehicles were already lined up for the next boat to Kingston. To the north, a jetty of massive boulders in the shape of a backward 'J' offered some protection from currents and wind.

I parked the car and we unloaded our gear, she smiling with excitement, me filled with dread. The moment of truth had arrived. With a lump in my throat, I began wrestling with my wetsuit, hoping Cassie would be too busy putting hers on to notice.

Of the many lessons in life, I'd learned when things get off to a rocky start it's best to move away from the cliff because things are only going to get worse. I should have paid attention. Cassie easily slipped into her wetsuit as if it were made of silk while I had to tug at mine. When I looked up, she smiled sweetly as if enjoying the wait, commenting about the gorgeous view of Mt. Baker. I pulled harder but my perspiring skin made the fabric even more stubborn.

When I finally zipped the last zipper, Cassie was chatting about *gulls*. I needed to invest in some talcum powder.

When it came to the heavy air tanks, though, my workouts paid off. I slipped my arms into the straps, lifted the tank and let it slip down over my back a few seconds ahead of Cassie. With a newly bolstered ego, I put on hood, goggles and gloves, picked up my flippers and waded into the icy water, Cassie right behind me.

As soon as the water reached my waist, I leaned back to allow the buoyancy compensator to keep me afloat so I could put on my flippers. But in my worry over the wetsuit, I'd under-inflated it and immediately sank to my eyes. The shock caused an involuntary gasp that sucked seawater into my lungs. Panicked, my feet shoved off the bottom, launching me out of the water like a breaching whale. Holding both hands over my mouth, I coughed uncontrollably and loudly, tears and mucous streaming from my eyes and nose. Cassie gently helped me back to shore wheezing and hacking like an old man. If she ever went out with me again, it would be out of sheer pity.

It took several minutes to clear my lungs. With assurance from Cassie that this kind of thing happens to the best of divers (she was being nice), we re-entered the water and swam to one of the resting docks 75 yards from shore. Below us, according to the park's brochure, lay a thriving marine community. We put our regulators between our teeth and dove in.

Descending side by side felt incredible, as if our bodies had already found their rhythm without ever having touched. Keeping my face angled toward her, I tried to commit to memory everything about this moment; her long legs bending in sync with mine, her slim waist and hips twisting ever so slightly with each kick, long arms barely grazing her sides. She looked as fluid and graceful as the water surrounding us.

We'd reached a depth of 20 feet when a school of Sea Perch, gold-colored bodies flashing stripes of metallic blue, passed on either side of us. We watched them disappear behind some rocks, from which a bug-eyed face peered out. Curious, we swam over to investigate and found a Copper Rockfish, its large head dwarfing a beautifully patterned body of brown, yellow and white swirls. Its erect spiky dorsal fin reminded me of the hairstyles worn by kids who called themselves "punks."

As we hovered, our undulating flippers parted long strands of eelgrass, exposing a variety of crabs; brown Dungeness wider than my hands to pebble-sized purple crabs with attitude. Cassie found a hermit crab with hairy legs and waved it in front of my face. As a joke, I removed the regulator and opened my mouth wide – and she promptly stuffed it into my mouth, mischief in her eyes. I pulled it out before its pincer found my tongue but the experience proved too much for the creature – it ejected from its shell like a pilot from a burning plane. We watched its naked curled body tumble into the sandy silt.

Seeing concern in Cassie's eyes, I swept aside the seaweed in search of the now homeless hermit, uncovering a beautiful sea slug with orange-tipped protuberances, but no crab. I nestled his former home in the sand, open side up, in case he returned.

We swam toward a long, rectangular shape I guessed to be one of the side-walls of a submerged dock, its silhouette covered with dense clusters of plumose anemones. At this depth, these creatures were almost 2 feet tall, their creamy white tentacles waving like pom-poms at a Friday night football game.

I was feeling like a bird soaring above a magical garden when enormous torpedo-shaped forms moved beneath us. Cassie pointed, gave me a thumb's up and *swam after them!* Clearly, she'd never read about sea monsters.

I kicked hard to catch up but when I reached the side-wall's corner, I hesitated, looking for her bubbles. Where had she gone? I nervously glanced behind me suspecting another prank, but saw only bristling sea urchins and an impressive Sunflower Star moving across the bottom after them.

I turned back and almost dropped my regulator. Several gaping jaws with sharp teeth faced me, only yards away. Even more intimidating, the bodies attached to the jaws looked huge, nearly five feet long, with powerful tails fanning back and forth. I tried to recall the brochure's descriptions of fish and guessed these to be the park's famous Lingcods.

A form moved behind the giants and they shot off in different directions, leaving a swirl of silt in their wake. From this cloud emerged the sweet goggled face of Cassie, eyes dancing with excitement at her encounter. I wanted to hug her but instead pointed to my air gage and up toward the surface; our adventure had come to an end. She nodded and we ascended together, our shoulders lightly touching. Despite the 52-degree water and thick wetsuits, it felt like fire streaking through me.

We packed our gear into the trunk of my car, showered and changed in the park's public restrooms. When she emerged, her long damp hair made little rivulets down her blue tank top. Her faded cut-off shorts were held up with an equally worn leather belt. I wore slacks and a bright red and yellow patterned shirt.

Walking to a nearby restaurant, Cassie excitedly recounted what she'd seen, her hands as expressive as her face. I leaned in close to listen but my real intention was to smell her hair and skin, anticipating what she'd feel like in my arms.

Our candlelit table overlooked the Puget Sound with Mt. Baker's snowy slopes in the distance but for the first time since arriving in Seattle, I forgot to look at the view.We shared a delicious meal of cedar-planked salmon and coconut prawns, laughed about first dates and worst dates, and completely forgot others were in the room.

She stretched her arms and yawned. "Well, this has been a great day but I need to get home. Lots to do and Mom needs help running the shop."

Glancing at my watch, I couldn't believe two hours had passed since our dive.

"You're right, it's late and I've got a buddy to walk before working tonight."

I paid for the meal and joined her in the restaurant's entryway, intending to open the door for her, but she reached for the handle first. My hand covered hers and she shyly retracted it. "Oh, sorry, I'm not used to...thank you."

On the drive back, I experienced another first – staying *below* the speed limit and showing goodwill toward rude drivers. I merely waved them on, not wanting to miss a single word Cassie spoke.

When I parked in front of her house and we climbed the steps to the front door, the conversation grew quiet. Why did this part always feel so awkward? I decided to be bold and reached for her hand. "Snoopy's developing early signs of bath-anxiety and frankly, I'm worried. Another date would help alleviate his symptoms but I told him I didn't know what you'd say."

Cassie laughed and gave my hand a tight squeeze. "Well, then, for *Snoopy's* sake, we better have another date." With a wink, she turned and walked through the door, leaving me suppressing a mad desire to yell and jump for joy.

But later that afternoon, when I entered the office to begin an evening shift, the stern face of Henry Stone brought me crashing back to earth.

He snarled in disgust, "We're short cars so you and I are patrolling together. And I'm driving!" Tossing the keys into the air, he snatched them to emphasize ownership. I followed him and warily slid into the passenger seat.

"So, where we eating tonight?" I asked, trying to sound cheerful.

Henry turned the key. "It's too early to think about dinner."

I leaned back – it was going to be a long, miserable night. He drove behind the depot, edging the car through a narrow, short tunnel to a vacant building known as the U.D. Office. Inside were stored test boards and radio equipment used by the railroad decades ago. Outside, a yellow light bulb above the front door acted as a beacon for bugs, transients, drug dealers and prostitutes. But not tonight. The building's windows were unbroken and both doors secure. We proceeded to a longer tunnel on the other side that connected the waterfront to the depot for freight and passenger trains.

Two sets of tracks ran between the rounded walls that reeked from the diesel oil splattered across its surface. With flashlights in hand, we entered the cold, dank interior. After several sweeps with our lights, Henry whispered, "Looks clear. Let's check the west end."

We returned to the car and I sensed, rather than saw, movement beneath the Fourth Avenue Bridge, on the opposite side of the tracks. Its large concrete pillars provided an ideal hiding place for people who didn't want to be seen.

"Henry, I think someone's…."

"I saw him."

We'd both been in the military and fought in Vietnam. Our training took over as we automatically put distance between us. Henry held his flashlight in front of him with one hand, his other resting on his holstered gun. Knowing our lights made us targets, I held mine to the side.

Beneath the bridge, the hairs on my neck raised. A footstep somewhere close. I swung my flashlight's beam and a man's face appeared.

"We're with the police department. What're you doing here?"

The man wore clean clothes and neatly combed hair – an appearance not usually seen among trespassers. "Just out for a stroll." His tone and demeanor were too calm.

I stepped closer, suspicious about what he might be hiding. "Keep your hands where I can see them. Are you here by yourself?"

"Yes, I'm alone. And I really don't want any trouble."

I noticed a bulge in his jacket. "What's in your pocket?"

Henry moved to a position behind him.

"Nothing."

"Then you won't mind if I have a look, will you?"

The man's expression underwent a dramatic change. His eyes darted back and forth and then he bolted; or at least he tried. Henry grabbed his arm and twisted it across his back. The man screamed and came around at Henry with his free arm but I stopped it and together, we wrestled him to the ground, kicking and yelling. We'd just cuffed and pulled him to a standing position when a form suddenly hurtled out of the darkness, knocking into my side. Henry held onto the first suspect while I scuffled with the new arrival, my light lying on the ground where I'd dropped it. When I felt one of the pillars against my shoulder, I swung his body hard into the concrete. I heard a loud exhale before he slid to the ground. Finding my light, I cuffed his hands behind his back while Henry scanned the area for anyone else who might be hiding. It gave us time to quiet our pounding hearts.

"Where'd that guy come from? I didn't see him 'til he was on you."

"Believe, me, I was just as surprised as you were."

Henry pulled a plastic bag filled with white powder from the first suspect's jacket pocket. "You boys weren't doing a drug deal, were you?" he asked in mock surprise.

"That's not mine, and these cuffs are too tight," the well-dressed man complained.

"Yeah, so are mine. I'm gonna file police brutality against you jerks." My attacker was a wiry little guy in camouflaged pants and shirt.

Henry called the Seattle Police for transport to jail while I checked the first man's cuffs. Blood stained his wrists so I loosened them but when I turned him back around, he spit on my cheek and chin. I wanted to punch him senseless.

"You do that again, I'm taping your mouth shut," I said through clenched teeth.

City officers arrived and placed both men in their caged patrol car. But before leaving, one took us aside. "The guy who's bleeding says he has that disease we've been hearing about -- AIDS. Better make sure you clean any blood off you and your cuffs."

"He's the guy who spit on me. I don't suppose we could charge him with attempted murder?"

"Nice try but the prosecutor won't go for it. You better stick with drug dealing and assault on a police officer."

Back in the car, Henry's attitude changed. He held out his hand. "Dean, you're alright." I shook it, hoping Henry and I would work out after all.

We drove back through the short tunnel, my mind distracted by the encounter with AIDS. I happened to glance at the tunnel's deck paralleling us about four feet above the ground when I saw shadows move. "Henry, we've got someone on the platform."

We jumped out and directed our flashlights along the stained concrete wall, revealing a strange huddled mass of bodies – and it was moving. Heaving ourselves up and over the edge, we stepped around broken glass and piles of garbage.

"Police Department. What's going on here?"

Three faces looked up; two were white and male, the third, Native-American and female. The absence of clothes below their waists answered my question.

Henry barked out orders. "You two stay put and you, lady, get dressed. We need to talk to you."

She clumsily untangled herself from the men, rolled over onto her back and began pulling a pair of pants over one leg. But her limbs were flailing in slow motion like an overturned turtle so whatever progress she made was soon undone. She began to swear and yell at herself until one of the men told her those were his pants. Muttering incoherently, she felt around for another pair and somehow managed to hoist them to her waist. She made her way to where we waited, leaning heavily on the tunnel's wall.

"Are you here against your will?" I asked softly.

Her dark eyes squinted into the beams, her breathing loud and labored. "I wass okey dokey 'till you come long. We havin' a pahty, a lil pahty, an' dese men brung da wine an' I'm da fun."

Her slurring showed she'd had a head start on the drinking. With the stench of urine and rotting garbage heavy in the air, I couldn't imagine anyone feeling in the mood for anything in this rat hole.

"Okay, you two, get your clothes on-- now!" Henry yelled.

The men dressed quickly and reached for something behind them.

"Leave those bottles, you lost them." Henry's menacing tone convinced them it was non-negotiable. They jumped down from the platform and casually walked away.

The woman swayed closer, her body odor and foul breath causing us to step back. "Whass wit you guys breakin' up my pahty?"

"You're not going to party here anymore," Henry replied, "And if you do, you're going to jail where there's no booze."

"I'm Crazy Mule!" she yelled, "An' I' pahty if I wanna an' you're not goin' ta shtop me."

"Well Crazy Mule, before your next party, you need to take a bath -- you stink!" Henry held his nose.

She turned to me. "How'd you like to pahty wit me, hansome?"

"Yeah, handsome, what's holding you back?" Henry was clearly enjoying this turn of events.

"The sad truth is, Crazy Mule, I can't dance half as good as Henry here."

She laughed the exaggerated manner of the inebriated, nearly falling over. We helped her down from the platform and watched her hobble out of the squalid tunnel; her pants inside-out and twisted around her bulging stomach. Knowing what she traded men for liquor, I couldn't help comparing this scene with one from over a century ago, when her ancestors lived on these northwest shores. Then, Crazy Mule would have walked straight and proud, an Indian maiden of the Suquamish tribe whose connection to the sea and its seasons provided them with everything they needed.

Back then, she would have given her heart to one brave, their union blessed by a wise chief so respected by European settlers, they named the city of Seattle after him.

"Damn it, who pushed me ovah, dumb injun." Crazy Mule had stumbled and fallen to her hands and knees. "Lookie, lookie what I foun'." Spying cigarette butts on the ground around her, she began scooping them up between uncoordinated fingers and stuffing them down her blouse. With each find, she'd gleefully chuckle as if she'd found treasure.

She managed to get back on her feet, swaying precariously until she gathered enough momentum to stagger away, unaware of the bloody scrapes on her hands and elbows. Her long black hair hung dull and frayed, creating an uneven line across her back.

She eventually disappeared from view down a narrow access road, just another drunk Indian living on the tracks.

Chapter 9

Known as the Emerald City, Seattle's landmarks, waterways, and islands attracted tourists from around the world, especially during the warm summer months. Different languages floated out from sidewalk café's, people thronged specialty shops and art galleries, and families with young children, souvenirs in hand, strolled along the waterfront.

But the real proof tourist season had begun could be seen in the increased traffic. Taxis, shuttle vans and red transit buses competed with "Ducks," WWII amphibious landing craft that transported laughing, waving tourists through city streets and across Lake Union's waters. Our monorail, touted as the world's first, carried crowds high above congested streets to Seattle Center's most popular sights: the Space Needle and the Pacific Science Center.

While appreciating this boon to Seattle's economy, I found myself avoiding downtown. And then it hit me - why not utilize the surrounding water to get away from the crowds? I began checking the newspaper and one Sunday, the Seattle Times' classified section listed a 21-foot sailboat moored at Friday Harbor at a price I could afford.

Wanting to make a special trip of checking out the boat, Snoop and I picked up Cassie and her toy poodle, Potpourri, early one morning. We drove north for two hours to Highway 20 and then west to a ferry terminal in Anacortes, a quaint main-street town on Fidalgo Island.

We'd been dating for three weeks now, meeting for lunch, dinner or a walk nearly every day. On the rare occasion our work schedules prevented us from seeing each other, we'd have long talks on the phone.

"I hope this sailboat's what I've been looking for," I said, "but if not, this is a great way to spend a summer day."

She smiled, my heart did its usual flip-flop and I stifled the words I knew were too soon to say; I'd fallen in love with her.

Driving onto the ferry behind lines of people and their vehicles, we were soon on our way to the San Juan Islands where Friday Harbor is the county seat and a favorite destination for commercial fishing boats and private yachts. The archipelago lies northwest of Seattle, accessible by boat, air or the Washington State Ferry that services the four main islands - Lopez, Shaw, Orcas and San Juan. Surrounding them were nearly a hundred smaller islands, many with private homes and docks, others visible only during low tide.

Leaving the dogs in the car, Cassie and I walked hand in hand to the front of the ferry, drinking in the unobstructed view of white-topped waves and dark rounded silhouettes on the horizon. Gulls entertained us with incredible aerial displays for pieces of food thrown from the upper decks.

"I've dreamed of owning a boat ever since I went sailing with a friend in Nebraska." Seeing her skepticism, I added, "There *are* bodies of water in Nebraska big enough to sail on, but this," I nodded at the ocean, "is definitely bigger."

I gave her a tight hug and she lay her head on my shoulder. "You'll make a great sailor."

Bursting with confidence, I envisioned sailing around the world, just she and I and our dogs. We'd dock at exotic locales or anchor offshore and swim to an isolated strip of beach.

"This is Lopez Island. All drivers please return to your vehicles." The captain's announcement interrupted my reverie. We remained at the bow to watch the ferry push up against a landing dock. Around us, several bicyclists waited for an employee to lower the ramp that connected the ferry with the island best known for its flat terrain and friendly residents. Once the bikers pedaled off, vehicles disembarked, new ones boarded and we left Lopez, the captain steering from the opposite end so the ship always went forward.

It didn't take long before the next island--Shaw--came into view. To our amusement, a nun in a dark brown habit and orange safety vest waited at the landing dock, her hand on the button to lower the ramp. She looked to be in her 60's, wearing glasses and a shy smile at the people scrambling to take her picture. We learned this island's nun-run terminal had been established when the Catholic Church purchased the tiny general store adjacent to the dock in the 1970's. And whoever ran the store greeted the daily ferries.

After a few passengers walked onto the car deck from Shaw, we were once again underway, this time headed for the largest island, Orcas, recognizable on a map by its horseshoe shape. A brochure promised a panoramic view of islands, mountain ranges and the ocean from atop Orcas' Mt. Constitution, the highest point in the islands. Many cars and passengers unloaded and came aboard at Orcas Village before the ferry moved smoothly across the deep blue seawater to San Juan Island.

We rejoined the dogs and when it was our turn, drove across the ramp and found a place to park close to Front Street. The view from the main intersection of Friday Harbor resembled a living postcard. Victorian-style buildings overlooked a picturesque marina where enormous yachts dwarfed smaller boats passing in and out of slips. Tall, straight masts rising above clean-lined hulls rocked in sync with waves and wakes, setting off a clanging of ropes and riggings. It was music to my ears.

As we walked the main dock's weathered planks in search of the boat for sale, Cassie noticed anemones growing just beneath the water's surface. She lay on her stomach, her beautiful face reflected in the water, and softly brushed the plumes with the tips of her graceful fingers. When each anemone felt her touch, it wrapped pink fleshy tendrils around her hand. I stood mesmerized by how innocently she sat on the edge of wonder without being self-conscious.

She looked up with a giggle. "Sorry, couldn't resist petting the wildlife." I pulled her to her feet and held her close, gazing into her eyes with earnest. "Don't ever change, Cassie."

She must've seen something in my expression because she blushed and stammered, "Ummm, we better find that guy with the boat."

The sailboat turned out to be exactly what I'd hoped so the seller and I shook on our deal. He agreed to have it delivered to Seattle the following week which gave us a few hours until the ferry returned. Snapping leashes on the dogs, we took lots of pictures along a trail that hugged the island's edge where it dropped into a sun-speckled ocean.

We eventually made our way back to a grassy slope overlooking the harbor. Cassie sipped espresso while our silly dogs jumped and played around us. This scene would forever be etched in my mind.

The next day, still high from being with Cassie, I began my work shift with a routine inspection of an in-bound train entering Balmer Yard. As it slowed to a halt, a big burly man leapt out of a boxcar and lumbered away from me.

I called out to him, "Hey, there, stop where you are."

He turned and faced me, his 6'5", 250 pound frame casting an immense shadow. Callused hands pushed back a worn captain's hat from his lined forehead, revealing wisps of gray hair. His pants, shirt and jacket were surprisingly clean for someone who'd been riding the rails. Tilting my neck back at an angle, I searched for signs of aggression but saw none. "I'm with the Railroad police and I need to see your ID."

"Oh yeah, I was warned about you guys." His smile seemed sincere.

"Did you also hear it's illegal to ride trains?"

He shrugged his broad shoulders. "Didn't know how else to get here." He pulled a driver's license from a wallet in his backpack. "Here's my ID, sir."

I noticed his license listed an east-coast address. "You're a long way from home. What brings you to Seattle?"

"Ran into some tough luck back home and heard Alaskan skippers were needin' crews. So here I am, hopin' my luck's gonna change."

Noticing his wedding ring, I asked, "Did you leave your wife?"

"Had no choice. We didn't have the money to travel and I wasn't about to bring my wife and kids on a freight train. But soon as I get a job, I'm sendin' money back home so they can join me. And I'm countin' the days."

He impressed me as an honest man making the best of a bad situation. I handed him back his ID and gave him directions to the pier known as Fishermen's Terminal where Alaskan boats regularly docked. I had no doubt he'd find work--strong, willing men were much sought after in the fishing business.

Genuine gratitude shone in his eyes. "Thank you, thank you," he repeated, pumping my dwarfed hand in his.

"Just get that family of yours out here as soon as you can."

His grin widened. "Yes sir!"

Watching him walk away, I felt an impulse to do more for this stranger who I normally wouldn't have thought twice about helping. I'd noticed his empty wallet in the faded backpack that bounced lightly against his back. He couldn't have much in the way of possessions or food. Taking a twenty-dollar bill from my pocket, I wadded it tightly in my hand. "Hey, wait a minute. You dropped something."

He turned around, a puzzled look on his face. "When you took out your ID, this must've fallen out."

Studying the crumpled bill in his hand, he held it out to me. "It's not mine."

I kept my hands at my side. "It's yours, friend."

He stared at the money for a long time. And then, with a nod and a touch of his cap, he walked away.

The radio crackled. "Burlington-Northern Yardmaster to Special Agent."

Yardmasters were exactly what their title indicated: in charge of all trains moving within the yards, unlike dispatchers who were in charge of trains outside the yards. Balmer to the north, Stacy Street on the east side and South Seattle each had a designated Yardmaster to handle the continuous stream of trains needing crew changes, detaching and/or adding boxcars, flatcars or tank cars for cross-country shipment to and from Seattle. Their offices were in elevated towers high above the tracks with windows on every side. Cameras mounted on light poles enabled the Yardmaster visual access to every section and if he needed a better angle, he could move the camera from his office.

"This is the Special Agent."

"Seattle Police Officer Sergeant McClain wants you to meet him at Golden Gardens Park immediately."

Curious about this unusual request for a personal meeting with someone outside the railroad, I drove the 15 minutes to the well-known park bordering the Puget Sound. When I arrived, I maneuvered my vehicle next to the familiar blue and white patrol car.

"Sergeant McClain, I'm with the railroad police. My name is…"

The sergeant waved his hand in front of his face, cutting off my words.

"Listen up – I don't have a lot of time here. A homeowner's claiming something is happening in the woods near her place." He paused for effect, looking over his shoulder as if we were spies trading secrets. "When the sun goes down, a man starts howling."

"Uh, that's very interesting but my jurisdiction is…"

The sergeant slapped the side of his car. "Hah! That's the best part. We checked the map and it's on *railroad* property. Besides, I don't have time for piddly-ass complaints from the rich folk on the hill. I've got *real* criminals to catch."

Unfortunately, some city, county and state officers shared his attitude toward our department. Railroad police were sometimes seen as inferior, despite the fact we were one of America's earliest law enforcement agencies, organized and trained by the brilliant Scotsman, Allan Pinkerton. Our commissions extended across the U.S. and Canada, more in line with Federal Marshals. My defenses started to rise.

"Well, Sargent, you better show me the area cause I don't want to keep you from doing whatever it is you do." And by the looks of his protruding belly pressed against the steering wheel, I assumed it included taste-testing at the local bakeries.

Motioning for me to follow, he turned his car around and drove a distance of maybe 100 feet. We hadn't even left the parking lot. He pointed to a steep wooded hillside on the other side of the road where expensive homes lined a ridge.

"How long has the, uh howling been going on?"

"About two weeks now…hey, you gonna use a wooden stake or just trap him?"

He cackled at his own joke but I ignored him, quietly studying the hill. He slammed his car in gear and drove off, but not without a final comment. "Let me know if he bites!"

Muttering, I grabbed my standard equipment -- pistol, radio and steel flashlight – and walked across the street. With no visible trails to follow, I had to push my way through thick underbrush and thorny blackberry vines. The closely spaced trees prevented me from climbing in a straight line so every few minutes, I'd have to stop and get my bearings from the road below. The higher I climbed through the vegetation, the more I wondered what or who might live up here, completely hidden from the rest of the world. Only a few dim shafts of sunlight penetrated the branches above, keeping the air damp and cold.

Forty-five minutes passed. Exhausted from tripping and stumbling my way up the incline, I decided this had to be the sergeant's idea of a prank. Disgusted with my gullibility, I began the arduous descent when I noticed a small clearing. Since any break in the brush would make it easier, I clambered diagonally across the hill and into a primitive camp made with plastic tarps stretched between four trees. Scattered around and beneath them lay wind surfing boards, bicycles, ice chests, lawn chairs and colorful stacks of beach towels. "Someone's been helping himself to people's things on the beach."

I remembered recent complaints of theft at Golden Gardens. "But why would he give away his hiding place by howling?"

A branch cracked behind me. I turned to face an emaciated man with frizzy bleached hair coming directly at me, insanity in his unblinking eyes. His pockmarked cheeks were puffing in and out like a bullfrog on speed, but his strides were wide and uncoordinated, making it easy to trip him. He slid face first at my feet.

"I'm with the police department and you better calm down right now!"

The man scrambled to his feet and lunged, but once more, his actions were clumsy and rushed. I knocked him down again. "Calm down or you're going to get hurt."

He got up on hands and knees and bared his teeth. Did he really believe himself to be a wolf or did he just want me to believe it? When he leapt, I stepped aside and tripped him again. "You're not a quick learner, are you?"

I grabbed his arms from behind, placed my foot in the middle of his back and pulled. His snarls turned into high-pitched yelps. I cuffed him and sat him upright. "Just what do you think you're doing?"

"These woods is mine an' I'm gonna keep it thet way." So the wolfman could speak after all.

"Well buddy, these woods are *not* yours and neither are these items you've been collecting."

He tilted his head, opened his mouth and let out a mournful howl. Our conversation had clearly come to an end so we slid and stumbled our way down the hill, me keeping a firm hold on his cuffed hands. When we finally emerged from the brush, sticky strands of spider webs and leaves stuck to our hair and clothes but I didn't bother brushing them off.

We crossed the street to the car, where I pushed him to a squatting position by the rear wheel. "You pee on these tires, you'll be wearing ankle cuffs. Got it?"

He curled back his lips and growled. I radioed dispatch, but had to shout when he started barking at the passing cars.

"This is the Special Agent – tell Seattle's Sergeant McClain I found an *un*real criminal for him to transport."

Chapter 10

"What a perfect day," I sighed, sitting at the stern of my new sailboat, hand on the tiller, sails snapped full. The bow cutting smoothly through the waves created an exhilarating ride across the surface.

Beside me sat Cassie, head back, eyes closed against the bright sun, long blond hair blowing across her face and my shoulders. Snoopy and Potpourri were stretched out over the railing; ears flapping against their necks as they sniffed at scents carried on the breeze. I felt like the luckiest guy in the world.

Cassie opened her eyes and met my gaze. Wrapping her arms around my neck, she brushed her lips against my ear. "I'm so glad you thought of going to Blake Island today."

"So am I…Snoopy's been missing Poo-Poo (our nickname for Potpourri)."

Cassie playfully slapped my arm. "And what about me?"

"Oh, yeah, Snoopy's been missing you too." I ducked, knowing I'd get a reaction from her but when I looked into her eyes, I became serious. "I couldn't *wait* to be with you." Leaning over, I kissed her delicious lips for the hundredth time that morning.

With a squeal, she hugged me tight. "I love being with you, Dean."

Blake Island lay nestled in the Puget Sound, about eight miles southwest of downtown. According to legend, Chief Seattle had been born and raised among its tall pine forests and sandy shoreline. The island stayed in private hands until becoming an official state park in the early 70's, with miles of trails for hikers and bicyclists. But the island's most popular attraction was Tillicum Village, where salmon dinners were prepared and served by Native Americans in an authentic long house. Lucky ticket holders arrived by private boats or tour boats throughout the summer and fall to enjoy scrumptious feasts and traditional dances.

When close to shore, I dropped anchor while Cassie unpacked our lunch of fried chicken and potato salad – one of my favorite meals. With paper plates balanced on our knees, Cassie took my hand and bowed her head to say grace but I never heard a word. My senses were in overdrive at her touch.

As soon as we heard "Amen," the dogs and I dove into our food before she'd even lifted her fork. And, as always, the dogs finished first and then strategically positioned themselves at our feet to give us 'the look,' a combination of pitiful starvation and undying hope.

To resist giving in, I distracted myself with the scenery – to the west, beyond Blake Island, were the snowy Olympic Mountains, more jagged than the Cascades. Behind us, the picturesque skyline of Seattle. Above were a few wisps of clouds. Below, the water…and directly in front of me two pairs of pleading brown eyes. I couldn't take it anymore. I asked Cassie to pass me the barbecue sauce. As soon as she turned, I tossed Snoop and Poo-Poo pieces of chicken -- they'd never tell.

With lunch over, I pulled up anchor and navigated the boat alongside the island's public dock and tied up. We found a trail and spent the next few hours hiking and learning about native plants from the interpretive signs along the way. Mid-afternoon found us on a secluded beach, Cassie snuggled against my chest, dogs curled at my feet.

"Hey you, we need to head back home," I whispered in her ear. She stretched her arms and sighed.

"You're right, but promise me we'll do this again, and soon."

"How about every week for the next 50 years?"

She giggled as if it was a joke and I let her believe it. We returned to where we'd moored, boarded our sailboat and prepared for the trip home. Using the motor to get out into open water, I maneuvered the hull to take advantage of a stiff westward breeze. We raised the mainsail and jib, feeling proud as they billowed into graceful curves against the sky, assuring us a steady pace back to Redondo Beach. Once underway, the dogs retreated into the cabin for a nap while Cassie settled at the bow with a blanket and pillow.

An overwhelming sense of peace came over me. I closed my eyes and listened to the waves, the boat's gentle rise and fall lulling me into a relaxed state. My limbs began to feel heavy...I tried in vain to hang onto the tiller. Soon, my arm slipped off just before my head rolled forward onto my chest.

I don't know how long I slept but when my eyes flew open, loud whooshing sounds were coming from somewhere close. I bolted upright and searched the horizon, relieved when I saw the familiar West Seattle landmarks. But Cassie, wide-awake and pale, sat transfixed on something behind me.

I turned around -- and stopped breathing. A racing regatta of sailboats was headed straight for us, with two 60-footers in the lead running bow to bow. "Cassie! Lower the sails while I start the motor!"

Slamming the hatch shut to keep the dogs below, I pulled hard on the starter rope until the outboard sputtered to life. Cassie had the mainsail down and was securing it around the boom with trembling fingers. I pushed the motor's handle so we were at a right angle to the oncoming racers, hoping they'd see us in time to adjust their course.

"I don't think we can get out of their way in time!"

Cassie looked up from stuffing the smaller jib sail into a nylon bag. "Would they really ram us on purpose?"

Rationale told me they wouldn't but the lead boats bearing down on us said otherwise. Their elegant bows rose sharply out of the water only to dip back down in perfect rhythm with the waves and each other. With just yards separating us, both continued to sail, not giving an inch, grim determination on each skipper's face.

Cassie buried her face in my chest. "I can't watch!"

The first boat streamed past our stern in eerie silence, her full sails a magnificent sight if it weren't for our precarious position so close to her side. We were now squarely in the path of the second. I held my breath and Cassie. But at the last possible moment, the captain varied his course so as to pass within inches, spraying water onto our deck.

Meeting the skipper's eyes, I felt the utmost respect for his superior skill in avoiding someone that had literally fallen asleep at the wheel. Graciously, he tipped his captain's hat and then resumed his position, eyes forward, face to the wind.

Overwhelmed with relief at our close call, we made it back in record time under power, grateful we wouldn't be in the local news. When we reached Redondo Beach, I tied my sailboat to an offshore buoy and transferred belongings and dogs into a smaller skiff. "Dean, *promise* you'll bring a thermos of strong coffee next time."

"I've got a better idea. How about you learn to sail?"

"Only if you learn to make coffee."

We shook on it and she helped me pull the boat onto shore. With a kiss and a tight hug, we said goodbye until tomorrow. Watching her walk across the street to her mom's home, the diminutive Potpourri prancing at her side, I missed her already.

Checking in at the office, I found Henry waiting for me with what resembled a sincere smile. "Looks like we're patrolling together."

"Sounds good to me, Henry. You driving again?"

He threw me the keys. "Nope, you are."

Catching them above my head, I asked, "By the way, where we eating tonight?"

With a shrug, he replied, "You name it."

Driving up and down bumpy access roads, we tentatively made small talk about family and the railroad until interrupted by dispatch. "Special Agent, we just received a call from Amtrak telling us they hit someone on the east-bound main line tracks, between First and Fourth Avenue."

"Dispatch, this is Special Agent. Our ETA is 10 minutes."

Though local police completed reports on injuries and deaths involving the railroad, we still had to conduct our own investigation. If the accident resulted from employee misconduct, the problem could be corrected, but when pedestrians wandered onto the tracks, there wasn't much an engineer could do to avoid a collision. With cars weighing up to several tons each behind an engine, it could take up to a mile to come to a complete stop.

We found the passenger train idling on the main line with several people huddled behind the last car. Just beyond them, between the rails, a body lay face down, its twisted limbs jutting out at unnatural angles. At first glance, we could tell the corpse had been rolled as evidenced by deep cuts marking the victim's back, shoulders and head. His scalp lay peeled back to expose a wide crack in the skull. A severed arm and foot lay outside the tracks.

"We better call the coroner, Henry, and see if we can figure out what happened."

A man spoke up. "I'm the conductor of the train that hit this guy. Dispatch already called for paramedics and Seattle police."

"Good," I replied, "Can you tell us what happened here?"

"I didn't see anything. I was riding in a passenger car."

He gestured up the tracks. "The engineer's still in the cab. You should probably talk to him, but he's pretty shook up."

Leaving Henry, I strode past several cars to the head engine where I found a middle-aged man behind the controls, staring blankly out the window. He didn't hear me enter. "Excuse me, sir." He jumped.

"I'm Special Agent O'Shea. You okay?" He exhaled and weakly shook my hand.

"Do you feel like answering some questions?"

"Go ahead." He went back to staring out the window.

"What happened?" A long silence. I lightly touched his shoulder. "If you'd like, we can do this tomorrow."

His voice shook. "We'd just come around that corner, goin' 'bout thirty miles an hour, when we saw this guy lyin' cross-wise on the tracks. His head was on one rail and his feet on the other. Just before we hit him, he looked directly at me and then..." He rubbed his eyes.

"Did he make any attempt to get up?"

"Nope. I was hopin' the plow would move him but..."

Modern freight and passenger engines had a steel plate in front, similar to the scooped blade of a snowplow, which had replaced the fan-shaped, cowcatcher of yesteryear. If anything sizeable ended up on the tracks, it could often push it to either side. But in this case, the victim had been pulled beneath the engine and rolled by each car passing over him. At some point, his body had been tossed close enough for the wheels to cut off an arm and foot.

"I kept soundin' the horn and ringin' the bell, while I put the train into emergency stop. But the guy just *lay* there..." The engineer's voice trailed off.

"The city police will be here shortly. They'll probably ask you the same questions."

When I returned to Henry, two paramedics were checking the torso for vital signs in order to declare him officially dead. They were still performing their examination when Seattle police arrived to question the conductor. With nothing to do but wait, I scanned the surroundings with my light, surprised to find a transient sitting in the weeds.

"Henry, we might have a witness. Let's go talk to him."

The man's weathered skin looked like a piece of dried apple, but if typical, he would be younger than he appeared, by maybe ten or fifteen years. Transients lived dangerous, isolated lives and when paired with addictions -- the most common being alcohol and tobacco -- they aged quickly. We rarely saw any past 60 years old.

He didn't stand when we approached. "Excuse me, sir. We're railroad police. Did you see what happened here?"

The man looked from us to the body. "Yeah, I seen what happened. Somebody got run over by a train."

"Did you actually see him get hit by the train?"

"Nope. He was layin' on them tracks when I first come up here an' I assed him what the hell he was doin'. Must've scared him cuz he jumped up an' run away. But he must've come back an' done what he did cuz now he's over there dead."

I wrote the report according to the transient's story, questioned the remaining employees and compared notes with the city police. Everyone agreed it appeared to be suicide. The train crew re-boarded to continue their run, the officers and paramedics packed up and drove off, and we were left to wait for the coroner.

Henry and I sat in the car discussing the weather and work, as if normal conversation could mask the abnormal scene lying just outside. After two uncomfortably long hours, the coroner arrived and pronounced the obvious. We assisted him and his aide in bagging the body parts and headed to the nearest all-night Denny's for dinner.

When our meals arrived, I shoveled scrambled eggs and ham, smothered in ketchup, into my mouth but Henry's hamburger sat untouched on his plate.

He watched me, frowning. "How can you eat after what we just saw?"

I shrugged, "I'm hungry." But the truth was I'd found a way to disassociate from those things that triggered depression or panic by convincing myself they didn't matter. What I didn't know was how long I could hold back this emotional dam before it spilled over into other parts of my life.

A call came through from dispatch. "Special Agent, a train conductor passing through the west-end of the downtown tunnel reported a naked man running around inside."

Henry shot me a look of exasperation. "Dispatch, we'll be right there."

I clutched my stomach. "A *naked* guy…now I feel sick."

The one-mile tunnel's west-end met the busy shopping area of Seattle's waterfront, a popular place for tourists and locals. We made a quick scan of the parking lot near the tunnel's mouth as well as the north side of the tracks, but didn't find anyone, clothed or naked. At the yawning entrance, our lights barely pierced the blackness.

"Maybe he's further inside," Henry muttered. "Better check it out."

We followed our moving beams, taking shallow breaths to avoid inhaling too deeply of the diesel fumes. Dripping water echoed with the crunch of our uneven footsteps alternating between rough wooden ties and loose gravel.

"I don't think we're going to find…."

Henry's words were cut off by the unmistakable 'singing' tracks make when a train is close, a kind of buzzing, chirping noise like cicadas on a hot afternoon. Except we were in a narrow space, two blocks from where we'd entered.

I turned and sprinted, my light jumping wildly in front of my feet. Henry panted right behind me. "If you fall…I'll run…you over."

Keeping my eyes on the opening, I willed myself to make it, ignoring my burning, suffocating lungs. The engine's deafening roar now bounced off the walls around us and the ground shook beneath our racing feet. I didn't dare look back; I didn't want to know if we weren't going to make it.

When we exploded into fresh air, our legs collapsed and we tumbled to the side. The train emerged mere seconds after us.

Between breaths, I said, "If our streaker's…in there…he's covered in soot…and stone deaf."

"Special Agent, are you at the west entrance of the tunnel?" It was the engineer from the train we'd barely out-run.

"Yes… we… are," Henry confirmed, his chest still heaving.

"There's a guy with no clothes on west of your location, by a parked vehicle."

Henry swore. "What!?! We're…almost run over…and he's by our car!" He stormed off with clenched fists and sure enough, a young naked man sat in the weeds near our front bumper. At least we could skip the physical search and go straight to the questions.

"Hey buddy, what're you doing out here with no clothes?" I asked.

The man looked up with bloodshot, swollen eyes, startled. "Who, who are you guys?"

"We're railroad police. Now answer our question."

The man leaned forward with his chest on his knees, gingerly rubbing the top of his head. "Not sure. Was partyin' with some friends and got really wasted. I remember makin' some moves on a girl and next thing I knew…"

A mischievous gleam appeared in Henry's eyes. "How long you been like this?"

"If this is Saturday, the party was last night."

I shook my head. "If you only knew what could've happened to you out here, passed out and naked."

He groaned. "That was definitely my last party."

I snorted, "Yeah, right. Next Friday night, you'll be trying the same thing on a different girl."

Henry and I knew we couldn't send him away in his current state of undress. The local mission would be closed but we knew Goodwill had a drop-off site in a nearby lot.

"Tell you what – we'll go pick out some clothes so you can get to a phone. What's your shoe size?"

"Thanks, man…I swear this won't happen again…I wear a ten."

We soon returned with an ensemble we'd personally selected just for him, a quarter to make a phone call and directions to the *second* closest pay phone.

He dressed and crossed the well-lit street, glancing nervously back at us.

We waved goodbye to our party animal, satisfied with how sharp he looked in size 44 green pants, bright red suspenders, an extra large Mickey Mouse T-shirt and two-toned bowling shoes, size twelve.

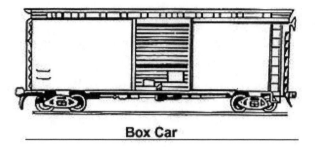

Box Car

Chapter 11

I awakened one early fall morning like I did every morning: with visions of Cassie filling my head. But when I learned she had a full schedule, Snoop and I headed for one of our favorite places -- Saltwater Park.

Facing the blue-gray waters of the Sound, the park lay halfway between Seattle and Tacoma, two rival cities that had literally buried a hatchet here. On clear days, the Olympic Mountains rose up across the sea's expanse and just off shore, an artificial reef had been built for divers to explore and creatures to inhabit.

I parked where the upper trail began and let Snoop run off leash through a towering wooded slope that overlooked the beach. My steaming breath reminded me summer's zenith had passed as I stuffed my hands deeper into my jacket pockets. Remnants of a lingering coastal fog floated around us like wisps of smoke, leaving drops of moisture on bark and leaves.

Snoop kept up with my brisk pace, checking for smells in the cold morning air and at the base of every tree we passed. Somewhere in the forest, a woodpecker's rapid staccato drilling echoed among the cedars and fir. Eventually the upper trail ended at a viewing area where I could look out over the restless waters of the Sound. It still took my breath away.

I patted Snoop's head. "Let's head over to the lower trail." His ears perked up, eyes intently looking into mine, tail wagging. I liked to think it meant, "Why sure, I'd love to walk there with you."

We raced back to the car and drove to another parking lot from where a paved pathway meandered along the shoreline. Walking with my canine friend of many years to the music of the sea always gave me a sense of wellbeing.

When Snoop and I reached a bulkhead of large rocks, I paused to watch the waves explode into fingers of white spray that seemed to reach for the sky. But as one wave rose, I saw something floundering near its crest and then disappear. Telling Snoopy to stay, I carefully picked my way over the slippery boulders for a closer look, the crashing surf soaking my face, hair and clothes. Close to the edge, I got down on my hands and knees and peered down into the swirling, hissing seawater, shocked to see a face looking up at me.

An enormous dog, its front claws gripping the rocks, paddled weakly with its back legs against the receding and surging tide. His big brown eyes pleaded for help.

"How did you end up down there?"

Sliding my feet into the water, I managed to wedge them into the wall against the pummeling sea. Freezing water filled my shoes and in seconds, I could no longer feel my toes. Using one hand to hold the ledge behind me, I bent over and grabbed the loose skin around the dog's neck only to be knocked sideways by an icy wave.

I straightened up to catch my breath and study the situation. The dog's size, tawny color and dark mask identified it as a Mastiff – just my luck. He must have weighed 130 pounds, if not more. Even if I could get a better hold, I'd never be able to pull him out of the water with one arm and numb feet.

I slid down closer to the dog and cradled his massive head in my hands. The dog's skin felt cold and his legs were moving in a mechanical motion. I had to figure out something fast.

I stood up to check on Snoop. To my surprise, he'd caught the attention of a family in the picnic area, barking wildly and running around them in frantic circles.

"I need help over here!" I yelled above the roar of the waves.

A man left the group and walked tentatively toward me, no doubt wondering why he could only see my wet head and shoulders.

"There's a dog in the water and I can't pull him out."

He sized up the situation. An unspoken understanding passed between us and we knew what to do. Waiting for a break between the waves, I quickly lowered myself back into the water, praying my shivering legs would hold up for just a few more minutes. With a heave, I pushed the dog's hindquarters up and forward while the man, lying on his stomach, grabbed the dog's neck with both hands. We hoisted the waterlogged animal high enough for his back legs to get a foothold and he clambered the rest of the way on his own. Water streamed off his heaving flanks, noisily splattering on the ground.

The man held out his hand and pulled me up. "Is this your dog?"

"No, I found him like this."

Standing on either side of the dog, we guided him haltingly across the bulkhead and onto the grass, his bedraggled tail hanging limply between long wobbly legs. Two young boys approached us timidly, their eyes wide at the sight of the enormous dog between us. A short stocky woman with a caring face produced a fuzzy blanket and soon all three were briskly rubbing the dog. The Mastiff gazed at them in unabashed adoration. "Can we keep him, Dad? Pleeeease, dad, can we?"

I don't know…" His hesitation gave them hope.

Trying to tip the balance in the boys' favor, I said, "Be a real shame if he survived the ocean only to be put down because no one wanted him."

I fervently prayed the man's resolve would soften, knowing I wouldn't be able to bring the dog to the pound. Instead, Snoopy would end up with a playmate half the size of my living room.

The dog's soulful eyes seemed to read the man's heart because his drooping tail moved ever so slightly. His sons softly patted the dog's head and he tenderly licked their cheeks.

I shook the man's hand. "Well, I'll call Animal Control. Thanks for your help." With Snoop at my side, we headed back down the trail but as soon as we passed the first bend, I sneaked back. The parents and their kids were walking across the parking lot, the Mastiff following behind. When they arrived at a small station wagon, the man opened the hatchback. The dog never hesitated. He stepped into the back of the car as if he'd always belonged to them, followed by two squealing boys. The man turned in my direction and spotted me. With a shrug of his shoulders, he waved goodbye.

Hugging Snoopy tightly, I said, "Now *that's* what I call a happy ending."

That evening, when Cassie heard our story, we were rewarded with kisses, hugs and praise. But as luck would have it, work called. With Henry on vacation, I decided to bring Snoop along to keep me company.

After checking in, I drove behind the depot to see if anyone might be hanging around there. In my side view mirror, Snoop's head stretched out the rear window, curly ears flapping against his shoulders.

I found the short tunnel and its ledge empty of trespassers but at the U.D. office, someone leaned against the building's front door. Driving closer, I could make out a man with a lit cigarette in his mouth, a large bottle cradled in one arm and an open book on his lap. He didn't even look up when I closed the car door, appearing quite relaxed in posture and demeanor. As soon as I recognized his smoking brand as the 'Maryjane' variety, I understood why.

"Railroad police!" I spoke loudly.

With bloodshot eyes, he waved at me, spilling wine across his pants. He cheerfully slurred, "Good mornin', offssur."

"Actually it's good evening – what are you doing out here?"

"Readin' the Good Book."

In the setting sun's light, I could make out "King James Version" stamped in gold on the book's worn spine. Although the man had the typical appearance of a transient; grease-smeared face, scruffy beard and dirty hair, he didn't have the usual backpack. His only belongings appeared to be what he held: a reefer, a bottle, and a Bible.

Nodding toward the book, I commented dryly, "You've got some good reading there but it doesn't seem to jive with what you're drinking and smoking."

The transient removed the joint from his mouth, lifted the bottle and said with enthusiasm, "God made 'em so I'm jes enjoyin' His blessin's."

I had to laugh. His logic would have made sense back in my drinking days.

"You're right, God did make everything, but I don't see you smoking those blackberry bushes over there. Besides, that book also tells you to take care of your body."

He sucked hard on the cigarette, his eyes never leaving my face as he held the smoke deep in his lungs. When he finally exhaled, he took a quick swig from the bottle, wiped his mouth and said, "Then I need ta ssstop readin' the Good Book." He slammed it shut and let it slide off his lap.

"Your choice but what you're going to do is put out that joint, dump the wine and head back to the streets – now!"

He sat forward and blinked at me. "What'd you sssay?"

"Put out your cigarette." He rubbed the glowing paper remnant against his pants.

"Dump the wine." He knocked the bottle onto its side, the contents forming a thin red stream flowing down the concrete step. "Close enough. Now get up."

Moving in slow motion, he took awhile to get his feet beneath him. I handed him the address of a local mission. "When you sober up, ask the people at this mission to help you better understand that book you're reading."

"I juss migh do that." Clutching his Bible, he got as far as my car. With great effort, he turned to face me. "Ya know, you bulls shouldn't…"

A fury of barking erupted behind him. When he turned and saw Snoopy's head and front paws leaning out the window, he stumbled back with a high-pitched scream.

"Whaaassssatt?"

"Can you keep a secret?" The man nodded without taking his eyes off Snoop.

"Our department had to make budget cuts so our K-9 unit couldn't afford full-sized dogs. We had to order these minis but don't let his size fool you. He can still tear your legs off." I placed a hand on Snoop's head and said in my sternest voice, "Stop-attack."

The man teetered off, muttering to himself, but I knew the transient grapevine would soon be buzzing about Seattle's bulls having K-9. I only hoped his stoned mind would forget such critical details as size and breed.

When I climbed back into the car, Snoopy jumped over the seat and into my lap, obviously pleased with himself. Scratching his ears, I mused, "Henry better not be gone too long now that I know he can be replaced. What do you say we head to the waterfront and see what we can find?"

I drove back through the short tunnel and across the depot's parking lot, able to see crowds of people milling around the lobby through the glass doors. At King Street, I turned right but hadn't gone more than a block when the radio crackled.

"Amtrak Agent to Burlington Northern Special Agent."

"This is the Special Agent."

"There's an out-of-control man in the depot who just punched somebody and now he's fighting with employees. Seattle police have also been called."

Hearing the urgency in his voice, I assured him, "I'm only a block away, I'll be right there." But before I could turn my patrol car around, a city police car appeared, speeding directly toward me. Rather than explain, I slammed my unmarked vehicle in reverse and kept ahead of them as we traveled bumper to bumper. When both cars braked in front of the depot, the two city officers jumped out with raised eyebrows in my direction. I told them, "Railroad police. I'm responding to the same call," and we entered together.

The usual bustling crowd of patrons now stood frozen in place, like statues caught in various poses, all facing the same direction. Shrieks and high pitched cursing echoed off the walls and ceiling from somewhere close. We elbowed our way through the unmoving mass and found three Amtrak employees wrestling with a well-dressed, thin man on a bench in the center of the lobby. And the employees were losing.

"Police. Back away so we can take over."

Visible relief crossed the workers' flushed faces as they released
their holds and stepped away. But the thin man acted like he didn't
realize they'd let go because he continued punching at the air with
savage intensity, his narrowed eyes glittering with hatred.

We leapt into action. I grabbed one of the man's bony arms
and tried bending it behind his back, surprised by his strong resistance.
One of the city officers pushed hard against the man's chest to keep him
seated while the second officer held him in a neck-lock. With his one
free arm and legs, the deranged man hit and kicked the poor officer in
front of him.

"Grab his other arm -- he's hitting me!"

"I'm trying! I'm trying!" I said between gritted teeth, exerting
all my strength.

We continued wrestling for some time, trying to control his wildly
flailing limbs. At one point, I actually felt my body lifted off the floor so
that only my toes touched the marble -- where did he get his strength?

After several more minutes, I could feel our energy
beginning to wane while the man's escalated with his insanity. Our
breathing had become labored as sweat streamed down our faces and
necks. The surrounding crowd still wore expressions of shock like
wax figures in a museum.

"Choke him out Steve or we're going to lose him." The officer in
front had finally had enough.

Ideally, a chokehold causes the subject to pass out in a matter
of seconds but I had a gut feeling this guy wasn't typical. Officer Steve
struggled to wrap his arm around the man's neck from behind, trying to
apply pressure on both sides.

Suddenly, the man jerked his head around and put his face close to mine. With foamy spittle dripping from the corners of his mouth, his glazed eyes fixated on mine. A deep gurgling noise seemed to rise up from somewhere deep inside of him, bursting from his mouth in a primal, haunted scream. Nausea waved over me and I turned away to break eye contact.

"God help us," I whispered.

I redoubled my efforts to bend his arm and finally succeeded, allowing Steve to maintain his chokehold long enough to restrict blood flow to the man's brain. His breaths became short, raspy panting, and then he slumped forward.

Pulling his wrists together to cuff him, we added a flex cuff around his ankles for additional security. The three of us lifted him onto a wheelchair as he regained consciousness.

After an initial check for injuries, including the three employees still standing nearby, we heard the rest of the story. Apparently the subject, a normal appearing traveler in a suit and carrying two suitcases, began yelling at an elderly man in sunglasses and leaning on a white cane, accusing him of "staring at me and thinking dirty thoughts."

When he abruptly left the depot, the blind man and his terrified wife believed the situation had resolved itself. But instead, the man dropped his luggage by the front door and returned to shout at them, appearing more enraged than the first time. When the blind man attempted to explain his disability, the attacker punched him hard in the face, knocking him down. The wife's screams alerted depot employees who bravely tried to subdue him, which is where we came in.

I found the traumatized couple huddled together on a bench at the opposite end of the lobby. They looked like anyone's grandparents: he tall and lean, she soft and plumpish. Both were dressed in their Sunday best for traveling, except his shirt now had blood sprayed across

it and her hair hung in disheveled strands around her face. He held a
bloody kerchief across his nose while his wife gently patted his hand,
tears trickling down her powdered pink cheeks. I'd always had a soft
spot for the elderly and seeing how shaken these two were, filled me
with indignation.

I knelt beside the husband and touched his trembling arm. "How
are you doing, sir?"

He cocked his head toward my voice. "Oh, we're all right, aren't
we Mother? We don't want to press charges, just want to go home and
forget all this happened."

I returned to where the deranged man sat quietly, but by no
means calmly. A palpable tension emanated from him, like a coiled
snake waiting for its next victim. The officers read him his rights but
when we tried to question him, he refused to answer.

With nothing left to do, I watched the city officers put him into
the back of their patrol car along with his luggage. He turned and pressed
his face close to the window, his hard, shining eyes burning into mine.
If spiritual battles for human souls really did take place, this man would
be one of Evil's victories.

A gust of wind came up, blowing dirt and litter across the
sidewalk in tight swirling motions. Glancing upward, the night sky
appeared empty, a black canopy of clouds eclipsing any lights from the
other side. I pulled my jacket tighter around me but it didn't help – the
cold still seeped through my clothes and got under my skin.

Chapter 12

Fall had begun tentatively, alternating between warm sunshine and cold rain, as if wresting for control from a reluctant summer. But by late September, the season had made its arrival permanent in the blushing leaves and sightings of migrating whales.

My relationship with Cassie had also started out with some uncertainty but the time had come for a change -- a permanent one.

Cassie arrived at my home like she did most afternoons, Poo-Poo beside her and a bag of groceries in her arms. Since I loved to cook, and she didn't, she'd bring the ingredients and we'd both clean up afterwards.

But on this particular evening, Poo-Poo moved awkwardly, her rounded belly out of proportion with her petite body. Exactly 62 days earlier, she'd been introduced to a flashy male named *Reno's Silver Dollar,* and they'd mated.

In anticipation of telling Cassie how I felt about her and our future, I failed to notice Poo-poo retreat under the table during dinner. By dessert, her rapid panting didn't register anything out of the ordinary.

"Uh, Cassie, there's something I want to talk with, tell you actually..."

I held her hand but avoided her eyes for fear I'd forget my rehearsed lines. Instead I focused on a napkin close to her elbow.

"I think it's time, Dean."

I breathed a sigh of relief. "So do I, but I wanted to be sure..."

"Well, I'm very sure – do you have some old towels?"

"I'm so glad you uh…*towels*?"

She pulled back her hand and jumped up from the table, her chair nearly tipping over. "Poo-Poo's in labor – what are *you* talking about?"

I remained sitting, trying to make the mental shift from proposal to puppies while Cassie ransacked my kitchen drawers. When she found towels that qualified, (I didn't tell her they were my nice towels) she scooped up Poo-Poo and made a nest around her on my kitchen floor. Sitting cross-legged beside the pile, she stroked the tiny dog's sides with her fingers, cooing softly.

Snoopy entered the room and tentatively circled, curious about the trembling face peeking back at him. He seemed to sense something amiss and approached cautiously, sniffing Poo-Poo's ears and gently licking her face before resuming his restless pacing. I came out of my daze and joined Snoop on his trek around the room, thankful Cassie's skills included canine midwifery. Eventually, Snoopy found a place on her lap and snuggled in. If only there was room for one more – me.

Poo-Poo gave a soft moan, her sides tightened and out slid a black, wet blob. I knelt beside Cassie to watch, surprised at the feelings surging through me. Touched by the tenderness of the moment, I leaned in to kiss her, pausing when I heard an unfamiliar sound. I never should have looked. Poo-poo's needle-like teeth were eagerly crunching away at the umbilical cord before slurping down a grotesque placenta. By the time she started licking the slime coating off the newborn, the initial stirrings of wonder and awe had been squelched. I retreated to the couch, afraid to ask how many more puppies there might be after this one.

Snoopy, however, stood over the puppy, head cocked to one side, intently watching. After several minutes, Poo-Poo leaned back and another puppy appeared, no bigger than a chipmunk. After she performed the same rites, the chocolate brown pup squirmed beside the first.

Poo-Poo shakily got up and went to the front door. "Is she done?" I asked hopefully.

"No, our little mama needs to go outside and take care of business. But with both of us here, she'll be fine."

Cassie stood in the front door's frame, watching Poo-Poo sniff around while I studied this girl who loved me. What were the chances of a guy from a small town in Nebraska even meeting such a class act from the Northwest? And then to discover our hearts were so in sync that my life and future no longer meant anything without her. But telling her would clearly have to wait.

After several minutes ticked by, I nervously joined Cassie. With the porch light illuminating my rain-soaked front yard, we could see Poo-Poo behind a bush, sniffing at something. We made our way to her and found a pup lying still in the damp grass.

"Looks like she couldn't make it back in time. Dean, you pick up mama and I'll take this little guy inside."

Once in the house, Poo-Poo returned to her towel nest and pushed out the last puppy, another chocolate, making her the mother of four. Three of the pups found teats to suckle but the one born outside, a tiny male, barely moved. Cassie wrapped him in a washcloth (I didn't tell her it went with my nice towels) and placed him on a hot pad on the kitchen counter. While she checked on Poo-Poo, I couldn't resist peeking at the perfectly formed face framed by two perfectly formed, miniature ears.

"He'll be fine," Cassie whispered behind me.

His short nose bobbed in our direction and he made the softest of whimpers. With the tip of one finger, I lightly rubbed his silky head. "Welcome to the world, little guy."

Once the pups fell asleep with full tummies, I helped Cassie load the new family into a box for the ride back to her home. Hugging her tightly, I wished I didn't have to go to work. "I can't wait to see you again." I touched her face and gave her an extra long kiss despite the rain falling on us.

She slipped her arms around me and leaned her head against my neck. "Is everything alright, Dean? You seemed distracted tonight, though with puppies popping out on your kitchen floor and front yard, I can't imagine why."

We both laughed and she waved as she drove off. Not until I saw her car's taillights disappear at the end of my street, did I dare answer, "No, sweetheart, I'm not alright -- not until I marry you."

The rain hadn't let up by the time I arrived at the office for a solo graveyard shift. Hanging my wet jacket on a hook by the door, I picked up the roll call from the top of a stack of papers in our In-Box. These daily crime summaries were especially helpful when they included photographs of suspects who were armed and considered dangerous. But on this particular night, the bulletin contained a disturbing incident about a teen-aged boy.

According to the notice, he and his girlfriend had managed to sneak into a boxcar with several transients headed to cities known to be generous to panhandlers (another term for beggars). In the transient world, Seattle was not considered "easy pickin's," in large part to the city's organized public awareness campaign. Throughout the downtown area, signs informed visitors and residents that missions providing food, shelter and clothing were available to the homeless. Giving them money, even a quarter to call the mission (a favorite line of panhandlers) only enabled them because transients would pool their money together to buy a cheap bottle of Mad Dog or White Lightning. People also didn't realize that transients often declined to check themselves into missions because of sobriety requirements.

The police bulletin described what had happened once the train pulled out of the yard: the transients knifed the boy in the stomach, disemboweling him in front of his girlfriend. A few miles out of town, they threw his body off the train and turned their attention to the traumatized girl, holding her hostage for several hours while they repeatedly beat and raped her. When her captors dozed off, she risked a dangerous escape by jumping off the moving boxcar in the middle of the night. She'd followed the tracks until reaching a town where she made a frantic 911 call from a payphone.

The young girl's horrific nightmare reminded me once more of the public's naïve image of harmless hobos cooking a can of beans over an open fire. Those days were long gone, the rails now the domain of violent gangs, felons on the run, and thieves looking for easy victims. And as for hopping on a moving train, one misstep in keeping pace with the train's speed and you'd be pulled under and sliced by steel wheels carrying tons of freight. Noise from the engine would drown out your screams.

Beginning my patrol in Balmer Yard, I spotted two kids crawling into a boxcar. With tonight's bulletin fresh in my mind, I decided to convince them they really didn't want to ride this or any other train.

Parking some distance away, I walked quietly toward their hiding place. I could hear giggling and murmuring; no doubt they were excited about their daring adventure. I radioed the train's engineer.

"Special Agent to Engineer on train on eastbound main line."

"This is Engineer on train 164. Go ahead Special Agent."

"There are some kids on your train I need to remove. Don't move until I call and release your train."

"I'll wait for your call, Special Agent."

With my nightstick, I sharply rapped the metal sides of the car, knowing it sounded even louder inside. "Both of you, come out of there, now!"

They didn't move. I walked to the open door and carefully peered around the side, making sure they didn't have any weapons. Two youths, a girl and a boy, stood still, as if by not moving, they could become invisible. Switching on my high-powered flashlight, I shone it directly into their faces. "Come out here. I'm with the railroad police."

Relief crossed their faces as they picked up their backpacks and jumped the four feet down to the ground. The girl's long dark hair framed a very pretty face and she wore the typical tight jeans and shirt of her generation. She glared at me with furrowed brows and a frown, her arms crossed tightly over her chest.

Her boyfriend, on the other hand, revealed his insecurity. With thumbs looped in his pockets, he refused to look me in the eyes, smirking and mumbling jokes. Noting his slight build and lack of whiskers, I didn't want to even think what the transients would have done to him.

"Move away from the train and place your packs on the ground." I called the engineer on my portable radio. "Special Agent to Engineer on train 164. I've removed your illegal riders and we're clear of the train."

Releasing its air brakes with a loud hiss, the train began to move, each car lurching forward, gaining momentum.

I turned my attention back to the kids. "I need some identification."

The girl pulled hers from her jean pocket, but the boy remained defiant. "Why should I?"

I leaned in close to him. "Because I said so."

He flipped his shaggy bangs from across his eyes and pulled his license from his back pocket. While I copied their information onto our field contact cards, he grew restless. "Hey man, if you're a real cop, why aren't you catching real criminals?"

I ignored him, continuing to record their information. "We don't need your protection -- we know what we're doin'." He spit onto the ground near my feet.

Putting their licenses in my pocket, I stepped toward the boy, nightstick in hand. "So you think you're a tough guy, huh?"

He leaned back and gulped, caught off guard by my changed attitude, but then regrouped. He pointed his finger in my face. "Yeah, I'm tough enough."

Using my free hand, I pushed his chest hard, knocking him off balance. With each step – me forward, he backward - I shoved him as I punctuated each word.

"Are-you-really-tough-enough?"

The girl stood rooted to the ground, her mouth open. The boy's eyes narrowed and he let his anger make a poor choice. Pulling back his fist, he took a swing at me. Easily side-stepping him, I jabbed the soft part of his stomach with the end of my nightstick, knocking the wind out of him. He doubled over and landed hard on his side. Gasping for breath and clutching his stomach, tears welled up in his eyes.

"Got anything else to say?" He shook his head, an inkling of respect in his eyes.

Turning my attention to the girl, I asked, "Is this your first time riding a freight train?"

"Yes…sir."

"If you're going to travel on trains, chances are very good to excellent you'll be raped, beaten or both. You're at the mercy of whoever finds you and when they're done, they'll probably kill you or throw you off the train in the middle of nowhere. Who's going to stop them?"

I helped the boy stand up. "And how would you protect her when you couldn't even protect her from me…and I'm the good guy."

The girl wiped her eyes and sniffed softly. "I didn't mean to make you cry but don't *ever* let anyone put your life in jeopardy."

I made a final appeal to both of them. "Look, the gangs on the trains have their own law and there are a lot more of them than us and we can't be everywhere at once. If I ever catch either one of you in the train yards again, I'll throw you both in jail and press every charge I can against you. Understood?"

"Yeah…and I'm sorry..sir," the boy stammered.

Since both were eighteen, I didn't call their parents. Watching them walk off railroad property, I felt relieved they wouldn't be in tomorrow's bulletin.

On my way back to the patrol car, a heavy-set man carrying a backpack stumbled across the tracks. He stopped to fumble with his backpack's straps but the motion knocked him off balance and he flopped to the ground like a heavy sack of concrete.

"I guess I'm not done out here," I muttered.

Quietly approaching from one side, I scanned the ground with my flashlight for any weapons. Seeing none, I let my presence be known.

"Railroad Police. What are you doing here?"

His face squinted into the light and I recognized him as someone I'd already warned about trespassing and riding trains. I preferred giving warnings, rather than tickets, for transients who weren't considered dangerous to save city police from having to drive our pot-holed access roads to transport a misdemeanor. But when trespassers ignored my warnings, I didn't feel quite so merciful. "I told you a couple of weeks ago to stay off railroad property. What part didn't you understand?"

The man rolled his eyes and threw his hands in the air. "Yeah, yeah, yeah. I undahsshtood you...sho what?"

"So you're NOT going to catch a train out of here and you're NOT going to be on railroad property again – right?"

His head wagged back and forth as he flung his arms up and down with each slurred word. "How'm I shupposed tuh know thish ish yur propaty?"

"Open your backpack and show me what you're carrying."

I braced myself in case he tried to get physical but his enormous weight and high level of alcohol were keeping him off balance.

"What if'n I don'wanna?"

"Then I'll cut it open and you lose the pack. It's your choice but either way, I'm going to see what you've got."

Swearing loudly, he slipped off the straps of his canvas rucksack and turned it upside down. Out slid porn magazines, a blackened cooking pot, food-encrusted fork and knife, dirty clothing reeking of body odor, a large butcher knife, a dented coffee pot and an axe handle. On the tracks, we called the last item a "gooney stick," a common weapon among transients.

Taking a step back, I reached for the grip of my pistol. "Push the knife and gooney stick away from you."

He clumsily kicked both objects in my direction. "Now get the rest of your junk and put it back in your pack." Picking up the handle and knife, I radioed police records, hoping they had a warrant for his arrest. But no such luck – I had to let him go.

He stood and angrily slung his backpack over one shoulder, spilling magazines and his coffeepot back onto the ground. Hearing the clatter, he began shouting obscenities and foul details about what he'd like to do to me, ending each statement with the finger. But mid-cursing, he abruptly turned and fell forward, hitting his head squarely on a steel rail. I waited for him to get up but his massive body lay still across the tracks.

I knelt beside the form and put a finger against his neck for a pulse, hoping not to find one -- the paperwork would be much easier. But unfortunately for the social services providing him disability payments, meaningless rehab and free medical treatment, he would live to offend people another day.

"Dispatch, this is the Special Agent. I need an ambulance at Balmer Yard, on the eastbound mainline. I've got a passed out drunk with a gash on his forehead."

"Okay, Special Agent, I'll make the call."

I paced back and forth, trying in vain to stay warm in the cold rain. I stopped to stare at the silent hulk whose clothes were now soaked. A dark trickle of blood dripped from his head and down the sides of the rail. I felt a twinge of guilt for wishing this man dead and yet, how wrong could it be to love the loveable and hate the hateful? And besides, people like him were the reason we had crime and corruption in society.

Satisfied with my rationale, I turned my back on the transient so I could think about my future happiness without distraction.

Chapter 13

Fall's rain merged into winter's, making the two seasons almost feel like one, except for the progressively shorter days. The puppies grew quickly as puppies do, spending much of their time nursing and sleeping in a big box in Cassie's bedroom. I tried to propose on two more occasions but each time, they managed to upstage me with their irresistible antics and playfulness. As soon as they were eight weeks old and weaned, all were sold except for the silver runt with the thick curls we'd named Bobby.

At the fitness club where Cassie now worked, a Seattle television station had asked her boss if one of his employees would demonstrate exercises to prepare viewers for snow skiing. The manager had chosen Cassie. The crew filmed her one afternoon, talking to the camera with her positive energy and natural enthusiasm for helping people. I couldn't have been more proud of her.

When Christmas Eve arrived, I wanted to make it extra special so I proposed and she answered "Yes!" We spent Christmas day calling friends and family to share the good news. By late afternoon, when the gray day turned into an early night, we cuddled in front of the TV to watch *It's A Wonderful Life*. And that's how it was going to be for us – I just knew it.

Once New Year's Day passed, people resumed their stressful attitudes over making a living as if the recent saturation of "goodwill toward men" had never happened.

During the months of January to April, Cassie and her friends and family kept busy with caterers and florists, dress shops and tux rentals, invitation specialists and hair salons. I just kept out of their way, hoping the plans didn't include my wearing anything frilly or pink.

For my last shift before the wedding, I'd promised Cassie I'd keep a low profile and not get into any scuffles. Bruises and swollen knuckles weren't photogenic and these pictures were to last a lifetime, like our marriage.

The radio crackled. "Special Agent."

"Go ahead, dispatch. This is the Special Agent."

"We have a young white female here at the depot, claiming she's been assaulted."

"I'm on my way."

I had a gut wrenching fear it would be Dana. For the last few weeks, railroad crews had been reporting a pretty girl walking the tracks at night in a "flowery" dress and sweater, but no coat despite the cold weather. We'd frantically drive up and down dark access roads, spotlighting yards and their brushy borders, searching for her. But most nights, she found us before we found her, badly beaten and raped.

We'd then do an all-over search for a nameless, homeless perpetrator among hundreds of possibilities while an ambulance raced her to the nearest hospital for the standard medical exam. Within a week she'd be back.

Learning Dana was a college student with her own apartment made her actions all the more perplexing. Her attractive face, sweet demeanor and nice clothes reminded me of the Ivory Soap girls I saw on TV commercials. She clearly belonged in mainstream society where people lived in neighborhoods and slept in clean beds. None of us could fathom why she purposely sought out dangerous interludes with predators.

When I arrived at the Amtrak Agent's office, my fears were realized. Dana sat on a chair, sobbing into mud-streaked hands, in a dress that now hung ripped and torn from her shoulders. Bloody mucus ran from her nose and over her swollen lips and chin. When she looked up, her smeared make-up encircled her eyes, adding to the haunted aura that seemed to emanate from her.

I took my usual place across from where she sat and waited for her to tell me what happened. She refused my offer to get her tissues or a cloth to wipe her face, shaking her head vehemently at any kindness on my part.

When she did begin to speak, the words sounded dull and flat, as if describing violent acts committed against someone else's body. She avoided eye contact.

I angrily pushed my pen against the paper, recording what she said while suppressing the urge to ask, "What's *wrong* with you?!"

There had been three assailants on this particular night and one had held a knife to her neck. But when I pressed for details, she ended the interrogation like she always did; curling up in the chair, arms wrapped around her legs and rocking.

When I heard the ambulance's siren, I leaned over and gently touched her arm to get her attention, but she'd mentally drifted off. "Dana, we will do *everything* we can to find these scumbags, but if I ever see you near the tracks again, *you will go to jail*! Do you understand?"

I stood to leave when she began humming softly, her voice sounding tiny and high-pitched. "Daddy, daddy, it's okay. I know you didn't mean it."

Her words stopped me cold. Dark secrets between parents and children were unheard of in my small Nebraska town. I'd learned of such things only after leaving home and moving to a major city. And even then, I couldn't comprehend the image of a parent wounding the very soul of their child.

I spent the rest of the shift searching for suspects, stopping to check every shadow and movement, but to no avail. Transients lived by a code that included strong rules against snitching; if one did talk to us, it wouldn't be long before we'd find a body or they'd just disappear.

At the end of the evening, I completed the report, feeling frustrated at not finding a suspect and rage at the monster who'd created this nightmare for Dana. I hoped a separate hell awaited him.

My wedding day began with birds chirping, dew-covered webs draping the lawn, and a hint of sunshine behind the clouds. I drove to Calvary Chapel and entered through a side door, as instructed. Escorted to a small room in the basement, I endured a procession of female relatives sent to inspect my hair, tux and shoes. After passing muster, I went upstairs to stand beside the minister, a trim man with a dark moustache and a twinkle in his eye. I suspected he derived endless enjoyment performing ceremonies for eager brides and panicked grooms.

Reminding myself to breathe, I glanced around at the decorations. Cascading flower arrangements, satin ribbons, and elegant candles had transformed the enormous sanctuary into a place of color and light. A piano began playing somewhere to my right, setting off an uncontrollable shaking in my legs.

Each bridesmaid came down the aisle in that stilted, unnatural gait reserved for weddings. The music stopped and the person I most needed to see appeared in a breathtaking vision of white lace and golden curls. Her eyes caught mine through a shimmering veil.

As if in a dream, she floated toward me. Awestruck by her beauty and my incredible good fortune, I stared at her with a lovesick grin, forgetting everything we'd rehearsed. The minister cleared his throat and scattered laughter from the congregation brought me back to reality. I stepped forward and put her hand around my arm.

Cassie led me to the unity candle, a waxy symbol of two becoming one. Our heads bowed in concentration as we lit the matches and then the candle's wick. Cassie's veil softly moved against her cheeks, wafting above the flame – and then it caught on fire. A black and orange edge crept upward, the congregation gasped, but I was now back on familiar territory. I snuffed the burning veil with my bare hands and we returned to stand in front of the open-mouthed minister.

Throughout the ceremony, Cassie's nudges cued me for when I should kneel or stand. Finally, the vows and the announcement I'd waited all my life to hear.

"I now pronounce you husband and wife."

Lifting what was left of Cassie's seared veil, I cupped her face in my hands and murmured, "I love you Mrs. O'Shea," before sealing it with a kiss.

Following the obligatory cutting of the cake and greeting our 200+ friends and relatives, we left the reception an official married couple. We'd decided a week of camping and exploring the Olympic Peninsula would be the perfect honeymoon, for which Cassie's mother had graciously loaned us "Helga." In her former life, Helga had been a bread truck but after Lucy bought her, she put in a bed, sink and propane stove. For bathroom privileges, we'd have to rely on campgrounds and truck stops.

Taking the ferry to Kingston, we passed Underwater Park where we'd had our first date, and watched the shoreline fade into the distance. Once we disembarked and drove across the Hood Canal Bridge, our last link with the mainland, we were truly alone.

From Highway 101, we took a detour and enjoyed our first meal as husband and wife in the Victorian seaside community of Port Townsend. In the 1800's, visionaries had built this town in anticipation of being a major port for the railroad. But when the railroad stayed on the east side of Puget Sound, the city went into decline until the establishment of a paper mill. From 1915 to 1980, a rail line operated between the mill and Port Angeles, its trains rumbling over trestles that crossed streams churning with salmon.

We found a campground at Fort Worden, a beautiful state park with a beach that extended to Wilson Point where a red roofed lighthouse stood. After an evening stroll in the sand, shadowed by curious Harbor seals lolling in the sea, we fell asleep to the rhythm of the waves.

The next morning we headed west to Port Angeles, the gateway to the mountainous interior. Turning south on Race Street, Helga strained at her maximum uphill speed of 17 mph when we began our winding ascent to a place called Hurricane Ridge. But once there, we were left speechless at the incredible view of snowy peaks and glaciers amassed on the other side of a swooping valley of mountain grasses and wildflowers. From the Visitor's Center, we hiked through a stunted pine forest from where we could see Vancouver Island across the ocean.

Each morning, I'd awaken early so I could watch Cassie sleeping beside me. This beautiful person was now my wife and she loved me! Too bad I couldn't say the same for the loathsome bread truck. With each turn of the road, and there were lots of them, she'd sway dangerously. Every bump reminded us her shocks were worn but her worst trait happened after we'd start to drive. As soon as the rpm's were high enough to get out of first gear, I'd shift and that's as far as we'd get - we'd be stuck in neutral.

I'd pull off the road, take a long wooden handle with a steel hook, open the hood, take hold of the shifting bar with the hook, and pull up, returning the transmission to first gear. I'd clamber back into the truck and start the whole process over again. When we did make it into second gear, I'd wrap my hands around the steering wheel and punch the accelerator, covering as many miles as possible.

But despite Helga's irritating quirks, the days and nights were pure bliss. All too soon, the honeymoon ended and we were back home, unpacking.

I called my boss, Jerry, to check in. "Anything going on I need to know about?" I immediately regretted it.

"There's been some burglaries at the Auburn Yard so we're starting surveillance."

"Uh, so, which shift do you want me to work?"

"The break-ins are happening after midnight so we need you 11 to 7-- *tonight*. Sorry, Dean, but we don't have anyone else."

Hanging up the phone, I gave Cassie a tight hug and reluctantly went off to work. After an initial drive around the yard's buildings, I found a discreet place to park across the street, next to a vacated bar. But after one hour, I could barely keep my eyes open.

Hoping a dose of night air would help, I jogged across the road, taking long deep breaths. I tried stretching out on a patch of weeds, letting the cold ground penetrate my clothes. After five minutes, I wanted to pull my hair.

I returned to the car and found a radio station that played old mystery theatre, just like my parents enjoyed when they were young.

The deep-voiced narrator set the scene, "It was a dark and stormy night…." A creaking door, a howling dog. Good, this would keep me awake. I loved a good mysss….

Sharp rapping startled me awake. Bright colored lights blinded my eyes. A voice spoke from somewhere close. Something large loomed over my car but I couldn't understand the words above that incessant knocking.

And then I heard them all too clearly. "Police. Roll the window down and place both your hands on the steering wheel." I groaned inwardly, dreading the humiliation that would soon be mine. After complying with his instructions, he asked, "What are you doing here?"

"Uh, I'm with the uh, railroad police and I'm on uh, surveillance."

I showed my badge and identification. He moved his flashlight from my ID to my face and back again. "So *this* is how railroad police do surveillance? Ha! No wonder the perps don't know about you guys – they never see you!"

I sank lower into my seat, feeling like I'd let my entire profession down.

"Do me a favor. Try staying awake like we do, you'll catch more bad guys that way."

Turning on his heels, he walked back to his patrol car, laughing out loud. I knew he'd be telling his peers about this for weeks to come. I felt awful.

As soon as the cloudy sky lightened enough to qualify as a sunrise, I went home and found my new bride setting breakfast on the table. Between mouthfuls of dry scrambled eggs (she'd forgotten to add oil) and crumbling bacon, I told her about an idea I had for the next surveillance and then stumbled down the hall and collapsed into bed.

The following midnight, I drove Helga to the surveillance site, giving her a chance to redeem herself. Cassie sat beside me, her lively conversation sure to keep me alert and awake. After two frustrating stops to unlock the transmission, we pulled up next to the vacant bar. Any burglars in the area would never suspect the rickety old bread truck.

Cassie lit the propane stove with a match. "I'll get dinner started while nothing is happening." With a kiss, she busied herself making fried chicken and buttery mashed potatoes.

"Now this is how a stake-out should be done. You and food, what more could I want? Besides, you're a lot prettier than Henry."

"I'll take that as a compliment. How many pieces of chicken do you want?"

"I'll have…"

Two figures appeared at the front door of the main office building across the street. They hesitated before disappearing inside. "It's time for me to go to work. Keep dinner warm while I go ruin someone's night."

She couldn't hide the worry in her eyes. "Please be careful – we're still newlyweds." I kissed her, gave her a wink, and stepped outside the truck. Pulling my jacket on, I re-checked my gun and cuffs and turned off my portable radio to keep my presence a surprise.

Quickly crossing the road and an empty lot, I crouched low beneath the window nearest to where the suspects had entered. Strangely, they'd turned on all the bright interior office lights -- these guys were either amateurs or seriously afraid of the dark.

I peeked over the ledge and saw two teen-aged boys rifling through desk drawers. They didn't appear to be armed. Finding the door ajar, I clutched my pistol in my right hand and kicked it open, but the boys were so engrossed in their search they never heard me. I coughed, kicked a box and aimed my .357 Magnum straight at them.

"Police! Party's over!"

They froze with their hands in the open drawers, faces pale with fright.

"Step away from the cabinets and put your hands above your heads. Slowly walk backwards towards me."

One of the boys spoke. "Uh, we work here. We're, we're cleaning."

I looked at the chaotic mess on the floor. "You've just added lying to the list. Now keep walking."

They haltingly made their way around the desks, glancing over their shoulders to avoid tripping. Their trembling hands confirmed my initial assumption of their novice status. When they were within a few feet, I told them, "Stop, get down on your knees and cross your ankles." They complied and I stepped forward and cuffed one boy's hands. "What you two call cleaning, we call burglary."

After handcuffing the second suspect, I called Auburn City Police on the office phone for transport to jail. Two cars soon arrived and the officers placed a youth in the back of each vehicle. But I noticed one stood back, a strange grin on his face. He finally approached and shook my hand. "I see you managed to stay awake tonight."

Recognizing him as the officer from the previous night, I laughed. "I had to come up with a plan so you wouldn't have to wake me again."

With that, I returned to where Cassie waited, feeling relief I'd reclaimed some credibility for our department and hopefully for me. When I slid open the bread truck's door, my bride greeted me with hugs and kisses and the smell of overdone chicken. Surveillance never looked so good.

Chapter 14

The warmer spring weather not only signaled the return of migratory birds but many of last year's transients, as well. Some of them remembered Henry and I and would get off the trains before they reached Seattle. One disgruntled contact went so far as to spray paint "HOT YARDS" on a bridge outside the city as a warning to others about our aggressive enforcement.

We began to hear rumors that our department had decided more territory could be covered with one officer per car instead of two, but we ignored these, confident our methods got the results the railroad liked to see in its reports.

Which is why I didn't expect to see my boss at the start of a night shift. Normally, Jerry would've been home with his family, finishing up dinner, watching TV. And he didn't greet me with his usual cheer, either. In fact, he remained standing in the doorway.

"Dean, meet your new partner, Eugene Dinkmeier, former MP in the Air Force."

"Uh, excuse me, Jerry -- *new* partner? Since when?"

"Since tonight. Now show Eugene how we do things around here."

A very tall man shyly stepped into the room, his rail-thin frame easily sliding between Jerry and the doorframe. His features were angular, with a long nose and pointed chin framed by a mop of curly red hair. Wearing a plaid sports coat, striped shirt and spotted tie, I would have guessed him to be a clown on his day off. I shook his clammy, limp hand.

"Uh, be glad to, Jerry."

Eugene seemed pleasant enough but his fashion taste would be like a giant neon arrow over our heads, flashing "COPS." Trying to be polite, I asked, "Do you have something less, uh *hip* to wear?"

"I've got another jacket in my car, but I thought we were supposed to wear nice sports coats."

"On a typical shift we are so when we call for back-up, it's easy to tell the bum from the railroad police. But tonight, we're going undercover to a beach party."

"A party on the beach? I love my new job!" He clapped his soft white hands together in a fluttering, rapid motion that made it hard to imagine him in the military.

On the drive there, I skipped the usual questions about his past and went straight to the evening's plan. "Our train crews have reported rocks being thrown at the auto carriers, breaking windows out of new cars and trucks. So tonight, we'll be fun-loving guys at a beach party and see if we can catch them in the act."

"Sounds *neat-o*." Eugene nodded with enthusiasm, his hair bobbing like a giant puffball.

Once I parked the car, I made sure our guns and cuffs were concealed in shoulder holsters; mine beneath a loose flannel shirt, his a tweed jacket. Hopefully, the kids would be too drunk and distracted to notice his pleated slacks and dress shoes.

We walked toward the glow of a bonfire on a narrow strip of seashore about half a mile away. Soon, we could make out lithe silhouettes against the flames, arms and legs moving to the beat of blaring music and hormones.

At the crowd's edge, I pointed out a keg set up on a wooden crate. "Let's make our way to the drinking center over there. It gives us a good view of the tracks. Now act natural, like you belong here."

I stepped into the circle of light and casually made my way, thumbs in my front pockets. Beside me, Eugene bounced like a jack-in-the-box, shaking his head out of sync with the music and giving high fives to anyone with a half-raised hand. Some swore, others muttered "Geek!" I suspected high school had been a lonely experience for him.

When we reached the keg, we picked up Styrofoam cups and pretended to drink, Eugene adding his own slurping and belching sound effects.

"Eugene, a train is due any minute. You watch that group of kids and I'll watch these over here, but keep one eye on me. If either of us sees someone throwing rocks, we need to arrest them and get out of here before the crowd knows what's happening."

Eugene replied, "Right-o! Keen-o!"

The light from an approaching train appeared in the distance. Nodding to Eugene, I moved away, keeping parallel to him so both he and the crowd were in my line of vision. I recalled one patrolman had recently been beaten at a party like this one. Fortunately, he'd only lost two teeth in his fight to keep his gun, but it reminded me how quickly these situations can turn, especially when large numbers of drunken youths were involved.

The train rumbled closer. A boy with his arm around a girl yelled, "Here it comes!" Letting go of the girl, he bent over and picked up some rocks. Another boy ran up with more rocks and dropped them at the first boy's feet. Together, they cocked back their arms and waited for the train.

I checked on Eugene but he seemed distracted by something. Stepping back, I saw a couple locked in a tight embrace, kissing passionately before a mesmerized Eugene. "Darn him."

I turned my attention back to the boys, ready to grab them as soon as they committed a crime. The train's engine roared past and both boys heaved several rocks in quick succession. One found its mark and broke the engineer's window. The teens whooped and cheered. The other rocks ricocheted back into the crowd at high speed but miraculously, no one was hit.

Taking advantage of the distraction, I sneaked up behind the boys and knocked them down, telling them they were under arrest. I cuffed one and looked around for Eugene. Where *was* he? With my attention diverted, the second boy slipped my grasp and ran away, yelling "Cops!"

But a miracle happened. He ran straight into Eugene, who actually did the right thing and cuffed him.

"Let's get them to the car before anyone realizes what's going on," I hissed at Eugene. We pulled the boys to their feet and slipped outside the bonfire's light. No one followed and the party soon returned to its original noise level.

"Hey man, these cuffs hurt!" one of the boys complained.

"They're not made to be comfortable. Keep moving."

When we arrived at the patrol car, Eugene read them their rights while I loosened each cuff a notch. "What's the big deal about throwin' rocks at a stupid train?" the complainer asked. "People do it all the time."

I radioed the train that had been hit. "Special Agent to west bound train going by Carkeek Park"

"This is the engineer on train 414. We were just rocked at Carkeek Park. They broke a window and some glass got into the brakeman's eyes."

The boys glanced at each other and then at me.

"*That's* the big deal – people get hurt." I lifted the radio to my mouth. "Tell your brakeman we've apprehended the people who threw the rocks and they *will* be going to jail tonight."

"That's great news, Special Agent," responded the engineer. "Let us know if you need us to testify at the hearing. You made our night."

The Yardmaster's voice broke in. "Engineer on train 414. I've called an ambulance for your brakeman. They'll be at the yard when you arrive."

Turning my attention back to the boys, I informed them, "Well, you two are looking at charges of vandalism, malicious mischief and assault. Time to call your ride."

"Special Agent to Yardmaster. Would you contact city police for transportation of two juveniles?"

"What's your location, Special Agent?"

Eugene picked up our portable spotlight, plugged it into the cigarette lighter and shone it on the street sign. "We're on Carkeek Park Drive, near the entrance to the park."

I relayed the information and we settled back to wait but Seattle City police pulled in behind us. We'd lucked out-- they were responding to a call about the same party.

Eugene and I walked the boys to the officers' vehicle, gave them our report and charges and said goodnight. Heading back to our car, I playfully jabbed Eugene's side.

"Hey, not bad for your first night on the job."

He smiled, pleased with how it had all turned out. And then we stopped in our tracks—dense smoke filled the inside of our car! We ran and opened two doors, coughing and waving aside the putrid billows. "Eugene! Can you see anything on your side?"

No answer.

"Eugene?" I banged on the roof to get his attention.

His face seemed paler through the curtain of smoke between us. He lifted an electric cord high enough for me to see what hung from its end -- the still turned on spotlight.

"Will I lose my job over this?" He pointed forlornly to a plate-size hole smoldering in the middle of the front seat.

I pulled off my shirt and motioned for Eugene to do the same. "Let's first make sure it's out." Covering our mouths and noses, we stamped out the embers and poured some sand in for good measure.

"Okay, Eugene, we now have a custom-made spotlight-holder within easy reach of driver and passenger, courtesy of you. And no, you won't lose your job over this."

We resumed patrolling but Eugene couldn't let it go. Every few minutes he'd groan, bury his face in his hands and lament how he'd almost set the company car on fire his first night on the job. After an hour of this, I suggested we find a place to eat.

"How can you be hungry at a time like this? I came *this close* to costing the company who just hired me, *thousands* of dollars. How detailed a report do we have to fill out? When the other guys hear about this, no one will want to patrol with me and..."

"Eugene! Calm down. You're getting worked up over...."

The radio's static interrupted us. "Seattle Special Agent."

"This is the Special Agent."

"Special Agent, the engineer on train 225 just reported hitting a man at Richmond Beach."

"We'll be there in 15 minutes." I returned the radio mike to its holder. "Eugene, we'll finish our talk later. Right now, you're going to see the worst part of our job."

When we arrived at Richmond Beach, we found a train idling on the tracks, a county sheriff's car and ambulance parked nearby. "Special Agent to conductor on 225."

"This is the conductor."

"We're at the parking lot behind your train. Where's the victim?"

"North about 100 yards. You'll see the crowd behind the caboose."

Eugene and I collected our equipment; rubber gloves, camera, flashlights and police gear. As we hiked to the end of the train, I told him what to expect. "We'll find the sheriff and see what info he has already. If he hasn't talked to any witnesses, I'll need you to find some and write down what they saw. I'll talk to the crew."

Eugene looked down and mumbled. "Sure thing, Dean, I'll try not to mess up...again."

At the accident site, several beams of flashlights danced in erratic circles around the stationary red light of the caboose, looking like an out of sync laser show. In the midst of this activity and noise, a crumpled body lay still between the tracks.

The sheriff found us and we introduced ourselves. "There was a party going on down at the beach," he told us, "And it appears this guy was heading back to his car when he was hit by the train."

"Have you had a chance to talk to the crew?" I asked the deputy.

"Just the conductor and brakeman in the caboose, but they didn't see anything, only heard the engineer yelling he'd hit someone and was going into emergency to stop the train. I'm on my way to the engine now. Want to join me?"

"Sure thing, and we can use this access road to drive to the engine, but I need a minute with my partner first."

Looking around, I saw Eugene staring at the body. "Eugene?"

"Huh?" He seemed in a daze.

"See those people over there," I nodded toward a small group.

"Yeah I see them."

"Ask if any of them saw anything. If there were witnesses, get names, addresses and phone numbers." When he didn't respond, I shook his shoulder. "Are you okay, Eugene?"

"Yeah, yeah, I'm alright."

"Good. And one more thing -- keep everyone away from here."

Before rejoining the sheriff, I shone my flashlight onto the body for a quick assessment. All four limbs stuck out at sharp angles from the torso with the head facing upward, eyes wide open, staring at the sky. Blood trickled from both corners of his mouth. He looked young, possibly still a teen.

Forcing myself into work mode, I took a deep breath and returned to where the sheriff waited. Somewhere tonight a family would be changed forever, their dreams for a son soon to become a never-ending nightmare.

"Has the victim been identified?" I asked as we drove to the engine.

"I've got his driver's license, which I'll share with you when I'm done here."

A train crew typically consisted of an engineer and head brakeman in the engine, with a conductor and rear brakeman riding in the caboose, if there was a caboose.

We found a lone man standing at the front of the train. "You the engineer?" I asked.

"He's still in the engine," a short man in coveralls replied, "I'm the head brakeman and I seen what happened. It was that kid's final act of defiance." With my pen poised above a pad of paper, I waited for him to explain but he merely looked from the sheriff to me.

"What exactly do you mean by his 'act of defiance?'"

Rain had begun to drizzle down on us, leaving tiny droplets on our hair and clothes. I pulled my collar up around my neck and held the notepad closer to my jacket, but the lines of ink were beginning to smear.

"Well, we got two sets of tracks here with trains goin' west bound on this track and east bound on that track." The brakeman clearly believed in explaining every detail, including the obvious.

"Our train was on this track, goin' westbound, when I seen this guy standin' right in the middle of the same track that we was on. But he wasn't lookin' at us, he was lookin' at an eastbound train goin' by on them other set of tracks. We started blowin' our horn, but he couldn't hear it on 'count of the noise from the other train, the one he was watchin'. Just before we hit him, he was flippin' off the crew of the other train as it went by. He must've thought they was yellin' at him to get off the tracks so that's what I meant by his final act of defiance."

"Is the engineer still in the cab?" I asked.

"Yeah but he's in bad shape." The brakeman answered.

The sheriff and I climbed into the engine where a figure sat behind the controls. Clearing my throat, I said, "Hello. I'm a Special Agent and this is Deputy Allen with the Sheriff's Department. Can we have a word with you?"

Without turning to face us, he began to talk. "He never saw us. He never even saw us! I set the emergency brakes and kept blowing the horn, but he didn't hear us and then we hit him and there was nothing I could do." After a long pause, he quietly added,

"After twenty four years, I've seen three suicides on the tracks but this kid just wasn't paying attention."

I spoke to the engineer. "You did what you could but I know it doesn't help the situation. And as for the other train, I'll contact the crew and get a written statement from them."

In an awkward show of sympathy, the sheriff and I patted the engineer's shoulder and quietly left the cab. We drove back to the caboose where I found Eugene intently watching the coroner bag the young boy's body. I tapped his shoulder and he jumped.

"We're free to go now – did you find any witnesses?"

Eugene shook his head and followed me back to the car in a melancholy mood. Once underway, he slumped in the burned out seat and looked glumly out the window.

"Eugene, I know seeing a dead person is tough the first few times but after awhile, you'll learn to shake it off. You have to, otherwise, it'll build up inside and you won't be able to let it go." He turned and in his face I saw the same look I'd seen in fellow soldiers after our first battle. I took a deep breath, hoping my words would help.

"Eugene, when I first saw death, it crawled under my skin and scared me too. I couldn't accept the fact I could be within its reach -- death was someone else's possibility, not mine. But after seeing buddies younger than me die in Nam, and kids like the one we saw tonight, die because of a simple mistake, I began to read everything I could about mortality, the afterlife and God. A lot of it is still a mystery to me but I do know the more I learned about a personal God, as opposed to an impersonal force, the less I saw dying as the worst that could happen to me."

He studied my face for a long time as the windshield wipers squeaked across the wet glass. Had I sounded too preachy? Too much like I had all the answers?

With a sigh, he resumed staring into the night, the rain-streaked window blurring lights and landmarks into shades of gray.

Chapter 15

I awoke to rays of late summer sunshine peeking through our bedroom blinds and playing across my face. Checking the clock on my side of the bed, I realized Cassie had been up for at least two hours while I'd slept in from working the night shift.

My audible yawning cued the dogs and before my feet touched the floor, three furry faces launched themselves onto our bed, snorting and wagging their tails. We had a wild, frenzied wrestling match that left the new floral sheets in a twisted pile. My day had officially begun.

I padded barefoot to the kitchen, passed the living room window and backed up. A dilapidated Volkswagen bus sat in our driveway, its loaf-shaped body squatting on undersized tires. I tried to guess which of our friends might be a closet hippie when a familiar - and lovely - pair of legs moved beneath the relic's carriage.

During our first months of marriage, I'd discovered Cassie didn't feel any obligation to follow the traditional roles of her gender. In fact, she looked for ways to defy them which is why, on this particular morning, I felt more amusement than surprise.

Strolling down the driveway with a cup of coffee, I banged on the dented shell of the bus. "Hey grease monkey, what're you doing under there?"

A giggle, a scuffle and an oil-streaked face emerged. "Dean, this is so exciting! Two guys sold it to me for just a hundred bucks. Can you believe it?"

"I can't believe it's sitting in my driveway." Giant patches of rust spread across the body like creeping brown mold. I didn't dare look at the engine.

"You'll see, I'm going to fix it up and sell it for seven hundred dollars."

With that, Cassie disappeared under the bus and I returned to the house to enjoy the morning paper. Life was especially good when the woman you married could also fix your cars.

Within an hour, Cassie had a list of supplies she'd need for her project. I jumped at the chance to go, curious how the guys at the local auto parts shop would treat her.

When we entered the store, my willowy bride stood in graceful contrast to the burly men in jeans and ball caps perusing shelves of chrome, tools and oil. Eventually, a male employee wearing a red vest and a tag identifying him as "Scotty" approached me.

"Can I help you find something, sir?"

With a nod in Cassie's direction, I answered, "Better ask her."

He turned to Cassie with a patronizing grin. "If you can describe what you're looking for, I'm pretty good at figuring out what you need."

"I'm rebuilding a '67 VW bus and I need a piston, ring set, gaskets and rod bearings. And could you look up a carburetor-rebuild kit for me?"

The young man's eyes widened and a smile spread across his face. "Yes ma'am!"

Between finding the parts and talking crankshafts with Cassie, he never stopped gazing at her with unabashed admiration. His world would never be the same.

During the next few weeks, I'd awaken to an assortment of bangs and clangs from our driveway. After my morning ritual, I'd make a cup of coffee and take it out to Cassie, placing it in her greasy hands. While sipping the steaming brew, she'd excitedly tell me which part she was working on and I'd nod as though I understood. When the last drop had been slurped, she'd plop the empty cup into my hand and disappear beneath the bus.

The day finally came when the VW had a coat of primer, a rebuilt engine and a second chance. We took it for a test drive around the neighborhood, made even more exciting by the missing floor beneath the pedals. But it didn't matter. As I watched the road pass beneath our feet, I felt proud of her. And true to her word, she found a buyer who paid $700 for the re-born bus.

Once Cassie realized how profitable her hobby could be, she began looking for neglected VW's with the same passion as garage sale fanatics. When shouting awakened me a few mornings later, I sleepily peered out a window to see Cassie guiding a tow-truck driver with one arm and waving at me with the other. I donned my bathrobe and watched them roll a metal beast off a trailer and into our back yard. She paid the tow truck operator and ran into the house to breathlessly summarize her find.

"These guys had this dune buggy parked in their backyard for *two years* and they told me if I could move it, I could have it for *free!* Can you believe it?"

Noting its multiple layers of mud, grass and spider webs, yes I could. But Cassie's excitement proved contagious and I had to laugh as she danced around her newest find.

"Looks like you've got your work cut out for you, sweetheart."

"Don't worry, Dean, I'll have it running in no time and we'll be four-wheeling around the countryside. It'll be so much fun!" Within the hour, a hosed-off, two-seat, dune buggy with a Volkswagen engine sat on blocks in our backyard, along with the familiar sight of Cassie's legs sticking out from underneath. After a few weeks of cleaning and replacing engine parts and brake line, the little dune buggy began to take on a personality with its bright yellow fiberglass body. And I had grown accustomed to the smell of grease on Cassie's hands.

One morning, while she toiled away, I thought an impromptu picnic would be a nice surprise. Under the close supervision of Snoopy, I began looking through our cupboards and refrigerator for ingredients and goodies. When I had what I needed, Cassie's father, Fred, dropped by for a visit. Noticing the checkered apron around my waist, he commented dryly, "You shore look cute in that apron, Dean. Now where's the one who should be wearing that thing?"

Pretending to blush, I teased back. "Oh Fred, you're such a flirt. As for the little woman, she's out back."

Fred peered through the kitchen window, just in time to see Cassie in grimy coveralls heave a part of the engine from the rear of the buggy. Glancing back at me, his forehead wrinkled over narrowed eyes. "Don't you kids have this marriage thing turned around?"

I shrugged and Fred started for the back door, muttering something about women who didn't know their place in this world. Putting the finishing touches on our lunch, I watched Cassie throw her arms around Fred's neck and gave him a big hug. When he saw me, he shook his head and waved goodbye.

Carrying an old blanket outside, I spread it on the lawn, placed the picnic lunch and a pitcher of juice in the middle and shouted, "Time for a break."

Cassie climbed out from under the buggy and ran to me with a squeal of joy. Leaping into my arms, she knocked me to the ground, overturning the basket. The dogs joined in, barking and jumping as Cassie tried to smear grease on my clean face. Rolling her over, I began tickling her until, breathless from laughter, she begged for mercy. I couldn't resist kissing her, which of course led to more kissing until the sound of munching brought me back to my original plan – our picnic! But it was too late. Three furry faces happily licked the last of our sandwich and cracker crumbs from their moustaches.

Pushing Cassie's hair from her face, I murmured, "Thanks to you, we both need a shower. And since you instigated this mess, you get to scrub my back."

She winked. "It's a deal."

With that, we kissed and stumbled our way into the house, leaving my checkered apron and her coveralls lying in a heap at the threshold.

When I left for work later that evening, Cassie was already asleep. As I often did, I paused to admire her sweet face nestled on the pillow, framed by her long hair. Touching her cheek, I whispered, "I love coming home to you."

Tiptoeing out of the house, I made the mental transition from husband to aggressive officer on the drive to work. Once in the office, I found my boss waiting for me.

"Hey Jerry, isn't it kind of late for you to be here?" I couldn't help noticing the dark circles beneath his eyes.

"Yeah, it is, so I'll make this brief. Patrolmen in Spokane are finding radios missing from vehicles on arrival inspections. So thieves must be getting on auto-racks (what we called auto-carriers) here in Seattle and we have to stop them - tonight."

I actually felt sorry for him, knowing his job included endless meetings and memos from higher-ups who dealt with numbers while sitting at desks in clean shirts. When damage reports came in from St.

Paul or Kansas City, or angry customers called with their demands, Jerry would be the one to handle them. No, I didn't envy him one bit.

Nor did he envy me. Catching thieves meant figuring out which carrier would be hit out of the hundreds going through Seattle on any given week. I checked the current schedule and knowing where illegal riders were most likely to get on, headed to the north end of Balmer Yard where I could view all trains arriving and departing.

Even though night had fallen, the yards were well lit with towering light poles, allowing me to scrutinize the evening's "hot-shot" train's auto carriers as it rumbled past me. These trains, also known as "through" trains, were given priority over other freight trains, stopping only for crew changes between where they were loaded and where they would be unloaded.

After twenty carriers went by, movement caught my attention. An enormous man wearing a tiny backpack ponderously jogged alongside the hot shot, heading my way. He managed to grab one auto carrier's ladder and, after a few precarious stumbles, drag his massive bulk up the rungs. Holding onto the underside of the second deck, he swung around the front end of the carrier and into its interior.

I spoke into my portable radio. "Special Agent to the train leaving north end of Balmer Yard."

No answer. The train began to pick up speed. "Special Agent to east bound train leaving north end of Balmer Yard."

The engineer responded above the din of the moving freight cars. "Special Agent, this is the engineer on train 478."

"You have a passenger I need to remove. Stop your train."

The carrier with the rider had now passed by, forcing me to run alongside the train to try and keep my eye on it. What made it difficult were the sloped, rocky ground bordering the tracks and the extra weight of gun, ammo, cuffs and radio around my waist.

"Special Agent, I'm stopping. Let me know when you're clear."

By the time I caught up, I had to take a few moments to catch my breath, and then I silently climbed onto the deck through the back end.

Auto carriers have either two or three decks running the full length of each train car. A single deck can hold six autos, allowing a three-deck carrier to transport up to eighteen vehicles. The sides of these carriers are constructed of sheet metal, with the front and rear ends open, providing easy access for thieves. Once aboard, they can pull radios out of vehicles at their leisure, knowing their crimes won't be discovered until the train reaches the next yard, sometimes hours away.

But before they get there, thieves will throw the stolen goods from the train, hop off once it slows down, and then drive back to retrieve the merchandise. Some worked alone but many worked in highly organized gangs.

Five, full sized, Ford LTD's were on the bottom deck, all facing the front of the carrier, which didn't allow much room between them and the metal sides. To make matters worse, the second deck was only five and a half feet above me, forcing me to bend forward while squeezing between the vehicles. I didn't like the tight space – it made the situation even more dangerous.

Beginning with the first LTD, I peered through the back window for signs of the trespasser before advancing sideways. Fighting feelings of claustrophobia, I wondered how he'd maneuvered around in here.

In the last Ford, a bald head atop massive, rounded shoulders bobbed up and down in the driver's seat, his sheer mass dwarfing the interior. As I crept closer, I could hear him babbling to himself – why did I always get the giants *and* the crazies?

I lunged forward and opened the driver's-side door. "Railroad pol…"

A mammoth sized fist slammed into my jaw with the power of a jackhammer, knocking my head against the carrier's steel side. The edges of my vision turned black and fuzzy, lights flashed and a deafening ringing wouldn't turn off in my ears.

Leaning heavily on the Ford's trunk, I willed myself to stay conscious despite my throbbing jaw. In a dreamlike haze, I saw my assailant reach for something in the front seat. My brain screamed, "Pull your pistol -- he's got a weapon!" but my arms felt strangely disconnected, hanging like useless weights at my side.

I braced myself for the worse but to my immense relief, he pulled out only his backpack, shuffled to the open end of the carrier and jumped off. Following him on wobbly legs, I gingerly slid off the carrier and stopped at the sight before me. The man's pants were missing their seat, exposing two large fleshy cheeks alternately rising and falling with each step. Didn't he know about underwear?

I drew my revolver. "Police! Stop where you are or I'll shoot!"

He turned around, his big bald head nestled in a depression between his shoulders. His eyes bulged as if he had a goiter. "The Marines are after me. I don't wanna fight the cat! AAAAUUUUUHHH!"

He swung his thick hands around his face as if at a swarm of bees, nearly falling over as he dodged and ducked the imaginary attackers. "They're all around me!"

Suddenly, he slapped his arms hard against his sides, shouted "About face!" and marched away, his screams in step with his stomping feet.

Holstering my gun because I couldn't justify shooting a crazy, I trotted after him, acutely aware of each jarring motion on my aching jaw.

Without a strategy to restrain him, I decided I might as well try an old-fashioned, all out, Cornhusker tackle. I picked up my pace and launched my short self into the air and onto his back, like a kicker on a 300-pound lineman. He never missed a stride. I frantically worked my arm beneath his chin while holding my legs out at an awkward angle to avoid brushing against his bare bottom. I wondered if he even knew he had a hitchhiker, but my chokehold eventually caused him to lose his momentum and bend over backward. As soon as my feet touched the ground, I quickly pulled him down.

"The Marines can see me! Where's the cat, I can't find the cat!"

I made a mental note to add ear plugs to my equipment. With much heaving and strain, I rolled him over onto his protruding belly. While I paused to catch my breath and wipe the sweat from my face, the teetering man made swimming motions with his limbs, his lumpy buttocks pointed upward like giant deflated muffins.

"I'm asking for a raise at review time," I promised myself.

Pulling his heavy arms behind him, it took several minutes to get his thick wrists close enough to cuff. When the first notch clicked shut, the man went strangely quiet. I radioed the engineer. "Special Agent to engineer on train 478. I've removed your passenger and we're clear of your train."

"Thanks Special Agent. Train 478 is clear to move."

I made one more call, this time to the Yardmaster, and asked him to contact city police for transportation to a psychiatric ward.

Turning my attention back to the man, I carefully annunciated each word. "I'm going to help you stand up. Do you understand?"

His placid face stared straight ahead. "Did you hear me? I'm going to help you stand."

Without answering, he shifted his weight and got his knees under him. Then, with a lot of effort on both our parts, we got him to a standing position.

Tenderly rubbing my jaw, I said, "I don't know what possessed you to slug me back there, but it was a bad decision." He showed no expression.

Grabbing one arm, I led him to the patrol car but we hadn't gone five steps when his pants slid to the ground in a heap around his ankles. I considered my options. He couldn't walk with his pants down, and I couldn't risk taking off the cuffs so he could pull them up. That left the worst choice – I'd have to pull them up for him.

"This is no way to earn a living," I muttered as I squatted down behind him to take hold of his pants.

Closing my eyes, I held my face as far away as I physically could from his filthy, foul-smelling backside. With a strong heave, I jerked his pants up until they hit a barrier - his bulging gut. Taking a deep breath, I tugged at them, moving them up and over the fatty roll and we resumed our walk. Until his pants dropped again.

"Now I know they don't pay me enough!" I shouted at him.

Using the very tips of my fingers to hold the tiniest edge of his pants, I went through the same routine, holding my breath and closing my eyes. When the side of my face brushed against his bare hip, I screamed in disgust. Once the pants were above his stomach, I pulled one of his fat index fingers through a belt loop and walked around to face him. Standing on tiptoes, I snarled up at him. "If you move that finger from your belt loop, I'm calling the Marines and they'll put you on the front lines."

"Sir yes sir!"

We marched to the car in perfect cadence.

Chapter 16

Our department's attempt to separate Henry and I proved futile – after trying to work with other officers, we resumed patrolling together and no one said a word.

On a cool rainy night, I entered the office where Henry waited, a sly grin on his broad face. I knew he enjoyed our partnership as much as I did because we preferred lots of physical confrontations—what we called a "good night."

Henry jumped up from his chair. "I've got the line-up of trains coming in. Let's go downstairs and check the depot for bums before we go on patrol."

His words flashed me back to one of our pastor's recent sermons, when he'd talked about treating the "least of our brothers and sisters" as a reflection of how we viewed God. Sitting in the pew with Cassie, I'd wondered if criminals and crazies fell into this category. But when I thought of how far their lives were from the divine and pure, I concluded he must be referring to the poor, disabled and elderly who lived among us in normal society. As we sang the closing hymn, "Nearer My God To Thee," I dismissed a nagging feeling in my conscience.

"Okay, but where we eating tonight?"

With a laugh, Henry asked, "Is that always going to be your first question whenever we patrol?"

"Hey, I need something to look forward to…besides deep, meaningful conversation with you, of course."

We laughed the easygoing laugh of friends. I'd found that time spent with the same person, especially in high-risk situations, formed a powerful trust. In Vietnam, when we depended on each other for survival, our squad felt closer than family. But what I'd believed to be an unbreakable bond ended when we each returned to the world and went our own way. Very few of us had kept in touch. By comparison, my marriage to Cassie seemed based more on who we were as persons, not just what we did together.

We pushed open the double glass doors and scanned the depot's lobby for any sign of troublemakers. In this place that never closed, people arrived, left and waited at all hours of the day and night, attracting pickpockets, panhandlers, and derelicts looking for a warm place to sleep. We felt especially protective over the more vulnerable senior citizens that often traveled by train.

Across the wide expanse of floor, we spotted a man wearing filthy mismatched clothes stretched out on one of several wooden benches lining the far wall. His eyes were closed and thunderous snoring arose from his slack, open mouth. We decided to give him a rude awakening but before we could, a young girl exclaimed, "Look Daddy!"

Glancing in disgust, her father took his daughter's hand and led her away. When we reached him, we understood why. The transient cradled an empty wine bottle in his arms, one leg hanging over the edge of the bench. A gaping zipper framed his exposed genitals.

"Hey buddy, wake up!" I shouted, holding my nose against the stench of wine and urine.

Henry smacked the bottom of the man's feet with his steel flashlight. The noise echoed off the high ceiling causing several people to look up from reading magazines. Henry gave another sharp rap and the derelict rolled off the bench, landing in a heap on the marble floor.

"Railroad police. Get on your feet."

The befuddled man scratched his scalp and used the bench to clumsily drag his body back up.

"Zip up your pants!" Henry bellowed.

The bum blinked at Henry and then at his pants. "Whash yure problum, osshfer?" His fumbling fingers managed to pull up his zipper.

"You are and it's time to go."

Henry and I each took one of the man's arms and guided him out the front doors.

"You come around here again, you're going to jail *without* your booze. Now hit the road." He stared at us as though searching for a response in his benumbed mind but when words failed to emerge from his moving lips, he gave up and staggered across the street.

Watching him, Henry sounded sad. "Usually they have more to say."

We turned to go back inside when screaming erupted behind us. The drunk had only made it halfway across the street, taking a stance in the middle of each lane. He rotated both arms like propellers while cars veered wildly around him, obscenities streaming from his mouth in nonsensical phrases.

Giving each other a high five, Henry exulted, "Now that's more like it."

Back inside the depot, an attractive woman who worked at the ticket counter motioned for us to come over. Well known to Special Agents, Honey Barr called our department on a regular basis, especially during Tony Penna's shift, to report minor infractions. She stood tall and curvy with unnaturally blonde hair worn straight and long. Her shirt's buttons strained to contain her large breasts. Honey's passion for tanning beds had left her skin a golden hue, like soft leather, with lots of tiny lines around her eyes and mouth.

"You got something going on, Honey?" I asked.

"Sure do….um, you working with Tony tonight?" She glanced hopefully over my shoulder.

"Nah, you're stuck with Henry and I. So what's the problem?"

"There's a drunk in the men's room passed out in one of the stalls."

She leaned close to me, lightly running her finger up and down my arm. A strong scent of musk wafted from her. "You'll say hi to Tony for me, won't you?" She gave me a meaningful wink.

"Consider it done, Honey." I smiled, wondering if our little interaction fell into the category of flirting or friendliness. I'd have to ask Cassie.

Sliding my arm out from under her hand, I looked at Henry and nodded toward the men's bathroom. Details didn't matter to him. If he could fight all day long and not do any paperwork, he'd have his dream job.

We entered the restroom together, our shoes squeaking on the wet, littered floor. The place reeked of ammonia. Stooping down, we looked beneath the only closed stall and spotted a pair of muddy boots dangling from the toilet. Empty wine bottles lay on the floor.

"At least his pants are pulled up. I can only handle one flasher a night," I said with relief. Pounding on the locked door, I shouted, "Police! Come out with your hands up!"

Seeing the question on Henry's face, I shrugged. "I've always wanted to say that."

We waited about thirty seconds, the deep snores of the unconscious wino on the other side confirming he'd heard nothing of what we'd said. Henry straightened up and shot me a look that meant we were done with the protocol portion of our job. It was time to kick in the door and get into his definition of police work.

In a mocking voice, I wagged my finger. "Now Henry, even drunk scumbags need their sleep."

He backed away from the stall and studied the situation, chin in hand. I knew we were about to apply one of his 'creative' strategies for lawbreakers. "Were you ever a tunnel rat in Nam?"

"Forget it, Henry! I'm *not* crawling under this door to get him out of there. You need to come up with a better plan."

"But you're the logical choice. You're shorter than me."

"Maybe so, but who knows what he's done on the floor in there."

Now we both stood back and analyzed the situation -- and then it hit me. "Let's each grab a foot and pull him out."

With that, we reached under the stall door, grabbed an ankle and yanked hard. The man came off the toilet with a "thump!" but his snoring didn't miss a beat. We dragged his legs until something stopped us.

"Can you see what it is?"

"No, but we've got him halfway - let's keep going."

With a "1-2-3" we leaned back and pulled hard but came to a halt at the same place. Our persistent efforts awakened the man. "Ow!!! My nutsh, yur killin' my...."

Squatting down, we immediately saw the problem. The metal post on which the stall door hung stood between the drunk's legs. Henry covered his mouth with one hand.

"Oops. The bum choir has a new soprano singer."

The man crawled back to the toilet, slurring obscenities. Henry yelled through the door. "Police officers. Get your things and come out of there."

We heard shuffling feet and then the jiggling of the lock. The door creaked open and before us stood an unshaven, foul-smelling man with bloodshot eyes, holding his groin area. "What'n hell ish goin' on here?"

Henry's eyes lit up – hostile confrontations were his favorite. He poked his finger in the man's face and answered, "You picked the wrong place to sleep, Mister."

The man swayed on unsteady feet and pointed back at Henry. "I'll shleep anywhere I damn pleash cuz I'm da bossh of meee."

Henry's face darkened. He pushed the belligerent man's chest hard enough to make him stumble back. "That's where you're wrong. Now clean up your junk and throw it away or I'll give you more to complain about than a sore crotch."

The man's bleary eyes squinted at Henry, no doubt trying to process the words through the stupefying effects of alcohol. His jaw moved up and down as he leaned over, clumsily grasped a bottle and dropped it in the trashcan. Once he'd cleaned up his mess, we escorted him out the front doors and left him on the sidewalk, still complaining about "dem damn bullsh."

Henry slapped me on the back with glee. "Man, that was fun! Except when we waste time doing things your way."

Since the depot now appeared free of problems, we checked out a patrol car for the remainder of the shift. Once buckled in, I tuned the radio to a Christian station as Henry drove out of the parking lot. I leaned back to savor the sweet strains of salvation in Jesus when the brakes screeched to an abrupt halt, throwing me forward against the seatbelt. "Hey! What's the matter with…."

Henry drew an invisible line with his hand. "*This* side of the car is under *my* control and that includes the radio." He punched buttons until rock music blared from the speakers and we sped off to Balmer Yard.

Henry and I had subjects we enjoyed talking about, like family, the day's news, the railroad and the best places to eat in Seattle. And subjects we avoided, like anything to do with faith and God.

When we'd first met, I believed him to be mean-spirited and cold, but the more we'd worked together, the more I realized he actually had a sensitive side. Of course, I could never tell him that. He was aggressive with lawbreakers and had zero tolerance for rude people, but when it came to his family, he proved a devoted husband and father. And as for our friendship, I had a hunch we both knew that beneath our conflicts lay a mutual loyalty and respect.

Near Balmer, we checked a line of Amtrak sleeper cars being stored on Burlington-Northern Property. Hookers liked using these for their clients but we didn't find anyone so continued to the north end of the yard. I pointed to an embankment up ahead. "Looks like we've got someone sitting under the bridge, above those boxcars."

"Yeah, I see him. I say we get him before he falls down the hill, hits the tracks and makes a bigger mess for us to clean up."

We scrambled out of the car and up the slope. I positioned myself above and behind the intruder, whereas Henry, eager for action, openly climbed the hill toward the stocky trespasser who acted unaware or unconcerned about Henry's approach. He wore a dark stained orange jacket, baggy grease-smeared pants, and dirt-caked boots. An empty bottle lay beside him, he held another in his hand. Long black hair hung past his bronzed face and grazed his shoulders, but something in his posture made me uneasy.

Henry stopped a few feet below the trespasser. "Railroad police. I need to see some identification."

The Indian stared long and hard at Henry, his knuckles tightening his grip around the bottle. Time stood still, each of us watching for the other to make the next move. Henry reached for the bottle but like a striking snake, the suspect grabbed Henry's necktie with his left hand and punched him in the face with his right. The hill's incline caused the Indian to lose his balance and fall onto Henry, knocking him off his feet. Both men tumbled end over end down the steep hill, the assailant keeping his hold on Henry's tie.

The boldness of the attack caught me by surprise. I half-ran, half-slid to catch up with them, reaching the bottom just seconds after they did. The attacker stood shakily to his feet while Henry, red faced and choking, frantically struggled to loosen his tie.

I threw myself onto the man's retreating back. The momentum shoved him hard against a boxcar's metal sides, giving me the chance to wrap my elbow around his neck from behind and pull one of his arms up high. Strangely, the man didn't utter a sound.

Henry managed to cut off his tie and now joined us, but when he saw me, he looked worried. "Dean, his blood's all over you."

My sports coat, shirt and hands were smeared red and my face felt sticky across my cheeks and forehead. "Yeah, I know, but I didn't want to let him go after what we went through to catch him."

His serious tone brought to mind the unspoken fear of contracting one of the many diseases carried in the transient population; hepatitis, TB and the scariest -- AIDS.

Just then, the man rammed his shoulder against me in an attempt to escape, unleashing a wave of suppressed anger at having his blood on my skin and seeing my partner nearly choked to death. I cursed as I tightened my grip.

Henry spoke sharply. "Hey! I can talk like that but you can't."

Immediately I felt ashamed, realizing with my profession of faith came a change in behavior, a change that proved a different focus. And the source of my reprimand humbled me – my agnostic partner.

Henry held the man so I could cuff him. "I better get something to clean my face."

"Good idea and while you're at it, call for transport."

Returning from the car, I carefully blotted a towel across my face, avoiding my eyes and mouth. The transient sat cross-legged on the ground, still quiet. Placing the towel across a deep cut on the back of his neck, I asked, "What's wrong with you?"

The man spoke in a flat tone. "I hate everyone."

"The feeling's mutual, pal," Henry snarled.

When city police and an ambulance arrived, it took several minutes to convince the paramedics my bloodied clothes were from the transient and not me. They carefully bandaged his wound and the police loaded him into their car.

I turned to Henry. "We'll have to stop at a store so I can buy a new shirt and you, a clip-on tie. I'll leave my coat in the trunk."

Once in the car, I glanced in the mirror and gasped. The smeared blood had turned to a brown color on my face, with darker spots beneath my eyes. Clumps of my hair stuck out at right angles, encased in dried blood. I needed a shower and quickly.

But before Henry could turn the car around, we received an urgent call from our fellow Special Agent, Tony Penna. He had three suspects on an isolated section of tracks that weren't cooperating and feared they were about to try something. Henry and I looked at each other, knowing we felt the same -- when one of us needed back-up, nothing else mattered.

We took off down the access road and onto city streets, breaking the speed limit and wishing we had high profile lights and siren.

We covered the miles in record time and came to a sliding stop, spewing gravel and dirt in every direction. Leaning against a retainer wall were three Hispanic men flaunting colorful tattoos and defiant expressions.

Tony strode to our car, keeping an eye on the trespassers.

"They're refusing to show me…what the *hell* happened to you?"

Without answering, I walked up to the three amigos, noticing a tensing of their posture at my appearance. They began to murmur back and forth.

"Are you giving this officer a bad time?"

For a few seconds, they stared at me, speechless. Finally, one asked, "What hoppened, Senor?"

I waved at my clothes and narrowed my eyes. "This is the blood of a man who refused to cooperate." I'd learned the quickest way to diffuse a potentially dangerous situation was to appear stronger-- or crazier-- than the troublemakers. And because it was their own code on the rails, they understood.

"We no want trouble, Senor."

"Si," another one spoke. "We no comprende what he say."

"Si, si, no comprende." They were nodding and laughing.

"Then show this man some identification." I motioned to Tony who stood beside me. In their frantic efforts to comply, they pulled pieces of paper from front and back pockets, dropping them and making mad dives to retrieve them. Finally, Tony held three ID's.

"We now know your names. If we ever catch any of you on railroad property again, you will be taught a lesson-- <u>before</u> you go to jail."

I asked Tony, "What do you want to do with these guys?"

The heaviest of the three made an appeal. "We amigos, no? You let us go, si? You no see us again."

I could see frustration on Tony's face since he suspected these men were behind a rash of recent assaults and robberies. But without evidence, we could only hope the fear of seeing me again would keep them away,

"You can go but I won't be so…" They ran off before he finished his sentence.

Waving goodbye to Tony, Henry kept a straight face until we pulled away. And then he slapped his leg and roared with laughter, leaning into the steering wheel. "The looks on those guys' faces, ha —you must've looked like the walking dead. I bet they run all the way back to Mexico!"

But my own laugh sounded hollow. For some reason, wearing someone else's blood to deter criminals felt more disturbing than clever.

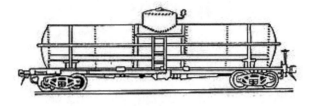

Tank Car

Chapter 17

After two years of marriage, Cassie and I bought our first home on the outskirts of Auburn, a suburb south of Seattle. Its access to countless trails bordering the beautiful White River promised lots of hiking adventures with our dogs.

Cassie still worked days at the health club while I preferred the 3-11 swing shift, when trouble was more likely to show itself. But this meant she'd be returning home each evening after I'd already left for work, so we agreed she should have a handgun for protection. I happened to own a small .38 caliber, five-shot pistol that would be perfect for her once she learned how to handle it safely.

So one gray winter morning, we packed a box of ammunition and the .38 for our first session of Handgun 101. We walked to a small clearing near the river where a slope would provide a buffer for bullets and a backdrop for three paper targets, each with a red dot in the middle. Cassie eagerly counted off twenty paces, put on safety goggles, and faced me expectantly.

I cleared my throat, trying to maintain some semblance of seriousness but her beauty still made me weak in the knees. "Never point your gun at anything you don't intend to shoot and always handle your weapon as if it's loaded."

I gave her the pistol with the muzzle pointed down and placed her hands around the grip. From behind, I took hold of her wrists and pressed my face next to hers.

"Mmmm, you smell better than any firing range."

Her silky hair against my cheek made me fight the impulse to cancel gun training for the rest of the day. But Cassie's excitement at learning how to shoot forced me to continue for at least a few more minutes.

She teased back. "Are you saying I smell better than gun powder?"

"No comparison." I continued the lesson. "Hold tight to the grip, point at the target and squeeze – don't jerk-- the trigger. Now give it a try."

I released my hold and stepped back, but not too far, expecting her to be intimidated by the kick from the first shot. The gun fired with a loud boom. Cassie giggled and proceeded to fire four more in rapid succession. Surprised at how quickly she caught on, I congratulated her on holding the gun exactly as she'd been shown. I helped her reload and she fired several more rounds.

Squinting at the targets, I commented, "It's hard to tell for sure, but your shots look pretty good from here. How about I give it a try with the second target?"

"Sure, Dean." Cassie handed me the loaded pistol in the correct position.

Now it was my turn to impress her. I'd been shooting guns since childhood and my high scores at police qualification tests confirmed my ability. I aimed the .38 with arms extended and fired five times while Cassie watched, wide-eyed. Reloading, I fired five more.

We walked over to check the targets, starting with mine. "Wow, you're really good," Cassie said, tracing the tight cluster of bullet holes with her finger.

"Well, we really can't compare, this is your first..." I stopped mid sentence. Several of Cassie's shots were clustered around the bull's-eye. "This *is* your first time, isn't it?"

She playfully mussed my hair. "Must be beginner's luck."

Well, let's try it again and see if you do as well." My ego felt a little shaky.

"You're on!" She positioned her feet on the shooting line, loaded the pistol and fired off five shots in perfect form. When I went to check, Cassie skipped past me. Her exuberant reaction confirmed my suspicion – she'd hit the target, two near the bull's-eye. Cassie did a victory dance and hugged me. "This is *so* much fun! We've got to do this again."

After firing several more rounds of ammo, we packed up what we'd brought and strolled hand in hand along the river. I pulled her close to me. "You're really something, Cassie. You rebuild motors and shoot like Annie Oakley. I got more than I bargained for when I fell for you."

She whispered, "I just hope I make you as happy as you've made me."

I kissed her passionately to show what words could not. Didn't she know just the thought of her brought a surge of feelings like nothing else? As we continued our embrace, my mind slipped into that delicious place of pleasure and I wondered if it was like this for other couples.

Arriving home in a dreamy state, we planned to continue where our kisses had left off, but the phone rang – it was my boss.

"I don't suppose this is a courtesy call to see how I'm doing, Jerry."

I sank down into the sofa, knowing there must've been a schedule change. Cassie began fixing lunch but I could see the disappointment on her face. Snoopy laid his front paws on my lap, his soulful eyes sensing the shift in my mood.

"Sorry, Dean, but we need you for a midnight stake-out. That crazy train buff from California is back. Last time he dropped a rock on the eight-mile fan, he broke a blade. We fined him but apparently he didn't learn anything."

I visualized Burlington-Northern's 7.8 mile tunnel high in the
rugged Cascade Mountains. Because of its unusual length, trains were
required to proceed slowly, resulting in trapped diesel fumes. The natural
air movement in shorter tunnels kept them clear but if a train broke down
in a long tunnel, the crew (and any illegal riders) would be exposed to
a toxic cloud. To remedy this, a powerful motorized fan, large enough
to cover the passage's east opening, had been installed. When trains
entered, it triggered the lowering of this fan, whose giant blades would
then create a draft strong enough to remove the deadly gases.

But in case the system ever failed, crews were required to carry
respirators while experienced transients wore wet kerchiefs across their
mouth and nose. Repairing the specialized fan would be extremely
costly, let alone replacing it, so I understood the urgency in Jerry's voice.
I just didn't like his timing. With a glance at Cassie, I sighed into the
phone. "Any description on this jerk?"

"He's driving a black Chevy Blazer with radio equipment to
monitor railroad and police calls. White male, 5'10", medium build,
50's, brown hair on sides and back of his head, bald on top. His M.O. is
to strike between 2:00 and 6:00 a.m. so I need you there from midnight
to sunrise. We have a restraining order on him so you can arrest him for
criminal trespassing and violating the order."

Hanging up the phone, I smiled at Cassie. "Bad news is I'm
working tonight, good news is I don't have to leave for hours." She
snuggled up against my chest. Lunch would have to wait.

Long after night fell and Cassie went to sleep in my arms, I
tiptoed over and around each occupied doggie-bed to get to the closet,
where I pulled on extra layers of clothes for the surveillance. At the door
I paused to look at my family, feeling content.

On my way out to the garage, I grabbed a large spool of nylon thread, some munchies and a can of pop. As soon as the car's heater warmed up enough to be comfortable, I drove through our darkened neighborhood and headed north to Everett, about an hour's travel time.

From Everett, I turned east on Highway 2, toward the black jagged peaks of the Cascade Range. Houses became sparser as the road's grade grew steeper. I drank the pop and stretched my arms over the steering wheel, catching a glimpse of lights through the windshield. I pulled over and leaned my head out the window – and caught my breath. A myriad of glowing, twinkling stars stretched above and around me like a black velvet canopy displaying heaven's diamonds.

"Wow, God, you really outdid yourself when you made all this."

Feeling less alone in the universe, I continued the twisting, upward climb until I recognized the Burlington-Northern turn off. My headlights bounced on the narrow, dirt road that divided a tall forest on one side and a tumbling stream on the other. Once across the tracks, the road ended abruptly at a supply shed. And beyond the shed stood the famous eight-mile tunnel.

I stepped out into the chilly mountain air, pulling on a hat, gloves, and my heaviest jacket. My footsteps and the stream's babbling sounded amplified in the silence of isolation -- not even a coyote or an owl could be heard. By the time I reached the tunnel's entrance, the dampness had seeped through my clothes. I couldn't stop shivering.

The passage's yawning blackness looked more like an impenetrable wall than a diesel-breathing mouth. Gazing upward, I saw the massive fan now requiring my protection. "What kind of psycho would drive all the way up here and drag rocks big enough to damage those blades up that hill?"

I suddenly wanted the man who'd kept me from sleeping in my own bed with my own wife to show up in the worst way tonight.

Returning to the car, I drove about a hundred yards down the road and backed into a stand of young pines, allowing me to see anyone driving by without them seeing me.

Now for my low-budget detection system. I counted off ten feet from the car, crossed the road and tied one end of the nylon thread to the trunk of a tree about three feet from the ground. Unraveling the spool as I retraced my steps, I looped it around a second tree and back to the car where I pulled it through the front passenger window. I carefully tied it around the empty pop can and set it on my dash. If I fell asleep, someone driving by would catch the thread with their grill or fender, which would knock the can over and wake me up.

I had just made myself comfortable in the front seat when unearthly groans echoed down the mountain, like a wounded monster. I heard a motor turn on and then movement – the fan! A train must have entered the opposite end, giving me a chance to see the blades in action. And they were impressive. Nearby trees were whipped and bent at right angles as if hit by gale-force winds. If I'd still been standing there, I would've been blown away – literally.

After several minutes, the fan retracted to its place above the tunnel's entrance, allowing a train to exit. "So that's how it works," I mused aloud.

Settling back into the seat, I munched on the snacks I'd brought, sang every song I knew, and debated the latest political issues with myself. Hours plodded on until I could no longer form coherent sentences - my brain had entered a state of sleep-deprived numbness, void of all logic. The stars blurred and my breathing grew deeper.

The explosion of shattering glass awoke me with a start, and I reached for my pistol, heart pounding. Blinking at the empty space that used to be a passenger window, the surge of cold air shocked me into alertness. Red taillights disappeared down the road.

Keeping my lights off, I followed, wishing the heater would work faster. Ahead, a small compact had parked beside the supply shed. The suspect had been seen driving a Chevy Blazer but perhaps he'd changed vehicles to fool us. Well, he'd be the fool this time -- I couldn't wait to slap cuffs on him and go back to my warm bed.

I eased to a stop right behind the car: no sign of anyone around. I carefully opened my door, glad I'd remembered to disable the dome-light button with a strip of tape. Creeping to the driver's side, hand on my gun, I leaned forward to look inside but movement in the back seat made me freeze. When I recognized what moved, my frustration vented.

"I've got a broken window, I'm freezing my butt off, all because two people want to get naked." Well, if I was having a lousy night, so would they. Shining my light through the window, I pounded my fist on the door. "Police!"

Immediately, two heads popped up. The shock in their eyes made me feel better – misery really did love company. The girl pushed the boy off of her and he rolled onto the floor. They hurriedly pulled clothes on with furtive looks in my direction.

"Come out through this door." I banged my fist to emphasize which one. "And make sure your hands are empty."

A skinny teen-aged boy emerged first, followed closely by an equally skinny girl. They slumped against the car.

"What are you two doing out here?" I asked incredulously.

"Nothin', just messin' around." The boy squinted into the light but the girl hung her head down in silence, long hair covering her face.

"Wrong -- you were putting your lives in danger. I'm up here looking for a criminal. What if he'd found you first?"

"We didn't know…we're just…" His voice trailed off.

I wrote down their names, address and phone numbers and made them a promise.

"Since you're both minors, I *will* be calling your parents and informing them about tonight. If I ever catch you near our tracks again, you're going to juvie. Now get out of here."

"Th-th-thanks officer, so-so-sorry," the boy said, shivering in his light clothing. They scrambled back into their car and sped off towards civilization and heated homes, leaving me alone once more on the mountainside.

After three more dreary nights of surveillance, Jerry called it off. But a week later Henry and I were in the office finishing a report when the phone rang.

"Police services, Stone speaking."

"This is Harborview Hospital's Emergency Room. We have a man with a fractured arm who's claiming he was knocked down by a *fan* belonging to the railroad. Can you confirm his story?"

Henry gave me a thumbs-up. "You bet we can—we'll be right there."

Chapter 18

The warmer summer months seemed to trigger a mass influx of transients from across the nation, the risk of freezing to death on moving trains no longer a deterrent. Henry and I were so busy warning, arresting and writing reports on the new trespassers and suspects, in addition to our regular offenders, that we'd developed good cop/bad cop scenarios to ease the stress of dealing with drunks for hours on end.

Entering the north end of Balmer Yard one late afternoon, we were waved down by a switchman standing by a cross-shaped, color coded switch used to move train cars to designated tracks. When we pulled up, he leaned into my window, pushing his ball cap off his forehead. "Just wanted to let y'all know we almost ran over a guy a coupla minutes ago."

"On purpose or by accident?" Henry asked, the corners of his mouth twitching.

The switchman missed the humor and replied with all seriousness. "Well, the train cars we're pushin' are on tracks so I'd say it was by accident."

He pointed to a set and continued. "The dummy was sleepin' on thet far rail. If I hadn't woke him up, he'd be a full head shorter."

Henry and I laughed at the man's choice of words but when we saw his puzzled expression, put on a serious demeanor with much coughing and throat clearing.

"Uh, so, what did he look like?" I asked.

"Taller'n me, bout six feet. Younger'n me, bout in his forty's. Fatter'n me, with slicked-back hair. An' he's missin' two front teeth."

Henry and I spoke at the same time. "Scary Larry's back?"

The switchman threw his arms in the air. "I dunno! I thought y'all were s'posed to figure thet out!"

I opened my mouth to explain but Henry drove off, leaving our confused switchman shaking his head. We didn't get far before we spotted movement inside a boxcar parked on a siding (side-track).

"Wonder who we got here?" Henry said, turning off the ignition. We approached on foot from opposite sides, shining our flashlights into the dark interior. Inside, a young Hispanic boy huddled in the corner.

"Police! Come out of there!" Henry said gruffly.

"Policia?"

"Si, Policia." I only knew a few Spanish words and if he didn't speak English, this would be a brief conversation.

The youth cautiously approached, clutching something to his chest. He wore an oversized shirt that hung to his knees and his pants were rolled up around his ankles. I motioned for him to open his hand so I could see what he held; a blackened rotting potato lay between his muddy fingers. He'd probably been surviving on whatever dropped off the trains, including spoiled produce.

"Comprende English?"

"No senor, no comprende." He pointed to a train and asked, "To Wenatchee?"

We heard this question often from illegals that had crossed the Mexican border to pick fruit in central Washington. Many started the journey without money or food and after riding freight trains for weeks, arrived in Wenatchee hurt or sick. And they were the lucky ones.

Once the season ended and the workers hopped a train for home or another job, gangs would prey on them for their hard-earned cash. If we found them after they'd been beaten and robbed, we couldn't offer much more than sympathy and a warning. The chances of finding a specific thief among hundreds who rode trains across the U.S., without addresses or real names, would be next to impossible.

Using hand gestures, I motioned for the youth to stay away because "banditos" would hurt him. He seemed to understand at least that part and followed me off railroad property. With a good natured "adios," he disappeared into the brush.

Continuing our search, Henry pointed to a large bulky figure clambering up the ladder of a gondola car, like a giant sloth. Once at the top, he dropped down inside.

The tops of gondolas were open for loading and unloading merchandise while their sides were lower than other train cars -- some were only five feet high. They were most often used to haul dense or bulky freight such as boulders, heavy machinery and railroad ties. My dad referred to them as "coal cars" because that's what they were used for in his day. When empty, they were a favorite hiding place for transients who didn't seem to mind the dust and grease.

Henry and I strolled around the gondola. "Hey Henry, do you suppose there could be a trespasser around here?"

"Gee, I don't know Dean. Let's find out, shall we?"

We each climbed the ladder on opposite ends of the car, reaching the top at the same time. We looked down into the gondola and covered our mouths with our hands, as if shocked. "Why look Henry, it's Scary Larry!"

Keeping our eyes on him, we dropped over the side and picked our way across the muck-covered deck. I stayed in front facing Larry while Henry stood behind him.

"Larry, Larry, Larry," I said, shaking my head. "What are we going to do with you?"

With a bored expression, he shrugged his big, round shoulders. "Ain't nothin' you kin do 'bout me."

Giving Henry a wink, I snarled back. "That's where you're wrong. Give me your ID – quick!"

Larry knew the routine and handed it to me. "Is this *everything* with your name on it?" I asked.

He was confused. "Ya' got my ID, what else ya want?"

"You don't ask the questions, I do," I said between clenched teeth. "I'm only going to tell you one more time – take everything out of your pockets and put them in your pack."

He resembled the obese Buddha statue that greeted us at our favorite Chinese restaurant, his protruding stomach resting on crossed, pudgy legs. Larry gulped hard.

"Why ya doin' this? I ain't done nothin' I ain't done before."

"Cause I don't want any identification found on your body."

Scary Larry's eyes bulged. "Wha, what're ya gonna do?"

"I'm going to solve all your problems. After today, you'll *never* have to worry about where you're going to sleep or find your next drink."

Feeling smug at how well the scene was playing out, I glanced at Henry but found him scowling. What could be bugging him? And then I remembered – I'd agreed to be the good cop this shift. Time for a role change.

I shook my head and lowered my shoulders. With despair in my voice, I choked out the words, "I don't think...I can do this. The last time made me sick for days."

Scary Larry turned to look at Henry, whose grin told me he understood.

"Ah, don't worry, Dean, it gets easier every time." Henry turned his full attention to the trespasser and shouted, "Com'on Larry, let's get this over with! Grab your pack and follow me outside."

The sudden change in Henry's tone startled Larry. He grunted as he lifted his sizeable bulk off the floor and waddled after Henry, heaving himself up and over the edge of the gondola. I followed behind, just as another patrolman drove up -- it was Eugene.

Henry and I nodded at each other; we now had a good cop to play to our bad cops. He just didn't know it yet.

Eugene rolled down his window, his curly red hair looking more bushy than usual. At least he'd learned to tone down his clothes, with the exception of ties – today he wore one with purple spots.

"Everything all right here, guys?"

Henry started to speak but I interrupted. "Just taking care of some loose ends." Opening the trunk of our patrol car, I pointed to Larry. "Give me your stuff and get in."

Larry stared in disbelief. He planted both feet wide apart and wagged his bloated face. "Hell no, I ain't gittin' in there an' there's no way you kin make me." By now, a curious Eugene had strolled over to watch.

"Larry, Larry, it's all in how you look at things." I motioned to the open trunk. "You've been wanting a free ride from the railroad – well here it is!"

Larry began to hyperventilate. "I won't come on yur propety agin, I promise."

Henry saw his chance to reclaim his role. He pushed his finger into the alarmed man's stomach and sneered, "You're right about that, Larry, you'll NEVER be seen again."

We'd now reached the point where the good cop is supposed
to step in and stop us. But Eugene had completely missed our cues. I
lunged for Larry's arm and began dragging him, Henry leaned close to
Eugene and whispered, "Stop us!"

Eugene's red eyebrows raised. "Me? Stop you two?" I almost
had Larry to the trunk.

Henry grabbed Eugene's spotted tie and hissed, "Yes! Now!"

Smoothing his crumpled tie, he hurried to where Larry and I
were scuffling. Timidly tapping my arm with a trembling index finger,
he said, "Dean-stop-this. May-I-talk-to-Mr.-Larry-in-private?"

I snarled at him. "What for?"

"Uh, I-just-do." He sounded like a robot from a science fiction
movie.

"OK, you got *half* a minute and then I want him *in* the trunk
before someone sees us."

Eugene led an anxious Larry away but still within our hearing.
"Mr. Scary Larry, these guys are crazy. No one will even work with
them...they should've been fired years ago."

Henry's head shot up and he swore under his breath.

Larry pleaded with Eugene. "Kin you hep me?"

"How fast can you run?" Eugene whispered.

"Right now, real fast."

"Start running and I'll hold them back as long as I can. But if
they ever catch you here again, you're on your own."

Larry took off in a pigeon-toed, heavy-footed gait, his baggy
pants making a whooshing sound as each leg brushed against the other.
His short arms stuck out from his sides, bouncing up and down with each
stride. We gave him a few yards and then screamed, "Don't let him get
away, he's mine, he's mine!" He made it over a small rise without once
looking back.

"What did you mean we should've been *fired*?!" Henry stood nose to nose with a stumbling, stammering Eugene whose flushed face matched his hair. I stepped between them and shook Eugene's hand. "Thanks for the help but don't quit your day job. Scary Larry's a better runner than you are an actor."

We resumed our patrol but hadn't left the yard before receiving a call from the Yardmaster. "Special Agent, there's been a collision between a car and an engine on Harbor Island. No injuries reported so we just need you to investigate and report."

"Yardmaster, we'll be there in about 25 minutes."

We drove over the bridge that crossed the Duwamish Waterway, connecting southwest Seattle with the tiny island used as an industrial area. Several railroad tracks traversed its span, allowing train cars to deliver freight to business warehouses.

When we arrived at the accident site, a switch engine sat idling on a set of tracks. Smaller than the more common "road engines" that pulled cars across the country, switch engines were used primarily in yards to move train cars to the correct track going to the correct destination with the help of a ground switchman.

We approached a small crowd standing around a man who kept moaning and cursing, while running his fingers through his hair. "We're with the railroad police. Can you tell us what happened?"

He pointed to a badly dented and crunched blue Ford Galaxy whose front fender still hung from a boxcar's ladder. "*That's* what happened."

"Well at least it's an old beater," Henry said.

"No! No! That's not my car—*that* one is!"

We followed his trembling finger to a sleek, two-door, Pontiac Grand Prix whose cherry red paint had been gouged across its entire right side. Hundreds of tiny shards from a smashed headlight and two windows glittered on the ground.

As we pieced together the incident, we determined that when the switch engine began moving train cars, the Ford's fender had caught on one of the boxcars being moved. Its owner had parked too close to the tracks. Before the ground switchman and engineer realized what had happened, the Ford had been dragged back and forth three times, banging into the Pontiac with each pass.

Henry whistled in amazement. "That's too bad, you had yourself a nice car."

The man spoke in a monotone. "I made sure I parked far enough away from the track so it wouldn't get hit. And then some jerk parks his piece of junk here. I'm in so much trouble."

Trying to cheer him up, Henry patted his shoulder. "Call your insurance agent and let them take care of it. At least you weren't in the car when it happened."

"It would have been better if I had! My wife saved for years to buy this Grand Prix. I wanted to show it to my friends so she made me promise nothing would happen to her baby….I'm a dead man."

Henry and I shuddered at the image of what waited for him at home. We didn't have grounds to fine the Ford's owner because the boxcar hadn't been damaged, but we did call a tow truck and have it impounded.

When our shift ended at midnight, I headed home, automatically maneuvering through late night traffic on East Marginal Way. But a lone figure on the median dividing the busy highway lanes caught my attention.

Making a quick U-turn, I turned on my emergency flashers and slowed down for another look. It was the Hispanic teen we'd found earlier in a boxcar. "Hey, amigo. Remember me policia." I shouted to him.

He cautiously walked over and when he recognized me, vigorously nodded. "Si, si, policia."

I motioned for him to get in and he practically dove into the back seat. He had to be hungry and he definitely needed a shower.

In a very tentative voice, he asked, "Wenatchee?"

I shook my head, "No Wenatchee."

He sat quietly while I thought about what I could do for him. Seeing a fast food restaurant, I pulled into the drive-through and ordered a bucket of chicken, coleslaw, and dessert. With the steaming food's aroma filling the car, I headed to a nearby hotel and motioned for him to wait.

A dignified silver-haired man in a suit greeted me from behind the reception desk.

"I need a room for one night for a friend who doesn't speak English."

"Just sign here and we'll take care of the rest." He didn't act surprised by the request.

"I'll pay now and if he needs anything more, give me a call so I can take care of it." I wrote my phone number on a card and handed it to him.

"No problem, sir and I'll make sure your friend's stay is a comfortable one."

Returning to the car, I picked up the food and motioned for him to follow me, giving him the key and letting him unlock the door. When he stepped into the room, he glanced around nervously.

I set the food down on a small table and led him to the bathroom. Pointing to the shower, I said, "Amigo, you smell bad." I pinched my nose and made a face.

"Si, si"

At the nightstand, I drew a picture of the sun, the number "12" and tapped the clock's face. "Twelve o'clock, manana, you vamoose. Comprende?"

"Si, Senor. Twelve, manana, vamoose." He smiled.

I then drew a picture of the hotel, the road out front and a bus station a few blocks away. "Bus to Wenatchee. Comprende?"

"Si, Wenatchee!" His smile turned to laughter.

Placing a twenty-dollar bill on the drawing, I said, "Adios, amigo and may Dios bless you." He watched me leave but before I reached the door, he blurted out, "Senor! Por favor!" Turning around, I saw tears tumbling from his eyes. He ran across the room and shook my hand vigorously. "Muchas gracias, muchas gracias. Vaya con Dios, amigo."

On the drive home that night, I felt the strangest sense of elation, and wondered why.

Chapter 19

Each morning after Cassie left for work, I'd fill three colored bowls with gooey chunks smothered in gravy and call out, "Chow time." Our canine trio would race across the linoleum floor, each sliding to a stop in front of their own dish. I'd snap the newspaper open and lean back in my recliner for an hour of relaxed reading.

But on this particular day, my peace was abruptly interrupted with frantic barking from Snoopy. He ran to the front entry, Poo-Poo and Bobby right behind him.

"Good boy, Snoopy. I didn't even hear anyone knock." I opened the door to an empty porch. Stepping outside, I scanned the front of the house while the toy poodles ran around the yard, stiff legged and alert. "Hmmm, must be a false alarm. Okay you two, let's go back inside." Shaking my head, I returned to the recliner.

The next day, it happened again. Just as I'd settled back to read the paper, Snoopy ran to the front door, barking fiercely. The poodles caught up with him, noses in the air, yelping their support.

"I must be losing my hearing." But once again, no one stood on the porch or anywhere near the house. And then it hit me -- the one who started the commotion hadn't joined us outside. Suspicious, I stepped back inside and peeked around the wall separating the entry from the kitchen. There was Snoopy, wolfing down the last bits of food from Bobby's dish.

"Snoopy!"

He immediately cowered and averted his gaze, the very tip of his tail wagging low between his back legs. "You're too smart for your own good, so the eating arrangements are going to change." I refilled Bobby and Poo-Poo's bowls and while they ate, Snoop lay on my lap with a noticeably bulging belly, no doubt working on another ruse to outwit the poodles.

The phone rang. When I picked up, I didn't recognize the trembling voice on the other end. "Dean...can you come get me?"

"Cassie? Are you okay?"

"No...I'm not..."

Hearing the fear in her voice, I slammed the phone down and made it in record time to where she worked. All sorts of possibilities ran through my mind but none made any sense – what could be wrong?

I made my way past treadmills and weight machines, to the new office she'd been so excited about. She'd picked out a nice desk and put up shelves for books and a big framed photo of us. A large window opened up to the gym so she could keep track of her clients while getting paperwork done. But when I arrived, the door was closed and the blinds were drawn.

"Sweetheart, it's me." I softly knocked and pushed open the door.

The only light came from a small lamp she'd purchased at a flea market one weekend. On the floor behind her desk, I found her sitting in a corner, trembling hands covering her face. I wrapped her in my arms. "Sweetheart, what's the matter?"

Her face looked pale and strained, her eyes flashing a terror I'd never seen before. She held onto me tightly and choked out the words. "I was in the locker room when a client turned out the lights, not realizing I was still in there. Someone had left a shower running so I went to turn it off but when I stood there...in the dark with the...water dripping down the drain...I suddenly felt panicked and ..."

"Shhhh, it's okay." I gently rocked her, pressing my face against hers.

"Something must've scared you, that's all." I lifted her chin with my finger so I could look in her eyes. "I've got an idea - how about a day off with your favorite guy? Get someone to cover your shift and let's head to the beach and try out that dune buggy of yours. What do you say?"

She wiped her tears. "Thanks for coming here. Maybe I do need a break." A weak smile returned to her face. "Let's do it."

An hour later, we were headed to Ocean Shores, a resort town where vehicles can drive on long stretches of sand. I'd volunteered to pack the picnic. When we arrived with the bright yellow buggy in tow, we found the beach gloriously deserted. Quickly disconnecting the car, we loaded our food and dogs into the front seat and took off, Cassie at the wheel.

The cool, salty air misted our faces as we sped near the water's edge. Cassie whooped out loud as she wove in and out, teasing the waves to try and catch her. With one arm supporting a huddle of anxious dogs and the other clutching the roll bar, I watched Cassie confidently handling the car she'd put together. Despite my white-knuckled apprehension, I felt proud of her abilities.

As the scenery passed in a blur of browns and blues, twelve sets of nails dug into my bare legs. "Do we have to go so fast?"

Cassie's eyes shone with excitement. Above the noise of the engine she shouted, "This was a great idea. Are you having as much fun as I am?"

"I doubt it but don't let that slow you down," I shouted back. "When are we stopping for lunch?"

"How about right now."

Cassie spun the wheel in a heart-gripping 360, spraying sand above our heads as the buggy slid to a stop. The dogs scrambled out before I'd even unbuckled my seat belt. "Hey, this looks like a good place for a picnic." I forced my voice to sound nonchalant, willing my legs to remain steady as I headed for a low mound. "We can use this as a table and spread the blanket next to it, over here."

I arranged plates and cups on the blanket and then placed our food on top of the sandy knoll while Cassie leaned back to soak up the sun, the dogs playing around her feet. Suddenly, Cassie cupped her hand over her mouth and imitated a bugle. "Charge!" She grabbed me around the waist and knocked me down, all three dogs barking and jumping over us. But I had a secret weapon – I knew Cassie's tickle spots. I twisted around and moved my fingers toward the side of her neck.

She laughed and screamed, "Don't tickle me, don't tickle me!"

"Give up?"

She looked at me seriously. "I love you."

I relaxed my hold and leaned over to kiss her but my lips met Snoopy's hairy head instead. The distraction was all Cassie needed to wrap her legs around my chest and knock me backwards. "Ha! I won two out of three. Time for lunch."

We ate our sandwiches and tossed pieces of kibble to the dogs, Cassie sitting cross-legged on the blanket as she talked about work. I leaned against the table of sand so I could watch her, relieved that whatever had frightened her earlier seemed forgotten for the time being. She was once more enthusiastic and animated as she described how much she loved helping people get healthy and strong in her position as a personal trainer.

"I was talking to this woman between sets at the club yesterday and she told me about a black powder club."

"What do they do?"

"It's a group of people who relive the days of the old west, using black powder muskets to shoot targets. Some of them use tomahawks and knives and have throwing contests. Since you're already good at throwing knives, I thought you'd like to give it a try. The part I like best is that you get to make your own clothing like the Indians did."

I dreamily pictured Cassie in a buckskin dress. "Sounds good to me. Why don't you find out when they meet and let's check it out."

As we spoke, I lazily made designs in the mound with my fingers. When I noticed an odd squishy feel, I dug deeper into the sand. The dogs ran over to inspect my work and began sniffing intensely. Suddenly a whiff of something awful hit us.

"EEEEEWWWWWW!"

Cassie and I jumped to our feet, holding our noses as we backed away. But it had the opposite effect on the dogs—they rubbed their faces and backs against whatever lay buried there, clearly euphoric. Taking a deep breath, I held it and stepped in for a closer look; a jawbone and eye socket coldly stared back. The tattered pieces of spotted gray hide clinging to the bone identified it as a seal – a very dead one.

"Dean, what is it?"

I gulped. "Uh, can dead seals contaminate food?"

She quickly gathered the remnants of our meal. "Dean, you're *never* picking our picnic spot again!"

I followed contritely behind her, carrying each reeking dog at arm's length to the dune buggy. After a quick ride back to the parking lot, we hitched the buggy to the car, transferred the dogs to the backseat and drove straight home with all the windows down.

My next shift with Henry began with a call from the dispatcher. A body had been found on the tracks. "I hate these calls. You never know what you're going to find."

Henry pointed to a small bridge arching over the tracks. "I bet we find the body under there."

We parked on a side road and walked across the bridge's aged wooden planks, feeling them sag beneath our weight. When we reached the halfway point, we looked down and just as Henry had predicted, a crumpled form lay between the shiny lines of steel. Henry returned to the car to request paramedics and Seattle police, since this section of tracks fell within city limits.

I slid down the rocky embankment and walked over to the body, or at least the biggest part of it. Each leg had been severed and lay a few yards away on either side. One arm, separated at the shoulder, was so flattened I didn't recognize it as human until I saw the curled fingers at one end, like a giant black spider fused to a piece of cardboard. The face looked upward and it looked young.

Henry came up behind me as I touched the cold skin of the corpse's neck.

"Definitely dead."

With his limbs scattered about and a wide-eyed expression on his face, he looked more like a mannequin that had fallen off the train on its way to a department store.

Footsteps behind us interrupted my thoughts. A heavyset man in striped coveralls and a taller, lankier version in the same attire approached us tentatively. "You the Special Agents?"

"Yes, we are. I'm Dean O'Shea and this is Henry Stone. Are you from the train that hit this...him?"

"Yeah, I'm the conductor and he's the brakeman. The engineer's back with the engine."

We stood silently while they stared at the body, as if the living were seeking comprehension from the dead. Finally, the conductor spoke. "He jumped off the bridge right in front of the engine. All I saw was this guy falling through the air."

The brakeman leaned over the torso and gasped. "Hey, I think I know this guy. He's a clerk at the railroad's yard office."

We were writing their information when two paramedics scrambled down the hill, followed by a city police officer. The medics exchanged a few words with us, assessed the body's condition, and returned to the ambulance. The officer began interviewing the conductor and brakeman to try and determine one of two possibilities -- suicide or homicide -- when the coroner arrived, brushing off his shirt and pants after hiking down to the tracks. A younger man followed with a collapsed gurney.

"I'm Dr. McGrath and this is my assistant, Robert."

We nodded and resumed our small talk, having switched into neutral to deal with the scene before us. The coroner unfolded a thick, black bag and with his assistant's help, methodically picked up each piece of someone's son, brother or dad. When they were finished, the bag was zipped shut and placed on the upright gurney. Dr. McGrath pulled the tight latex gloves off his hands. "Well, then, I think that's it for..."

Laughter burst out from the bridge above us. Three boys leaned over the railing, pointing at the gurney and jeering.

"We need to say something before we leave," I said to Henry.

He nodded and I led the way, scrambling up the embankment in a surge of adrenaline from the rage I felt inside. The boys were too distracted by the scene below to notice us. "Is there something funny down there?" I barked, trying to keep my anger under control. They were, after all, just kids.

Startled, they turned to face us. The oldest of the three shrugged. "It looked kinda funny seein' him in pieces."

I stepped closer to make sure I had their attention. "That body belonged to someone who was part of a family, maybe had kids like you. Would you be laughing if he was someone you knew?"

The boys looked at the ground and shuffled their feet.

Henry waved them off. "You kids get outta here and go on home." We watched them trot past the end of the bridge and a parked car with its driver's door hung open. No one appeared to be inside.

"Let's check it out," said Henry.

The vehicle was an old Plymouth littered with crumpled paper and plastic cups on the floor and seats. A note lay on the dash in child-like letters: Im tired of living a lie time to end this hell

Henry shook his head. "You'd think as long as you were breathing, there'd be something to live for." We returned to the tracks and gave the note to the police officer, agreeing it appeared to be suicide.

Once everyone concluded his role in a man's death, we resumed our patrol in a somber mood. As a soldier who'd fought so hard to survive, I couldn't comprehend someone throwing his life away. Could life really get so bad that death seemed the better choice? Or worse, the only choice?

A familiar voice broke the silence. "Yardmaster to Special Agent.'

"This is the Special Agent. What can I do for you today, Yardmaster?"

"Got a call from the switch crew. Some guys are fighting at the north end of Stacy Yard."

"We'll be there in fifteen minutes."

Henry drove faster, his jaw tight. Each situation demanded different energy levels and mindsets, leaving no time to process our reactions between calls. We'd developed an ability to detach from one and prepare for the next in a matter of minutes.

I sighed. "Looks like it's going to be awhile before we eat."

Henry grinned--he'd rather fight than eat anytime. "That's okay with me."

We pulled into Stacy Yard without seeing anyone, which meant we'd have to go find the troublemakers. Getting out of the car, we took a few moments to adjust the gear on our belts.

Train yards are dangerous places. Switch engines continuously move cars from one track to another, making it necessary to watch several tracks at once. Sometimes switch engines release cars to move along the rails unescorted. These roll slowly and quietly until they connect with a parked car down the line, adding the risk of being run over or caught between the two. To make matters worse, the space between tracks is narrow and some cars have equipment or freight hanging over the edges.

When we needed to get across a yard with long trains on the tracks, we'd jump between the cars by using the release levers and knuckles (definitely not in the company manual) while watching for engines pushing or pulling that particular line. If we did end up on the wrong car at the wrong time, the slack motion could knock us off or throw us beneath the wheels but we chanced it, wanting to get to the action in the least amount of time.

We didn't find anyone around the trains so we headed for an open lot past the tracks. Our hunch paid off. Two yelling, cursing men wrestled with the uncoordinated motions of the inebriated, the taller man's long black hair hiding his face as he squeezed the other's head in the crook of his arm. The shorter, stockier man danced around in an attempt to free himself, bellowing and punching his opponent's stomach with flailing fists. A direct hit finally broke the headlock and they fell to the ground, sending up puffs of dry dust. A third man sat cross-legged, watching them in stony silence.

"The show's over, boys!" I shouted.

The wrestlers continued rolling on the ground, trading punches in a kind of delayed action, oblivious to our presence. I strolled over to the lone spectator. "What's going on here?"

The disheveled man looked up. "You bulls?"

"Yup. Now what's their problem?" I asked, pointing to the fighters.

"Well, seein's this here's our first time in Seattle, we started drinkin' to celebrate but run out of juice so I got this here jug." He patted a gallon of wine perched on his lap.

"But before I cracked the seal, them two started fightin' over it. Guess their mama never taught 'em to share."

I checked the man's identification while Henry quietly watched the wrestlers. They didn't appear close to quitting despite bloody noses and cut lips.

"Henry, why don't you do the honors so we don't miss today's buffet specials."

"My pleasure."

Snatching the gallon jug from the unsuspecting man's lap, Henry untwisted the cap and positioned himself over the fighters. Lifting the bottle high, he turned it upside down and announced, "Welcome to Seattle, boys!"

As soon as the wine splashed onto the men, they forgot the fight, sputtering and yelling instead at Henry. Their clothes were now a trendy deep purple.

"What the hell.....I'm gonna kick yur ass." The stocky man staggered to his feet.

"No you're not." He spun around to look at me. "We're railroad police and you're not doing anything to anyone. Besides, my partner just solved your problem and there's nothing to fight about anymore."

We hurriedly wrote their information on contact cards, got them to their feet and escorted them to the edge of railroad property. "Enjoy your visit boys, and don't miss Seattle's Underground Tour."

I turned to Henry. "Now let's eat before something else happens."

We sped to our favorite Mexican restaurant, Azteca, near the waterfront. But no sooner had we dug into our giant burritos with extra guacamole and sour cream than the portable radio crackled. "Stacy Street Yardmaster to Special Agent."

I filled my mouth with an enormous bite so Henry would have to answer. "This is the Special Agent, Yardmaster. What can I do for you this time?" He hungrily eyed his plate.

"I need to talk to you in my office immediately."

"We're on our way."

We wolfed down as much as we could, letting the sauce drip down our chins, and left a $20 on the table. Fifteen minutes later, we entered the Yardmaster's cubicle, brushing corn chips off our shirts. He got right to the point. "One of our switchmen left his assigned portable radio in the lunch room today. By the time he realized his mistake, it was gone."

Henry snarled, "This is the big emergency – some idiot lost his radio?"

"A missing radio is serious but there's more." He lowered his voice. "Someone's broadcasting on the stolen radio-- in Spanish."

"So a Mexican stole it – so what?" Henry stated dryly.

The Yardmaster gave Henry a sharp look. "We've been able to translate some of what he's saying and we think he's at the Bush Hotel threatening someone. He keeps repeating the word 'morte' -- that's Spanish for 'death', you know."

We rolled our eyes and Henry swore. "Hell, he's probably saying 'norte' as in 'Follow me *north*, amigos.'"

The Yardmaster folded his arms across his chest, clearly not in the mood for jokes or debating.

"Okay, okay, how long has he been using the radio?" I asked.

"Off and on for about two hours now."

"Give us twenty minutes and then have someone broadcast continuously on that channel for an hour. Can you do that?"

"Yeah, I can have one of our guys do that. But why?"

Giving Henry a wink, I explained. "Henry and I will pay a visit to the Bush Hotel. We'll walk down the halls and listen at each door. When we hear your man's transmission, we'll have found the thief and the radio."

Henry and I both knew our chances for success were slim to none, but at least we wouldn't be bored – something we avoided as much as hunger.

We left the Yardmaster's office and drove down Jackson Street toward a six-story brick building with large letters painted across the top -- "BUSH HOTEL."

Completed in 1915, the historic structure had provided low-income housing for ambitious Chinese immigrants and Japanese builders during Seattle's growing years. But today, its tenants were mainly vagabonds and misfits.

We parked our car in Chinatown and walked the short distance to the hotel. Once we passed through the double doors and into the lobby, everything about it exuded old; stained, bland-colored carpet, aged reception desk, walls that badly needed new paint, the musty smell of cigarettes and body odor. Behind the counter, a potbellied man in a tight shirt watched a small TV. When we showed our ID's, he waved us toward the stairs without waiting for an explanation. This must happen a lot, I mused.

At the top of the steps, we found a hallway with the same stained carpet bordering rooms on either side. The shared common bathrooms were at the end of the hall.

"This isn't going to work, is it Henry?"

"Hell no, but we'll hear some interesting conversations. You take the left side, I'll take the right."

The yellow ceiling lights cast a jaundiced hue on the walls as I leaned close to each door, hearing the voices of people who inhabited an invisible stratum of society; prostitutes, addicts, transients. Behind one, a female voice screamed, "Higher, reach for the moon, higher!" From another, what sounded like several men howling. "I really don't want to know what that's about," I muttered.

Henry motioned for me to join him. "Listen to this one."

A woman shouted, "Yeah, that's right, you the best, baby. No one's good as you. I'm gonna keep you around, baby."

"Definitely paid for," I said.

We continued down the corridor straining to hear a railroad employee's jargon. But unexpectedly, one of the doors swung open, leaving my head inches from the barrel chest of a man in dirty brown pants and a sleeveless undershirt.

Raising two huge fists, he thundered, "What're you doin' here?"

Looking into his angry, bloodshot eyes, I stepped back and stumbled over my feet. He'd caught me off guard with a perfectly legitimate question. If only I had a legitimate answer. "Aaaahhhhhh, I'm selling magazines to pay my way through college." I scolded myself for a lack of creativity, especially since I didn't have any magazines.

The man glared at me in cold silence.

Trying to sound credible, I asked, "Would you and the Mrs. be interested in a subscription?"

"There ain't no Mrs. and I don't see no damn magazines."

Looking over my shoulder, I pointed to Henry several doors ahead. "There's my partner and he's carrying them. Now, would you be interested in fashion or interior design for your, uh, home here?"

The man's eyes narrowed. Pointing a fat finger at me, he warned, "Keep the hell away from my door." He slammed it with such force the thin walls shook.

I rejoined Henry at the end of the hall. We agreed to call it quits and headed back toward the lobby. But as we passed the angry man's room, the door swung open again. With hands on his hips, he scowled at us, a cigarette dangling from his lips.

Henry's temper flared. "You got a problem, Mister?"

"Yeah, I wanna see what yur sellin'."

"You wanna see what!?"

Henry's fist was halfway through the air when I stopped it, quickly pulling him down the hall and whispering I'd explain later. In the meantime, somewhere in Seattle, a Spanish-speaking man had a few more hours to enjoy talking on his stolen radio before it would need to be recharged. And we had the charger.

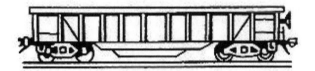

Hopper

Chapter 20

"Special Agent, this is dispatch. Someone in an office building near the intersection of Elliott Avenue and Denny Way just reported a man on a train car next to their building, screaming."

"This is the Special Agent. We're on our way, dispatch."

I glanced at Henry in the driver's seat as we sped to the waterfront location, knowing these calls gave him the same adrenaline rush they gave me as we mentally prepared for the unknown confrontation and danger.

Henry pulled alongside a set of tracks on which several boxcars waited to be unloaded. The tracks ran between tall, modern office buildings overlooking Elliott Bay, giving the lucky employees a view of ocean and islands from their desks.

Getting out of the car, we mirrored each other as we adjusted the gear on our belts and lightly touched our gun handles. From the closest building, several faces peered down at us from a second story window. "Hey Henry, looks like we're the entertainment."

"Then let's not disappoint them."

A high pitched shrieking erupted, like a wounded animal in the final throes of agony. It echoed off the buildings' facades and metal cars on either side of us. Henry and I nodded at each other and started down the line of boxcars; he took the left side while I paralleled him on the right. We found the first four cars empty.

My hand rested on my pistol grip as I rounded the end of the last train car at the same time as Henry. We stopped at the sight between us. A thin man wearing a red bikini sat perched at the end of the boxcar, legs dangling over the edge. Long matted hair clung to his cheeks and neck and from his wide open mouth emitted spine chilling screams. Multiple cuts from his thighs to his ankles were bleeding freely, splattering the rocks beneath his feet. His face, stomach, and chest were smeared with blood as if he'd been dipped in a vat of crimson dye.

Henry and I unfolded leather gloves from our belts and pulled them over our hands —we had us an official crazy. And when it came to techniques and protocol for the human mind gone awry, the company manual had yet to write any. We were on our own.

"Hey, stop screaming!" I yelled.

He didn't. Henry smacked the bottom of the man's feet with his long metal flashlight. "Shut up!" The man abruptly closed his mouth but kept his head back and eyes closed.

I carefully annunciated each word. "We're with the railroad police department. What happened to you?"

He turned to look at me, the whites of his eyes a stark contrast to his red skin and blue eyes. "Nothin' man."

I checked our audience in the second story window. They'd grown in number, some now standing on chairs behind the ones in front. I imagined this kind of drama – the socially acceptable versus the unacceptable – was a rare sight from where they sat day after day.

"Then how do you explain all these cuts on your legs?" I returned to my questioning.

Squinting, he tipped his head back. "I'm travelin' west."

"Tell you what, Mister. Come down off of that car and let's talk about it." I tried using a soothing tone in my voice like they'd taught us at academy but the man remained on his perch, peering down at us like a blinking red owl.

Henry opted for the non-academy method. "Get your ass off there now or I'll drag it off!" He added emphasis by banging his flashlight hard against the car.

Without hesitation, the man dropped to the ground, landing on the sharp ballast rock between the rails with bare bleeding feet. He didn't flinch.

Holding the man's arm with my gloved hand, I directed him to the side of the tracks. "Now tell us about those cuts and where your clothes are."

"I'm goin' west an' I cut my legs to wash my face cause I can't go west dirty an' I don't know why you wanna know 'bout my clothes cause I'm wearin' 'em!"

"Well, Henry, that clears it up for me. I think we need to get this man a ride going west, don't you?"

Henry returned to the car and made the call while I kept the conversation going.

"So, what're you going to do once you get out west?"

"I'll know when I git there."

"What do you do when you travel east?"

His eyes studied me intently. "I wash."

I offered to get him a blanket, but he refused, choosing to remain standing and exposed to the late afternoon wind blowing in off the ocean. He had no recollection of home address or family but said his name was "Chief Sitting Custer."

When the ambulance arrived, two medics approached us, wheeling a stretcher, and clearly apprehensive at the bloodied patient before them.

"These people are here to take you *west*." I said for their benefit, hoping they'd catch on to what we were dealing with. The medics nodded their understanding and carefully helped the man onto the gurney, while he repeated gleefully, "Goin' west, goin' west."

As soon as the ambulance's taillights receded into downtown traffic, Henry and I turned to give a salute to our audience, who were now waving and clapping wildly. Another crazy off the streets; they could all go back to their jobs where the view showed only normal people.

We drove onto Alaska Way, a main street bordered by railroad tracks on one side and a popular shopping area on the waterfront side. While checking for trespassers from the car, we saw a blue Chevy pickup weaving in and out of traffic.

"Looks like a drunk driver," Henry muttered.

The truck swerved and narrowly missed oncoming cars, only to over-steer back into the far right lane and then start the pattern all over again

"Times like these I wish we had jurisdiction in the city. By the time we call city P.D., he'll have hit someone." I didn't like feeling helpless. "Henry, the light's red so he's got to stop behind these cars. When he does, pull up on the driver's side."

The truck jerked to a halt, barely missing a taxi's fender. Henry quickly maneuvered our car alongside it. The driver, an older man with gray hair and half-closed eyes, bobbed his head forward and back between the steering wheel and the neck rest.

Quickly jumping from our car, I reached through his open window and slammed the gearshift into park. He was too drunk to notice, let alone react, so I turned off the motor and pulled the keys out of the ignition.

"How's it going, buddy? Looks like you've got engine trouble. You stay put and I'll call someone, okay?"

He looked at me through bleary eyes. "I shtay here?"

"Yeah, that's right. The repair guys will be here any minute." With that, I flung the keys over the guardrail and into Elliott Bay. As I settled back into the car, Henry's blue eyes flashed approval.

Grabbing the radio, I made a call. "Yardmaster, would you notify Seattle police that there's a confused man in a stalled car on Alaska Way."

Feeling good about one less drunk on the road, we headed to Azteca for dinner. On the sidewalk outside the restaurant's front door, we recognized a Native street person known as "Billygoat." Dressed in a tight fitting shirt and khaki pants, his puffy face and bulging stomach proved he'd been drinking and eating well. A single braid hung down his back.

"How're things going, Billy?"

"Okay for me but…" he looked both ways and motioned for us to step closer.

"Not good for you boys. Tribe's put a bounty on you two. They say you been too hard on us Injuns so they takin' a collection."

Henry laughed out loud. "The Indians are asking for money so they can offer a reward for us? Ha! Wonder if the people giving them quarters know that."

Henry pointed at Billy. "You tell them it better be a high price 'cause we're worth it."

Billy laughed, showing a wide gap between his front teeth. "Okay, I tell 'em to make it good price, mebbe ten dollahs each."

"You do that and we'll split it with you. See ya' around."

We found our usual table and ordered our usual dinner -- giant burritos and 3 refills of chips. Afterward, we drove to the vacant U.D. office and found a broken window and a metal locker pushed in front of the shattered window from the inside. We had visitors.

Henry parked the car and we climbed the steps to the front door. He pointed at the window just a few feet away. "Whoever put that locker there might still be inside."

Clutching the railing with one hand, he leaned toward the window and used the handle of his flashlight to break off any remaining sharp edges of glass from the frame. He then shoved the locker, sending it crashing to the floor.

"If anyone's in there, they now know we're here," Henry muttered, shoving his light back into his belt. With the agility of a trapeze performer, he clambered over the railing and launched himself into the air, his hands landing on the window's narrow ledge. The rest of his body hit the building with a gut wrenching "smack!".

Henry began to run up the wall, his body levitating slowly while his feet kept up a furious pace, scuffing wildly against the bricks. His face red with exertion, he heaved his torso through the window, making loud blowing sounds like the seals we often saw around the docks. He sagged against the ledge to catch his breath, arms and chest inside the building, butt and legs dangling out. With a lot of groans, Henry pulled the rest of his bulk up and precariously squatted inside the window frame. "Once I'm inside, I'll unlock the door to let you in."

He carefully twisted his body around to face the interior, and prepared to jump. My hand had been resting on the doorknob the entire time and I realized we hadn't bothered to check it. Turning the knob, I pushed it open and stepped inside just as Henry landed on the concrete floor. Disgust crossed his face.

Pointing a finger at me, he growled, "Not a word!"

I tried to hold in my laughter but it finally burst out in deep belly laughs. "Henry, I didn't know…. you could fly through the air…… and run up walls…. and how flat your butt looks…hanging out a window."

Henry scowled. "When you're done, we've got work to do." He stormed off.

The U.D. office consisted of two rooms, each about the size of an average living room, with a tiny bathroom adjoining the larger. For many years, railroad employees worked in these quarters, providing 24-hour communication coverage. But when new technology enabled trains and dispatchers to communicate directly with each other, the U.D. office became obsolete. Its employees were transferred but the equipment had been left behind to collect cobwebs and dust.

We checked the first room and found sleeping bags rolled out on the floor, surrounded by water bottles, magazines and canned food.

"Looks like someone's living here, Henry."

In the larger room, we found several pieces of radio equipment missing. "I knew someone would eventually find this stash," Henry muttered.

"Do you think the ones who stole the equipment are the same ones living here?"

"It wouldn't surprise me." Henry scanned the room. "People who'd hang out here couldn't be Seattle's brightest."

We heard voices and froze, our eyes fixed on a back door several feet from where we stood. The knob rattled and turned. I nudged Henry. "Look, another *un*locked door."

I slipped to one side while Henry pulled his flashlight out of its loop. The door swung open and two men stepped inside, heads down, talking with each other. As soon as they passed me, I kicked the door shut and announced, "Welcome home, boys. We've been expecting you."

Henry's flashlights exposed two startled faces. The taller man stood paralyzed, like a deer caught in headlights, but the other turned and bolted for the door. Using both hands, I shoved him hard and knocked him off balance.

"You're not going anywhere so settle down."

Henry spoke from behind the light. "Railroad police. If you want to stay healthy, don't move."

The man I'd pushed made another leap for the door. I side-tackled him, ramming my shoulder into his ribs. He cried out when he hit the door with his face and collapsed on the floor. I put my knee between his shoulder blades. "Didn't you hear my partner say we were police?"

He gasped and sputtered, "Alright man, I give up. Get off my back."

I helped him to a sitting position. "You try that again and you'll get more than air knocked out of you."

"Dean, you alright?"

Henry stood behind and to the side of the taller man who had an uncanny resemblance to Abe Lincoln with his dark beard and sad, haunted eyes.

"Yeah, I'm okay…"

My suspect scrambled for the door in yet a third attempt at escape. Pushing him back against the wall, I warned, "Do you need more convincing?"

His glittering eyes betrayed his rage.

We walked both of them outside and checked them for weapons. Instead, we found pliers and screwdrivers in their pockets, the perfect tools for removing radio equipment. "What are you two doing here?"

"Nothin'." The shorter man snapped.

I looked him in the eyes. "I'll tell you what you're doing here. You found some radio equipment and you've been stealing as much as you can carry to sell on the streets. You must've run out because you're back for more. Is that about right?"

Abe remained mute but the other couldn't keep quiet. "We ain't done' nothin' an' you can't prove it. So back off and let us go, pig." He spat at our faces.

Henry's temper had a hair trigger when it came to belligerent trespassers and I could tell he'd reached the explosion point. He stepped close to the man, standing nose to nose, like a drill sergeant before a recruit. "Looks like you got a problem, Mister, and I know just the cure."

"You can't do nothin' to me."

Henry pushed hard on the man's chest. "That's where you're wrong 'cause no one's around to see what happens." Henry grabbed his arm and pulled him back into the U.D. Office. When the man stumbled, Henry dragged him up the stairs.

"I ain't goin' in there with you." The man kicked and thrashed.

Henry grabbed the top of the man's pants and his collar and carried him to the door, kicking the door open so hard that it slammed against the wall. He pushed his captive into the darkened interior.

The taller man stood transfixed. "Are you sure you don't want to tell me what the two of you have been up to?"

"Ain't nothin' to tell," he said in a whisper, not taking his eyes off the door.

A loud crash from inside the building startled him. "Wha, wha, what's he doin' to him in there?"

"Not sure. My partner's got a temper and when we come across someone who mouths off, he kinda goes crazy." I looked down at my shoes, shaking my head. "And I'm afraid you're next."

He swallowed hard.

"But if you tell the truth, I'll stop him from taking you in there."

A succession of crashes, followed by cries for help, proved too much for Honest Abe. "Okay, man, here's what went down. We was lookin' for a train to catch outta town when we seen this building and decided to check it out. So, Scott, that's my friend, he broke out the window an' crawled through an' unlocked the door for me. We come across all that equipment an' figgered it was left behind so we been takin' it to a pawn shop."

"Tell me which one and we're done here."

"The one on First Avenue 'bout five or six blocks from here."

I yelled for Henry to come out and he emerged with a slightly ruffled but unharmed man who was now cuffed.

While waiting for Seattle police to transport, Henry brushed pieces of insulation and dirt from his shirt. "Our house cleaning got a little messy."

As soon as the police arrived, the shorter man saw his chance. "Officers, I want to file a complaint against these jerks for brutality. They roughed us up an' held us against our will an' falsely accused us an' illegally searched us an' cuffed us."

Our city peers politely listened to the accusations, glancing back and forth from us to him. Finally, one officer held up his hand. "Hold on, Mister, I think I've got the solution to your problem."

The complainer sneered at us. "I knew you Seattle boys would help us out. So tell me -- what do we hafta do to stop these railroad pigs?"

The officer annunciated each word clearly: "Stay-off-railroad-property!"

Chapter 21

"Henry, I'm riding the high-rail with Gordon today. Meet me in Everett at 6:00 tonight and we'll patrol from there." Within our jurisdiction lay miles of tracks without access roads, creating veritable no-man's lands. For these areas, we relied on a "hi-rail," a vehicle (usually a truck) with specially fitted, flanged steel wheels on the back and front ends. When driving on the street, these wheels would be locked in the 'up' position but when we needed to be on tracks, they'd be lowered. The front rail-wheels would lift the truck's front tires off the tracks while the rear rail-wheels kept the rear tires stable while they provided the power. The entire transformation took only minutes.

Hi-rail operators followed the same rules as railroad engines. The driver had to obey dispatchers' instructions and trains were always given priority. When trains did end up on the same tracks, the hi-rail would be directed to a spur or side-track to wait, often for long periods of time. But despite the chance for delays, I still enjoyed riding the hi-rail to check tracks along the waterfront, especially on mild summer afternoons like this one.

"Great, you get the scenic route and I get the depot," Henry muttered as he waved us off.

Gordon slowly drove the hi-rail out of Balmer Yard, the chatter on the radio nonstop. Although the tracks made steering unnecessary, it still looked odd seeing Gordon use both hands to arrange papers and sip coffee from a styrofoam cup. His tall, lanky frame left only a few inches between his mop of brown hair and the truck's roof, while his knees rested on either side of the steering wheel.

What I liked best about Gordon was sticking out from the top of his eyeglasses at a 90-degree angle -- clip-on sunglasses. The guy was a true optimist, considering how seldom the northwest saw sunshine.

Once out of the downtown area, we accelerated to 30 mph, which felt fast on the tracks. We'd been driving for about an hour, Gordon inspecting tracks for broken rails and debris while I looked for trespassers and hobo camps, when we reached an isolated stretch of beach where the Puget Sound lapped a sandy beach. To our right, beautiful homes perched atop steep banks rising 100 feet and higher.

"Wow, they must have a million dollar view up there, Gordon. If your job's ever open, let me know. I could look at this every day."

I craned my neck out the window to get a better look at the mansions lining the horizon when a rock the size of a baseball hit the track, making a loud clunking sound. Before I could react, another rock narrowly missed my head and bounced off the side of the truck, leaving a dent in the rear panel.

I shouted, "Stop!"

"What hit us?" Gordon asked, bringing the hi-rail to an abrupt halt.

Scanning the skyline, I saw three boys running across the hill, looking back at us.

"A rock meant for my head, and I'm going after the delinquents who threw it."

"Are you really going to climb that cliff?" he asked incredulously.

"If I don't catch them now, they'll get away with it. Any trains coming in the next couple of hours?"

"No, we're in the clear for at least that long."

I scrambled out of the cab to his final words, "I'll be here to pick up the pieces if you fall."

Pulling on leather gloves, I started up the incline only to slide back to the bottom.

"You really want to do this?" Gordon asked, leaning out his window.

"No, I don't, but I'm too stubborn to quit."

Throwing myself into the foliage, I grabbed a handful of tangled branches and pulled myself up. Step by step, I dragged each leg through thorny blackberry vines, keeping my fingers tightly wrapped around plants to keep from slipping.

I didn't dare look down until I had to stop and catch my breath. Big mistake—the slope looked even steeper from above. I weakly waved to Gordon. My arms were covered with tiny red scratches and my legs began to shake uncontrollably from keeping my muscles tense for so long.

From the ledge above, I estimated I was halfway. Huge mounds of rotting grass clippings now surrounded me, their musty stench making me nauseous. Apparently people in million dollar homes did the same thing as the rest of us —dumped their lawn waste out back and out of sight.

The sun had almost set when I heaved myself up onto a perfectly manicured lawn. Laying sprawled in the grass' cool dampness until my heart and breathing could return to normal, it occurred to me I didn't have a way down. My anger hadn't left much room for logic.

Slowly getting up on my sore feet, I turned to face an enormous home whose large windows reflected an incredible view of the orange and pink clouds resting on the Sound behind me. I stiffly walked across the expanse of green to one side of the home, hoping a pair of Dobermans weren't running loose. Following a path of white stepping stones through beauty-barked landscaping, I reached a circular driveway and stopped short. There, parked in perfect formation, were the cars of my dreams—a Lincoln Continental, a Mercedes, and a Cadillac.

"Wow, must be some party going on in there. And I'm under-dressed."

The front door swung open and a man carrying compacted trash, stepped outside. He didn't notice me, giving me a chance to look into the home where a group of well-dressed people, talking, laughing and holding drinks, occupied an elegant living room. And peering nervously from a window were three boys.

The man nearly ran into me before he noticed me, causing him to jump back and gawk at my appearance. Sweaty, scratched up men reeking of decaying grass must be a rare sight in his neighborhood.

"Uh, what can I do for you?" he asked, clearly suspicious of my presence.

"I'm with the railroad police." I pulled my badge from my back pocket.

He relaxed a little. "Why would the railroad police be at my front door?"

"We were riding in a vehicle on the tracks below your property when two rocks were thrown and one just missed my head. I believe the boys in your house right now are the ones who threw them and I'd like a word with them."

The man chuckled and shook his head. "Officer, surely you must have bigger criminals to go after. A couple of kids threw some rocks – big deal."

His minimizing the act frustrated but didn't surprise me. I heard it often from the parents of kids I caught on railroad property.

"I could've been killed," I said between clenched teeth. "The next guy might not be so lucky."

He waved at the gleaming cars. "As you can see, I've got company. I'll tell their folks and they'll take care of it." He extended his hand. "Thanks for stopping by, officer."

I stepped between him and the door. "I want to talk to those boys and their parents or I'm calling Seattle police to assist me. Your choice."

"Look, their dad's my boss and I don't want …."

"Did I hear something about three boys?" A very attractive woman in a gauzy red blouse and sleek black pants appeared in the doorway, her head cocked to one side.

"Yes, you did, ma'am. They threw rocks at a vehicle I was riding in and one almost hit my head."

She put her hand over her mouth and gasped. She stepped closer. "Did you see them throw the rocks?"

"No, but they were the only ones standing where the rocks came from. I know they're in there and I'd like to talk with them"

"I'm confused," she said in a husky voice, one finger brushing against her dark red lips. "Where were you when the rocks were thrown?"

"I'm a police officer for the railroad and I was riding on the tracks."

I showed her my badge. She touched it lightly, then looked at me with a smile that made me feel strangely flustered.

"I'm afraid those naughty boys are mine. Their father isn't home much… sometimes he's gone for *weeks*." Her eyes fixed on mine. "How can I make this up to you… just name it."

Clearing my throat, I felt myself blush. "Well, um, Mrs., I'm sorry, I didn't get your name."

"It's Rhonda Morrison, but please call me Ronnie." She slipped her soft hand into mine. "And what's your name?"

"I'm Special Agent O'Shea…and uh, Mrs. er, Ronnie, I'd like to talk to your boys…could you call them uh, right away, now would be best actually, so I don't disrupt the party… looking like this."

She still held my hand and gave it a tight squeeze. "You look just fine to me. I'll go get the little troublemakers." She slunk away, leaving a waft of perfume in her wake.

The homeowner glared at me before storming off to rejoin his guests.

Within minutes, Ronnie emerged with three young boys in tow, timidly peering out from behind her. The smallest had a finger pushed up his nose. She lined them up in front of me.

"Boys, this is Special Agent O'Shea. He's a police officer for the railroad and he wants to talk with you."

The youngest looked to be five or six and the oldest couldn't have been more than nine. Each wore a miniature dress shirt half tucked into miniature dress pants with matching shiny shoes scuffed with dirt. And each peered up at me with big round eyes.

Remembering the arduous climb to ensure justice prevailed, I opened my mouth to begin when a stately gentleman in a silk shirt and dress slacks joined Ronnie, slipping his arm around her waist. I nodded to him and turned again to the boys but a noisy shuffling distracted me. The entire party now streamed onto the front lawn, looking like models from a fashion magazine shoot. They formed a half circle around us, no doubt relishing the sight of the boss' kids getting into trouble with the law.

Looking back at the frightened boys, the embarrassed parents and delighted guests sipping drinks and munching hors d'oeuvres, my mind went blank.

"Uh, well, as your mom said I'm Special O'Shea, I mean, Agent Special O'Shea and I'm with the railroad special police…."

I bent down and asked the middle boy, "Do you understand what I'm saying?"

With trembling lips and chin, he said in a sniffling voice, "You catch…bad people. But I'm not…bad."

Straightening up, I chuckled. "That's cute, he thinks…"

The crowd's cold silence snuffed out my feeble attempt at humor.

Moving quickly to the oldest boy, I put out my hand. "And what's your name, young man?"

"Travis. Are you gonna take us to jail?"

The middle boy burst into tears. "I don't wanna go to jail. Mommy!"

"No one's going anywhere, I just want to know who threw the rocks."

The smallest pointed his finger at the other two. "They did it!" He turned and ran to his parents, tightly wrapping his arms around his mother's legs.

This wasn't going at all like I'd planned. These boys were obviously not the malicious delinquents I'd imagined. Wanting to end this quickly, I briefly explained the dangers of throwing anything onto the tracks because people worked on them every day.

"But I'm going to need help telling your friends. If I deputize each of you, will you be my assistants and tell your friends what you learned today?"

They looked up and nodded, wiping eyes and noses with their sleeves.

"Then let's seal the deal." I shook three sets of sticky hands, relieved a lousy situation had ended on a positive note. The disappointed partygoers strolled back into the home, resuming their laughter and chatter. Ronnie and her husband approached me.

"Tomas, this is Agent O'Shea."

"Glad to meet you, officer. I appreciated the way you handled our boys and I can assure you, it won't happen again. If there was any damage, here's my business card."

"Thank you, sir. There was some minor damage to our hi-rail and I'll get that to you. And speaking of the hi-rail, I need to get back so I'll say goodbye."

I turned and headed back across the lawn, the vision of my body sliding down the long steep incline going through my mind. Someone called my name—the surly homeowner. "Did you climb that cliff?"

"Yeah....is there another way?"

"Unbelievable! I never put a fence across there because I thought it would be impossible to climb. There's a path on the other side of the house we use to get down to the beach."

I jogged down the trail to where Gordon waited. When he saw me, he was visibly relieved. "Dean, if I hadn't seen you climb that, I'd never have believed it."

"That's the closest I ever want to get to mountain climbing. Thanks for hanging in there for me."

We resumed our ride to Everett, each bend revealing another amazing view of the Puget Sound. The dark, blue evening sky seemed to melt into the rolling waves while the jagged Olympic Mountains beckoned like Shangri La in the distance. Silhouettes of gulls stood in straight lines on rocks like sentinels of the sea. I wished Cassie were here to share this beauty with me...

Gordon interrupted my romantic thoughts. "Uh, you okay? You're kind of staring at me weird."

"Yeah, yeah, I'm fine." I sat up straight and looked out the side window, embarrassed I'd slipped into a daydream while with a coworker.

Gordon accelerated and we made it in record time. When I climbed out of the truck and thanked Gordon, he said, "Maybe next time your partner can make the trip."

When I joined Henry in the patrol car, he noticed my scratches and dirty clothes.

"What did I miss?"

"Just a few kids needing safety tips about throwing rocks. Let's go back to Seattle and see about dinner."

Seattle's waterfront is known for its many fine restaurants. And fortunately for us, the railroad tracks paralleled the business area, allowing us to check for problems while deciding on a place to eat. But tonight, dinner would have to wait – across from Pier 70, nearly twenty cars had been parked with their wheels up against the rails, their drivers not realizing a train can be wider than the tracks.

"Special Agent to dispatcher," I said into the radio mike. "We have several vehicles parked against the tracks across from Pier 70. If you've got any trains coming, hold them until we get this cleared up."

"Dispatcher to Special Agent. Train 164 is arriving in three hours. Let me know when the tracks are clear."

Henry pointed to a popular eating establishment where we could see people seated at candlelit tables through the windows. "I'll go in there and make an announcement to move their cars. If that doesn't work, I'll call city police and have them ticket the vehicles before towing them."

"I'll stay here and get license plate numbers, but don't expect city PD to prioritize our train schedule."

Henry crossed the street and disappeared into the restaurant. I pulled out a small pad of paper and tried to ignore my stomach's urgent growling -- this was going to be a long night. Suddenly, wailing sirens erupted as flashing red and blue lights atop dark silhouettes of cars headed my way. "I'll never complain about city PD again."

Four police cars braked across from where I stood, and surrounded Pier 70. When two more joined them, I wondered if they'd over-reacted just a bit.

Henry appeared with a line of people behind him. "Henry, what did you tell the police to get a response like this?"

"Me? I thought you called them. Everyone kept ignoring my announcements, even when I threatened to have their cars towed. But once we heard the sirens, they couldn't get up from their tables fast enough."

We approached the closest police unit. "Good evening, officer. We're railroad police -- what's going on?"

"Armed robbery down the street, suspects turned into this parking lot." He pressed down on his radio and spoke, "We'll move in from the front."

Waving goodbye, he said, "Later, guys," and drove off.

What a lucky break – we wished we could thank the criminals for their perfect timing!

When the last car backed away from the rails, our shift officially ended. We returned to the depot to hand over the patrol car and review with the next shift's patrolmen the criminals that were known to be in our area. We also had a "white train" due to arrive; they were literally painted white, carried military cargo and government guards to protect it. If these trains ever had to stop for a crew change, the guards would emerge from the engine and/or caboose to patrol on foot until ready to move on.

Getting home well after midnight, I stepped over a pile of leather pieces in the living room. I smiled, recalling Cassie's excitement at making her "frontier" outfit for the black powder club we'd recently joined. I quietly undressed in the dark and fell into bed.

After what seemed only minutes, I awoke to morning light and a close up of Snoopy's nose and tongue. Holding him back to prevent a face washing, I rolled him onto his back for a vigorous tummy scratch, his rear leg moving in rhythm to my fingers. When Bobby and Poo-Poo jumped up to join us, we were soon involved in a boisterous game between the pillows and the blankets.

"Ahem."

We stopped in mid-play. There stood Cassie, hands on her hips, head high, striking a pose at the foot of the bed. With a twirl, she walked back and forth like a model on a runway, dressed in a white rabbit fur vest, buckskin pants and moccasins.

"Well, how do I look?"

"Great!"

"I made you something too."

She handed me a pair of knee-high moccasins. Jumping off the bed, I gave her a tight hug and then pulled on the moccasins. "Wow, you *made* these?"

"Yes, and now I've got a favor to ask. Teach me to throw a knife."

I hurriedly ate breakfast, took my throwing knives from the dresser drawer and joined her in the backyard. I tied a small log with ropes to a pine tree's branches so it swung horizontally and positioned Cassie about ten feet away.

"Okay, hold the knife by the blade and concentrate on your target. And then, with a smooth motion of your wrist, throw the knife. Your hand should be pointing where you're aiming when you release."

I followed through and tossed the blade, which stuck, point first, into the log. Doubting I'd be able to make a second perfect throw, I told her, "Your turn."

Carefully taking the knife between her fingers, Cassie positioned herself in front of the target, looking like an Indian princess on a hunt in her new outfit.

"Don't be afraid to use force in your throw."

She nodded, cocked her arm back over her shoulder and hurled the knife with all her strength. The dagger's handle glanced off the log, imbedding itself in our gas meter. We stood staring dumbly at the protruding knife until a hissing sound shocked us into action – a gas leak! We raced into the house but in the entry, I stopped Cassie.

"I'll call the company while you change out of the rabbit fur and skins. We'll have enough trouble explaining why we stabbed our meter."

Chapter 22

Since the day we married, Cassie and I had agreed to live on a budget. And three years later, it paid off. In the fall of '85, we made a down payment on a two-story, fixer-upper in Renton, a nice suburb bordering Lake Washington's southern shore. Its repairs were cosmetic: new carpet, roof and paint, and if we did the remodeling ourselves, we'd soon have our first rental property.

Autumns in Seattle were the perfect season for finishing projects; the days were shorter but summer's warmth still lingered. So after breakfast one September morning, I drove past lawns sprinkled with pinecones and crimson leaves, and pulled up in front of our project house.

Seeing Cassie's car in the driveway, I knew she'd be getting a head start on the interior painting. I crossed the yard enjoying the crunching sounds beneath my feet but when I turned the front doorknob, I found it locked. And all the blinds on the windows were pulled down - what could she be up to now?

Using an extra key, I stepped into the entry to the sound of the oldies turned up loud, accompanied by my wife's off-key and improvised vocals.

"...and when I'm with you, Dean, the whole world looks my way..."

Stepping over drop cloths, cans of paint and a wooden ladder, I changed into a pair of old torn sweats I kept in the hall closet.

"Youuuuuuu take my breath away, oh yeah, oh yeah!"

I picked up a brush and headed for the living room.

"So shake it, shake it, Dean, com'on, com'on!"

Turning the corner, I stopped short at the sight before me: Cassie stood naked, singing her heart out as she dabbed at the trim around a window. I'd seen nude paintings before but this was my first painting nude.

When she noticed me, she giggled, obviously enjoying my reaction. "So…what do you think of the color?"

Her beauty still took my breath away but somehow I managed to speak. "It's the most beautiful color I've ever seen."

The next few hours forever changed my aversion to painting as we moved our brushes and grooved to the tunes, "au natural."

The following afternoon, we were ready to tackle something I'd been losing sleep over— insulating the interior walls.

"I'm sure glad you know how to do this, Dean." Cassie sat cross-legged on the floor, watching me with such confidence, I didn't have the heart to tell her this would be my first time.

"Piece of cake, Sweetheart."

Dragging rental equipment and bags of insulation into the house, I gave her a reassuring look before drilling some holes into the wall. Next, I placed a nozzle connected to a bulky machine by a long, flexible hose into the first hole. Cassie flipped the switch and soft insulation poured in, just like the picture in the manual.

"Go ahead and dump more insulation into the hopper."

Cassie emptied the last bag and I began to think about where to drill holes in the next room. My preoccupation kept me distracted so that when she kissed the back of my neck, I jumped, knocking the hose out of the wall. Fuzzy flakes spewed out everywhere, sticking to the carpet, walls, and ceiling. We scrambled to turn off the machine, knocking into each other and the hose but it was too late. Peering through thickly covered eyelashes, we resembled a pair of overgrown, fluff-covered chicks. Spitting insulation out from between her lips, Cassie said, "Oops."

We burst out laughing at each other's comical appearance, trying in vain to brush off the insulation. By the time I left for a midnight shift, we'd used several vacuum cleaner bags and Cassie still wore a halo of fuzz.

I found a note from Jerry on the office's main desk.

"Dean, you're on your own tonight, Henry's working Everett."

I grabbed a set of keys, dreading the thought of eating by myself, and decided to patrol South Seattle, since I hadn't been at that yard for some time. After waving to the truck inspector in the inspector's shack at the entrance, I parked in front of the office building where management and clerical staff worked during the day.

The first floor appeared undisturbed, so I proceeded upstairs where I found a man pushing a mop across the expansive floor. His scraggly beard, torn jeans, and long ponytail looked more like a transient than an employee. I made my way toward him, looking for some friendly conversation; night shifts really dragged when working alone.

"Hey, how's it going?"

The man spun around. "It's goin'. Who's askin'?"

"I'm Special Agent O'Shea." He ignored my extended hand. "Thought I'd see how you're doing tonight."

Dropping the mop handle with a loud "smack!", he placed both hands on his hips.

"How d'ya think I'm doin' if all I do is clean up after you people? While you wear nice clothes an' drive 'round all day, I'm up to my elbows in toilets."

I stood there stunned, caught off guard by his anger. My natural inclination would be to snarl back and then leave, but something impressed me to stay. Suspecting the source of his hostility might be about more than a demeaning job description, I tried to remember what our pastor had said last Sunday about "witnessing."

"That does sound unfair. You work all night long, alone, without ever hearing you've done a good job. It must be a tough way to make a living."

His eyes narrowed. "Yeah, day in an' day out, never changes."

I forced myself to show some empathy because I sure wasn't feeling it. "It doesn't make any sense, does it?"

"Damn right it don't, but how'd you know? Your kind got it made."

"Think so? There was a time when my whole life was in the toilet, not just my hands. On the outside, I looked tough like you, but on the inside, I was scared and didn't know what to do about it. I felt like I was sitting at the bottom of a deep pit, going nowhere."

Something flickered in his eyes. "That's 'bout it."

"Life seemed easy for others, but not for me, and me was all I saw. Depression and addiction have only one small window, slanted inward. So when God reached down and thumped me on the head, it brought me to my knees. I found He'd been there all along. I still have lots of questions, but at least I know where to go for answers."

The janitor shifted his feet, his dark eyes blinking fast. "I dunno, man, I gotta get back to work."

"Do you believe in God?"

He picked up the mop and turned his back on me.

I placed my business card on a desk "Here's my card. You can give me a call sometime if..."

He waved me off, elbows and shoulders moving in a jerky rhythm across the floor. I headed for the exit, feeling like I'd failed somehow.

"Hey, Special Agent man."

I saw my business card in his hand. "Yeah?"

"I jus' might check out this God of yours."

"You won't be disappointed…..friend."

The last word felt both strange and the right thing to say. I left the building wondering if my boss's note had been divinely planned. If I'd been with Henry, I'd never have sought out a surly janitor in the middle of a lonely night.

Returning to the car, I'd just turned the key when a man appeared, tapping on my window. "You the Special Agent?"

I nodded, rolling down my window.

"Just got a call from the Mechanical Department foreman. They got a bum in their lunchroom and want you to take care of it."

"I'll head over there right now. Thanks for the message."

The Mechanical Department, combined with the Material Department, was where staff worked days and evening shifts, repairing, maintaining and cleaning Amtrak coaches in open-ended buildings that resembled large carports.

Usually, no one would be there after 11:00 p.m. but tonight, an Amtrak train had been late getting in due to delays. I parked in front of the cafeteria and entered, letting the door slam behind me. The sound startled two men sitting at picnic tables on opposite sides of the room. I knew immediately by the dirty clothes and blank, drug-induced expression, which guy was the problem.

I walked briskly across the linoleum and stood behind him. "Railroad police. It's time for you to leave."

He came out of his trance. "I don't hafta leave here!"

"That's where you're wrong, Mister."

Grabbing one of his arms, I pulled him off the bench, but he managed to break free. With hands clenched, he swung around to punch me but I knocked him forward onto the table. His feet scuffled frantically on the slick floor as I twisted his arm to give him an incentive to cooperate. "Just calm down and you won't get hurt!"

"Ew got the ong man." With his face pressed against the table, he couldn't annunciate very clearly.

"I've got the wrong man? Can't you come up with something more original..."

"I werk ere."

"What did you say?" I released my hold on his head so he could stand up.

"I'm a railroad employee jus' like you!" He looked understandably upset, with a few bruises on his face.

"Who's your boss?"

"Jake Walker."

Straightening his shirt, I tried to make light of the mistake. "Hey, sorry about that, but when you tried to hit me, I went into automatic. Let's shake and forget it happened."

Ignoring my outstretched hand, he nodded toward the other man who still sat at a table, apparently unaware of the incident that had just taken place. "That's the guy you want. Been panhandlin' all day an' night an' won't leave."

I took a deep breath and strode across the room. The other man's eyes protruded at an odd angle like a frog with a goiter. When I saw red oozing ulcers covering his arms and face, I muttered, "Great - a crazy with something contagious."

He shifted ever so slightly as I positioned myself behind him. "What are you doing here?"

He didn't move. I shoved his shoulder and repeated more forcefully. "I asked you a question and I want an answer. What are you doing here?"

He turned to look at me, the rank smell of alcohol wafting up from him. "Jes eatin' my lunch."

"Do you work here?" I wanted to be sure this time.

"Yeah, an' my boss's the same as that guy's."

The front door to the lunchroom swung open and in walked the boss himself – perfect timing. Jake pointed to the man in front of me. "That's the guy. Get him outta here. I've told him to leave half a dozen times, but he keeps showing up and asking employees for money."

The transient flashed a toothless smile. "My drinkin' costs money, so leave me alone." Grabbing his collar to avoid touching his neck, I pulled him to a standing position and shoved him toward the front door, keeping my hand in the middle of his back. Once we reached the car, I retrieved my Polaroid and snapped a close-up of his pop-eyed, spotted face.

"Now listen closely. This picture will be on the bulletin board in this lunchroom. If you're ever here again, the employees will call the city police or me and you'll be arrested. Then you'll go to jail where they don't serve drinks. And you know what that's like, don't you? Now get out of here."

With a flip of his blotchy finger, he shuffled off to beg for his next meal. To make sure he left railroad property, I went around the side of the building to watch him and found a lone Indian standing next to an open dumpster.

"Hey, Chief, what're you doing out here this late?"

The young Native American's dark eyes bore into me. When he spoke, his voice was flat and devoid of emotion. "My name is Albert Red Horse."

He wore a bandana tied around his forehead and thick black hair down to his shoulders. His angular features and bronzed skin were the kind seen in Hollywood westerns.

"Okay, Albert Red Horse, answer my question – what are…"

A woman's head popped up inside the dumpster with food in her hands. Realizing the situation, I felt disgusted. "You mean to tell me you put your girlfriend into that garbage heap to find you something to eat?"

He didn't respond or even blink, wearing a stoic expression like an impenetrable mask. The petite Native woman shuffled through the waist deep garbage and handed what looked like half-eaten sandwiches to Albert. She then hoisted herself out of the bin without any assistance from him. Making no eye contact with either of us, she kept her head down and took her place behind Albert.

"Okay, both of you, take your dinner off the property and I better never see you around, or *in,* our dumpsters again."

They turned and walked away in silence. Like ghosts, even their footsteps were muted.

Continuing my patrol, I checked the U.D. building and the tunnel, finding them both clear. I proceeded along the tracks to where a large cottonwood tree stood alone, surrounded by thick brush and mounding vines. Transients were often found here sleeping, hiding, or trying to get out of the rain. Despite our department's repeated requests to have the tree cut down, it remained standing, year after year.

Kicking my way through the tangled weeds with a flashlight, I nearly stumbled when my foot made contact with a body. My light revealed a young man with a few days' growth on his face, leaning back on his elbows and clutching an empty bottle in one hand. His light colored shirt had a splatter of blood across the front.

When he realized my presence, he jerked his head up, giving me a glimpse of swollen, bruised, eyes. He'd obviously been in a fight and could barely see past the puffy flesh. Lacerations crisscrossed his cheeks and forehead.

"I'm with the railroad police. Looks like you're having a bad week."

He exhaled loudly and shook his head. "Man, oh man."

"Tell me what happened."

He furrowed his brow for several minutes and then spoke as if each part of the story was painful to recall. "I remember gettin' a bottle and this good-lookin' chick appeared outta nowhere an' asked if I'd like to party. I told her, 'Sure thing' and followed her an' then I woke up here, talkin' to you."

"Before meeting your dream girl, were you carrying any money?"

He rolled to one side and touched his back pocket. "Man, I had sixty bucks an' my drivers license."

"Looks like she had a boyfriend in on the scam. Be glad you only lost your wallet."

Guessing he hadn't been on the streets very long, I pointed to the bottle. "Why get drunk in the first place?"

"I got problems and drinkin' makes 'em go away."

"Looks like drinking made more problems this time. What's your name?"

His face went blank and then he blurted, "Dan Rayner."

"Well, Mr.Rayner, that bottle won't make anything go away. I know-- I've been where you are. Drinking just keeps you from growing up and learning how to handle life. When I made God my hiding place, I never regretted it."

He stared at me as if in shock, his lips barely moving as he whispered, "I heard all that before...my dad's a pastor."

"You must be breaking your dad's heart, and even worse, you're breaking your heavenly Dad's heart."

"Neither of 'em care." Daniel groaned as he stood up on wobbly legs.

"Do you really know that, Daniel? Have they told you to your face they don't care?"

"They don't hafta. I jus' know." He turned to go but I took hold of his arm.

"Don't you want to get medical attention for those cuts?"

He broke my hold and muttered, "Forget it."

I called out, "I'll be praying for you, Daniel." But he never looked back

<hr/>

A few weeks later, while on patrol with Henry, we received a call from Tony Penna. "I've got four guys getting off the train at South Seattle. They're drunk and I need back-up."

Henry punched the accelerator and we made it in record time, braking to a stop between four trespassers and Tony. "These guys giving you problems?" Henry asked as we jumped out of the car.

"That guy over there has a temper and started a fight with these three. But they don't want to do anything about it so I'm kicking them loose after I get their information."

I shined my flashlight on the troublemaker and immediately recognized the pastor's son, Daniel. His eyes were no longer swollen and his cuts had healed, but he still wore the same bloodied shirt. I poked my finger into his chest.

"Daniel Rayner, what do you think you're doing?"

"You, you know me?"

"I've been praying for you like I said I would."

Henry snorted. "Even if I believed, I wouldn't waste my time on this loser."

I kept looking at Daniel, ignoring Henry's sarcasm. A light of recognition flickered across his face. "Oh, yeah, I remember now... you're that Christian cop."

"And you're the guy running away from your father."

"You really been prayin' for me?"

I nodded.

Daniel's face contorted as he rubbed his eyes. He extended his hand and whispered, "Don't stop, man...please don't stop."

And I didn't, making it a daily commitment to pray for both the prodigal and the janitor, two men who crossed my path one memorable night. I never saw either again -- the janitor died in a motorcycle accident shortly after we met -- but I've often thought of them, hoping each found his way back home.

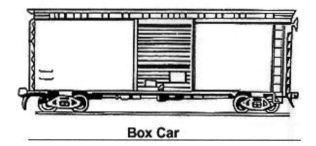

Box Car

Chapter 23

"Hey Henry, where we eating tonight?" I asked, climbing into the passenger seat of the patrol car.

Henry, in his usual place behind the steering wheel, raised his eyebrows. "I know we need to decide the important things at the beginning of our shift, but let's think on it for a couple of hours."

With our start-of-the-shift dialogue complete (which I suspect we viewed as good luck), we began our eight-hour policing assignment -- find trouble and take care of it.

We drove the dusty, rutted road paralleling Balmer Yard, finding only employees on the property. "Pretty quiet around here," Henry grumbled. "Let's see if we can find some action at the tunnel."

Driving past Seattle's waterfront, we parked the car in front of the tunnel's west end. Stepping over discarded beer cans and syringes we made our way to the entrance, using our flashlights to peer into its depths. But no faces peered back.

"Looks like we're in for a boring night." I knew my words would annoy Henry. He swore and kicked a bottle, sending it skidding across the gravel. He didn't find the situation funny at all.

"Let's check out…"

Noise from the other side of the tracks caught our attention. Thick brush separated and a shockingly thin man emerged, zombie-like, walking straight for us.

Henry's scowl turned to a grin. "Now, this is more like it."

The man's hair hung in curly wisps against his sunken cheeks and long scrawny neck. His ripped T-shirt and soiled jeans were several sizes too big. As for his age, he could have been 20 or 60.

"Hold up there, buddy," I called out.

He stopped abruptly, blinking into our lights with pinpoint pupils. The pungent smell of garbage wafted from his body. My guess was he'd been doing drugs for so long, he'd destroyed his mind and spirit, leaving behind the empty shell that now swayed unsteadily before us.

"Police department. What are you doing here?"

"Nothin' man." He spoke in a flat monotone, as if hypnotized.

"I think you were hiding in those weeds, shooting up. Show me your arms." Henry took hold of the man's bony wrists and turned them over, revealing translucent flesh draped over withered muscles. Meandering lines of needle tracks ran down both arms, many infected or scabbed over.

I looked into his lifeless eyes. "You've been using a long time. It's going to kill you, you know." Taking hold of his elbow with a gloved hand, I directed him to the car, letting him set the pace with his stumbling shuffle. "Now turn around and put your hands on the hood of the car."

Like a sci-fi movie where the dead come back to life, the man's body stiffened as if electrocuted and then he rose up on his toes and sprinted away. Surprised by his burst of energy, I had to chuckle. Clearly, his attempt to escape would prove futile; after all, I was muscular, well fed and worked out regularly in a gym. I half-heartedly trotted after him, fully expecting to find him collapsed a few yards ahead but to my dismay, the distance between us grew.

Determined not to be outdone by a malnourished addict, I kicked my pace into over-drive – and so did he. Breathing heavily from the full-out run, I watched in disbelief as his feet pumped furiously up and down, carrying his emaciated frame further and further away.

Just when I thought I might have to let this one go, a blur shot out from behind a shed. It flew through the air and tackled the stick man. Henry! I'd forgotten him in the chase —but how and when did he pass us?

I leaned against the shed's wall to catch my breath. When I saw the patrol car parked behind it, I immediately felt better.

Pulling the suspect's hands behind his back, Henry shook his head in my direction. "Looks like you might be out of shape there, ol' buddy."

"Hey, he had a lot of fear motivating him and the rest of the guys don't need to know about this."

Henry pointed at himself. "Who, me? I'd never tell."

We found only one spoon and a syringe in the man's pockets--not much to warrant his panic. But for some addicts, being in jail for just a few days without their drugs would be too long. We bagged and recorded the evidence, handed the man over to Seattle police and returned to the car.

"I'm telling you, Henry, fear causes adrenaline to surge through the body, giving people super powers."

"Of course, it does, Dean….that's why me and the guys will understand."

Back in the car, I turned the radio to Christian music. Henry promptly reached over to change the station. Expecting this reaction, I slapped his hand, causing him to pull back. He scowled at my shaking finger. "Did you forget? It's my turn to control the radio."

Henry sat back in the seat, hands tightly gripping the wheel while heavenly melodies filled the car. We drove to the other end of the tunnel.

"Looks like we've got customers."

Two men walked side by side, one well over six feet tall while the other couldn't have been more than five feet, his head not quite reaching his partner's shoulder. The taller man wore a white dress shirt and close-cropped dark hair, while his sidekick preferred all black and a long blond ponytail.

"Talk about the long and short of the matter," I smirked. "Let's see if their stories match as well as they do."

Henry and I moved away from each other, creating a gap between us. With our hands resting on our holstered weapons, we called out, "Hold up there, guys!" Railroad police."

Both stopped and turned to face us. "Bulls?"

Henry circled to one side while I watched the suspects. Suddenly, the man in the white shirt bent over and picked up a 2'x 4' board, lying by the tracks. Holding it like a baseball bat, he charged me with rage in his eyes.

It's amazing how the mind works in emergency situations. I instantly developed tunnel vision and saw only my assailant. My muscles tensed as I poised to react. When the plank came around, I ducked, feeling it whoosh over my head. This threw the attacker off balance for a second. Focusing my energy into my flexed right arm, I plunged my fist deep into the soft part of his stomach. I felt him come off his feet a few inches as his lungs belched foul smelling air. The man dropped the board, clutched his midriff with both arms and fell forward onto his head.

Glancing back at Henry to be sure he had the other one restrained, I squatted next to the wheezing man. "Just take it easy and you'll get your breath back."

Looking over at his partner, I asked, ""What's wrong with him?"

"I don't got no problems with cops. I don't know why Ricky took a swing at you but I'm sure sorry he did, Officer. An' I know he's sorry, too."

Once Ricky regained his breath, I let him sit up. "You created a problem for yourself coming at me like that."

"I didn't know who you were. Anyone can say they're a bull."

Ricky's fingers began fumbling with the buttons on his shirt as he tried to reach for something. I stooped down and placed a light chokehold around his neck.

"Just calm down," I said through clenched teeth. "I don't know what you're hiding under your shirt so don't move."

"You're hurting me, you idiot! I've got a colostomy and you knocked my bag off." Henry and I exchanged glances, his hand moving to his pistol. I released my hold.

"Okay, now slowly open your shirt and show me the colostomy bag." He pulled it open. Sure enough, a slim, plastic bag encircled part of his waist.

"Pig! Now I have to put it back into the hole."

"Watch your mouth or I'll add another problem to your list."

He spat. "I didn't know you were cops. You sure as hell don't look like cops."

Taking my police identification from my back pocket, I held it up. "Now you know what railroad cops look like."

"Well, Mr. Railroad Cop, I'm charging you with police brutality."

"Get in line. Now give me some ID and an explanation why you're here."

"We was takin' a short-cut," the other man broke in, still slouched at Henry's feet.

"The problem with that," Henry said as if speaking to a child, "is the short-cut is through private property and you made the mistake of trespassing with someone who's looking for trouble." The man shot an angry glance at Ricky.

After obtaining their information, we decided it'd be too much trouble to arrest them. "We're giving you both a break even though you don't deserve it. But this will be your only warning."

Henry added, "Next time, you're going to jail and I don't care what kind of bag you're wearing."

"Yeah, yeah, we're eternally grateful."

With those final words, Ricky strode angrily away, holding his shirt and a dangling colostomy bag in one hand, his cohort trotting behind to keep up.

"Now that we have two more satisfied customers, let's have dinner at Andy's." I happily settled into the front seat of the car, already knowing what I wanted to order.

Andy's Diner on Fourth Avenue was a popular eatery for both city and railroad police. It gave us a chance to compare warrants since criminals often traveled across both our jurisdictions. By the time we pulled in, three city police cars were already parked in the lot.

Our favorite tables were located in a real train car built into the restaurant. When we passed our city peers, we greeted them with a nod.

As soon as our food arrived, Henry and I stopped talking and dug in. But halfway through our meal, one of the officers, Tom, received a call over his portable radio. Our tables were close enough to hear their dispatcher.

"Dispatch to Unit 407. We just received a call from the manager of the Bush Hotel stating he was assaulted by two railroad police officers. He's requesting contact."

Tom looked at us and spoke into the radio, "I'll take care of it." He watched us closely while we pretended we hadn't overheard. "I don't suppose you two have been to the Bush Hotel today?"

We continued eating with gusto until Henry asked, "Were you talking to us, Tom?"

"I'm looking at you, aren't I?"

"Tom, you know we only patrol on railroad property. The only scuffle we had tonight was with a midget and a beanstalk and there's no way one of them is a hotel manager." I pushed my empty plate away and sat back in the chair. "And besides, if one of them really does run the hotel, what's he doing in our yards with a lousy attitude? You know how sensitive Henry here is."

Tom snorted. "Yeah, right! I'll check it out and get back to you if there's any truth to it. Later, guys."

We paid our bill and stepped out into the cold, rainy night, zipping our jackets to keep warm. "Before doing reports, let's check out the big cottonwood," Henry said, hating paperwork even more than I did.

As soon as he turned the key, the words of a Christian song filled the car,

"Oh God, you're the King of Kings..."

Henry backed the car out and casually turned down the volume, thinking I wouldn't notice.

"Yes, let's check it out," I answered, turning it back up.

"Through your love and through your Son..."

Henry tore out of the parking lot and into the late night traffic.

"You save each and every one..."

As soon as we turned onto the dirt road leading to the lone tree, Henry saw his chance and turned off the radio. When I started to protest, he whispered, "We need the element of surprise."

"Now you're reaching, but I'll let you have this one."

When the cottonwood's massive branches came into view, he turned off the headlights and wipers, allowing the car to coast to a stop.

"See anything, Dean?" Henry whispered.

"Not yet."

Scanning the darkness, I noticed a flickering light at the base of the tree and in the encircling brush, the outline of a station wagon caught our eye.

We unclipped our seat belts and quietly opened the doors. "Why don't you see what's happening over at the tree and I'll check the car. And Henry...don't start without me. I don't want to miss the fun."

He grinned. "You've got thirty seconds."

Silently, we turned and headed to our respective targets. Peering through the wagon's back window, I saw only blankets and empty cans. I turned back toward the tree, keeping my profile low as I slunk into the weeds, pistol in hand.

When I reached the tree, I saw three men sloshing down beer beneath a lantern's yellow light. One looked as wide as he was tall, with long black hair hanging over beefy rounded shoulders. He wore an outlaw biker's sleeveless jean jacket. The second man's shaved head appeared marbled with numerous long, thin scars crisscrossing his scalp. The third, a burly man with squinty eyes, had a red bulbous nose above a thick moustache that hung below his lower lip. But my stomach lurched when I saw who sat between them -- two very young, very frightened sailors in uniform, looking fresh out of boot camp and still in their teens.

The biker held one of them between his fleshy arms, nuzzling the boy's ear with his mouth. The second sailor stood against the cottonwood's trunk, being prodded and teased by the other two transients.

Baldy raised a can of beer and shouted gleefully, "We's goin' ta show you boys how ta party all night long. Oh, yeah!"

From the darkness came a reply, "Party's over, boys. Everyone stay calm and keep your hands where I can see them."

Henry stepped into the circle of light holding his steel flashlight with one hand, his other resting on the .357 strapped to his side. The outlaws stared open-mouthed, their alcohol-saturated brains trying to grasp the sudden appearance of this stranger. Taking advantage of their shock, I stepped out from the brush directly behind them. "Railroad police. Do exactly what he tells you."

With the transients momentarily caught off guard, I motioned to the sailors. Recognizing their chance for freedom, they jumped up and scurried to my side.

"Get behind me. You're going to learn something tonight."

Noticing their trembling, I whispered, "It's over, you're safe now." Immense relief shone in their eyes.

Henry's voice thundered, "Make one move and we'll blow you away."

The three gawked back and forth, not sure which of us to focus on. Finally Baldy spoke up. "Hey, what's yur problem? We's just havin' some fun."

"These sailors weren't having any fun."

Keeping my eyes on the outlaws, I asked the boys, "How'd you two end up way out here -- with them?"

"They approached us at the waterfront, sir, " one explained in a wavering voice. "They said they'd take us to a party..." He began to gulp hard so the other continued.

"We were just assigned our ship and thought we could meet some girls...but when they brought us out here...." His words trailed off as he looked at their captors.

"We ain't doin nothin' ya stupid cop!" Baldy was shouting at Henry. "We jus' wanted ta give these boys somethin' ta talk 'bout when they got back ta their boat, is all."

"This is bull__!" The biker rose to his feet, aiming a torrent of obscenities at Henry. Baldy and Bozo started to get up to join him.

"Both of you, on the ground in kneeling position." When they didn't comply, I leveled my .357 Magnum and repeated the command. "On the ground, now!"

They dropped to their knees.

Biker had obviously taken the breaking up of their party as a personal affront and now had something to prove. He began advancing on Henry, shoulders hunched forward as he jabbed the air with thick, beefy fingers, punctuating each threat. Within the lantern's circle of light, a strange audience of circumstance - outlaws, sailors and police partner -- watched the drama unfold. But only I knew the next scene would be the final one, as Henry's wrath was about to be unloosed.

"Keep coming scumbag, so I can take you out." Henry tapped his long, steel flashlight in the palm of his hand.

When Biker stepped close enough, Henry rammed his fist hard into the man's chest, knocking him back. At the same time, the end of his flashlight butted the guy's chin with an unexpected result. The biker's body immediately went rigid, from his big feet to his wide, open eyes, remaining standing like a wax replica of himself. We held our collective breaths as raindrops plopped on leaves in a steady rhythm and tree frogs croaked nearby.

And then, as if someone called out, "timmberrrrrr!" the stiff, unbending form of Biker toppled backward like a giant sequoia, hitting the ground with a resounding "thud!" He was out cold.

"Well, that takes care of that," Henry said casually. "Now for you two."

"But we ain't done nothin' wrong," Bozo whined.

"Yeah, we can tell you're a couple of nice guys welcoming visitors to our city. What were you really going to do to these boys?"

"Jus' have a coupla drinks, play a few games." Baldy wagged his head as he spoke.

"Well, let's invite city PD to your little party and see what kind of warrants you creeps have." They immediately shut up.

After we handcuffed the three trespassers and asking dispatch to contact city police, Henry picked up an open bottle of beer. Standing over the unconscious biker, he emptied the contents on a spot right between the man's still open eyes. A spasm of coughing and gasping erupted as he tried to sit up, only to discover his hands were cuffed. He began to struggle and curse but when he looked up and saw Henry, he lowered his voice as if swearing at himself.

With the police on their way, I turned my attention back to the sailors. "Do you two have any idea how lucky you are? Usually, we arrive *after* the crime's committed."

They looked down at their feet. "We just want to go back to our ship and forget all this...we owe you both, sir."

"If you really want to thank us, promise you'll *never* do something this stupid again. You might not be so lucky next time... actually, I believe luck had nothing to do with it."

After giving us their information, they jogged down the road and back to their lives as proud members of our Navy and hopefully, wiser youth.

When city police arrived, we found our suspects only had warrants for minor offenses to which we added assault and criminal trespassing. They spent one night in jail and were back on the streets the next day, no doubt looking for victims to invite to their next party.

Chapter 24

"It's time to do something about the 4th Avenue warehouse. Gangs have moved in and they need evicting." Henry grinned at my news as we headed for the car one cold November afternoon.

"Sounds like our kind of job."

Burlington Northern had scheduled the vacant warehouse to be torn down by Thanksgiving, but before the crews and equipment could begin, any squatters had to be out. The reason for the order was the building's proximity to downtown Seattle – the railroad received frequent requests from businesses to destroy all potential shelters so derelicts wouldn't set up camp and scare away customers.

We parked behind the one-story, 300-foot long structure and walked to a concrete loading dock with several roll-up doors, one of which had enough space at the bottom to peer inside. Squatting low, I shone my flashlight across the darkened interior, the littered concrete floor stretching far beyond the light beam's edges.

"You ready?" I asked with an eager grin.

"Let's go for it."

We rolled the door high enough to slide beneath its metal frame and into the building. The familiar rush of adrenaline kicked in, heightening my senses for what, or who, we might find inside. Once my eyes adjusted to the darkness, I could see four walls forming a small, enclosed room at the opposite end of the warehouse. Henry saw it too.

"If we're going to find trouble, we'll find it there," he whispered.

Our footsteps echoed loudly...too loudly. I didn't like announcing our presence to potential criminals, especially if they had walls to hide behind. When we reached the door, I gently pressed my ear against the dilapidated plywood and held my breath. Not even a creak could be heard.

"If they're in there, they're not moving," I whispered, making a big deal about first checking the knob before we busted through. It was locked.

Motioning for Henry to stand back, I positioned myself with pistol and flashlight and then slammed my foot through the decomposing wood, knocking the door off its hinges. We charged into the room, ready for anything--except an empty room. The draining emotions felt like being star quarterbacks at the Super Bowl only to be told the game had just been cancelled.

Our lights revealed a torn sofa, a spindle chair and dirty clothes heaped around bottles of cheap booze. "Right place, wrong time," I stated flatly, giving the sofa a solid kick of frustration. Sharp pain immediately shot through my foot and up my shin.

"OW!"

"Don't tell me that couch got the best of you," Henry teased.

I limped over to the chair and swung it hard against the wall, satisfied when I heard its spindles splintering – until one hit me in the head. "OW! I can't believe this!"

Henry laughed. "The chair won that one too?"

Feeling my temple for any signs of a bump, my frustration turned to the cache of liquor. "I think we need to make sure they can't celebrate when they return."

"Now you're talking," Henry said. We peeled off our jackets, rolled up our shirtsleeves and with primal yells, threw bottles of Mad Dog, Night Train and Ripple against the walls. The exploding shards actually felt therapeutic.

I took hold of the last bottle by its neck, lifted it over my shoulder -- but stopped mid-throw. A sickening stench of urine hit my nose as liquid flowed over my hand and down my arm. I dropped the bottle and frantically pulled off my shirt without unbuttoning or inhaling.

"You just *had* to throw that last bottle, didn't you?" Henry sniffed the air and made a face. "Phew! Didn't your mama ever teach you not to pee on yourself?"

"Ha, ha, very funny. Let's just get to the depot so I can clean up."

"If you think you're riding in my car smelling like that, you're crazy."

"Oh, it's *your* car now." I strode quickly toward the exit, but Henry didn't move. Letting out an exasperated sigh, I offered him a deal. "Look, I'll put my shirt in the trunk and hold my arm out the window. Will that satisfy you?"

"You got yourself a ride, Mr. Pee-body."

As soon as we arrived, I jumped out of the car before he parked and headed for the Men's Room at the depot. Stripped to the waist, I vigorously washed my hands, arms and torso, ignoring the strange looks from patrons. Once I felt clean, I plunged my shirt beneath the running faucet, using paper towels to stop the drain. With handfuls of soap, I scrubbed the fabric for several minutes until satisfied. When I emerged from the men's room with a clean-smelling body in a wet, soapy shirt, I made my way to Henry.

"So now you're entering wet T-shirt contests?"

I held my hand in front of his face. "Not another word." At the front doors, we stepped outside into a blustery November wind.

"Hey, railroad police!" Two young men were running in our direction.

"Oh great. Looks like the pain-in-the-ass brothers found us again," Henry muttered. In their early 20's, Lyle and Kyle were well known pickpockets in the downtown area. And for some weird reason, they always wore matching fringed jackets with leather belts and enormous silver buckles.

But today, they didn't look their usual smug selves. Bits of leaves sprouted from their slicked down hair, ensnared, no doubt, by the thick layer of gel. Lyle's right eye had swelled and started to color. A thin trickle of blood oozed from Kyle's broad nose.

"Wonder what happened to the boys this time," I muttered to Henry.

"Hey, railroad policeman." Lyle's shrill tone always annoyed me. "We wanna file a formal complaint, right now."

Kyle continued. "We're standin' behind the depot when two cops started beatin' on us for *no reason*."

Lyle broke in. "Just mindin' our own business…"

Kyle pushed his brother aside. "*No* reason, man. Now look at us – our hair's messed up!" He wiped his bloody nose with the back of his hand.

"You mean to say you were just standing there?" Henry asked incredulously, "And for no reason, two city cops started hassling you?"

The brothers sighed with relief. "We knew you'd understand."

Henry took a pen and note pad from his pocket. "What did these cops look like?"

Kyle stepped closer. "Well, we really didn't get a chance to uh, see them…"

Henry's eyes narrowed. "What about a badge number?"

The brothers shifted their eyes nervously. "Uh, no, so they must've been undercover cops…yeah, undercover like you two."

"Well, then, we need to catch these guys," I said, shaking my head.

"That's for sure," Henry added, pen still poised.

Lyle and Kyle gave each other high-fives. "We knew you guys were cool."

Henry slipped his pen back in his pocket. "Because you guys were on railroad property, it's <u>our</u> job to beat you up. Those other cops were out of line."

Both men's faces froze mid-smile. Henry and I waited for the news to sink in. When it did, their faces contorted between shock and anger, Lyle cocking his head to one side to see out of his good eye. "What'd you say?!!?"

"We said it's our job to..." The brothers stormed off before we could finish our sentence, giving us the one finger salute over their shoulders.

"I bet they got caught with their hands in the wrong guy's pocket and he let them have it," Henry mused, watching their retreating backs.

"Sounds about right – so where we eating tonight?" We returned to the patrol car but no sooner had I buckled my seat belt than the radio crackled. "Engineer on the Stacy Street switch engine, calling the Special Agent."

"They're playing our song." I grabbed the mike. "This is the Special Agent."

"Special Agent, we've got a naked man at the west end of Stacy Street Yard who keeps running in front of the switch engine. We need him out of here before he gets hit."

"We're on our way. ETA is ten minutes." Giving Henry the thumbs up, I said with mock enthusiasm, "Oh boy, a naked crazy—our specialty."

Arriving at Stacy Yard, we found the switch engine pulling train cars but no naked bottom sprinting ahead of it on the tracks. We continued our search until Henry exclaimed, "Bingo!"

Sitting beneath a bridge near Marginal Way, a man stood pulling on a gray hooded sweatshirt. "At least he's dressed -- we can cross cruel and unusual punishment off our list of charges." I jumped out of the car. "Railroad police. What're you doing out here?"

The man hunched forward, arms held out to his sides. With over-sized bulging eyes, he resembled a surprised owl about to fly away. He let out an ear-piercing scream that echoed off the bridge above us, sending pigeons flapping in every direction, and ran for the street.

I got back into the car. "Why do they always run away?"

"Maybe he didn't like your wet T-shirt." Henry smirked, accelerating and sending a shower of stones behind the tires. We easily caught up with the subject who was doing an impressive job of maintaining high decibel shrieks while running at full speed. His arms flailed in wide circles, as if practicing the butterfly stroke.

"This guy's going to get run over and we'll be blamed for chasing him," Henry muttered.

"Then drop me off behind him and drive ahead and block his escape."

Henry slowed down enough for me to open the door and literally hit the road running. Passing the screamer, Henry slammed on the brakes, causing the car to slide sideways to a stop. Seeing his progress blocked, the man made a quick right turn. When I attempted the same, my shoes lost traction, sending me sprawling across the wet pavement.

Ignoring the road rash on my hands, I leapt to my feet and once more began to close the gap between us. We were now on a grassy strip alongside the road when the runner abruptly stopped and turned to face me. I collided into him full force, knocking us both to the ground but amazingly, his high-pitched screeching didn't miss a beat.

When I pulled him to a sitting position, he began to chant strange mutterings while his even stranger eyes darted back and forth like ping pong balls.

"Hafta run...dark train...black rain...sorry trouble...I'm bad... look inside."

"Just calm down, Mister. I'm with the police." He struggled against my hold on him.

Henry reached us and positioned himself in front of the still ranting man. "Hafta see...gray birds...white turds...no slide...wanna play."

"Shut up!" Henry shook the man's shoulders and he fell silent, gazing at Henry with a gap-toothed smile spreading across his face. His eyes widened. "Dad!" Henry jumped back as if bit by a snake.

I punched his arm. "Why, Henry, you ol' dog, you."

The man continued looking at Henry, awestruck, and held his arms wide, clearly wanting a hug.

"*I am not your dad!*" Henry bellowed into his face.

Elbowing him in the side, I reasoned with him. "Can't you be his dad until we get cuffs on him. And besides, I'm starting to see a slight resemblance here."

"*Not* funny, pal." He rabbit punched me in the gut.

Henry scowled, paced and took several deep breaths. "Okay... *son*....let's get these cuffs on you." The man eagerly held up his arms and allowed his wrists to be cuffed. Henry walked him back to the car while I ran ahead to call for transport. When Seattle police arrived, I gave a detailed report of the arrest, resulting in raucous laughter from the officers.

After placing the newly dubbed "Henry Jr." into the patrol car for a ride to a mental facility, Henry and I watched the departing car in silence.

Through the window, the man craned his neck to look back, a goofy, crooked smile across his face.

I buried my face on Henry's shoulder, making loud, sobbing sounds. "Why do they have to grow up so fast!"

He twisted my shirt and pulled my face close to his. *"Not-another-word."*

"Sure thing…..Pops."

We had dinner at Andy's and then headed to Balmer Yard, where we'd been getting reports about stolen car stereos. At the south end of the yard, we counted twenty auto carriers with new Nissans. According to the train schedule, it would be hours before any engines arrived to pull them east, allowing thieves time to steal.

The tracks at this end of Balmer had steep banks on either side, so Henry and I used an old bird hunter's trick. One of us would walk next to the train while the other paralleled him out of sight, at the top of the slope. If the plan worked the way we hoped, the suspect would see the one by the tracks and try to escape by running up the side where the other waited.

I won the coin toss to be the catch person at the top. Keeping in the shadows above and ahead of Henry by about fifty feet, my eyes strained for any movement on the train parked below. Henry had passed half the auto carriers when I saw a man jump from a car and scramble up my side of the ravine. Perfect! I ran to meet him but he spotted me and changed direction. We sprinted along the top of the embankment until I managed to get close enough to kick his shoe with my foot. This knocked him off balance and he came to a sliding, face-first stop. I applied pressure to his hand to keep him down.

Between breaths, I told him, "I'm with the railroad police. Calm down and you won't get hurt."

"Senor, senor, soy innocente, innocente."

"Great, you're an illegal who doesn't speak English." I cuffed his wrists and stood him up just as Henry's footsteps could be heard approaching us in the dark. "We're over here, Henry, and..."

The suspect made a run for it. But in his panic, the Mexican ran headlong into my partner. Henry grabbed the cuff chain with one hand and the man's long hair with the other, bringing him to a painful, neck-snapping halt. Maintaining both holds, Henry pushed the now subdued suspect to a street light, and seated him on the ground.

"What're you doing out here?"

"I don't think he speaks English, Henry."

Groaning in exasperation, Henry began communicating with his own version of Spanish and rapid hand gestures. But while watching the suspect, I noticed something strange about his hair. It moved! Leaning over for a closer look, a wave of shock and repulsion swept over me – tiny bugs swarmed his filthy scalp.

"Your hands, Henry, your hands."

"Why do you always think you can do better? He's understanding me."

I pointed to the man's scalp and made a scary face. Henry narrowed his eyes and took a closer look. I braced for his reaction. "Damn you! Don't you take el batho? Wash your hairo?"

Henry swore and kicked the gravel, closely scrutinizing his skin for crawling life forms. "That's it. I'm wearing gloves from now on. Alright, Jose, what have you got in your el pocket-o's?"

We pulled out two large screwdrivers, wire cutters and pliers. "Well, now, tools of a car radio thief – looks like we found our hombre."

Seattle Police arrived to transport the prisoner to jail, but because of some unexpected time constraints in their department, we'd have to accompany the suspect to the station and do both the report and booking.

Dreading the extra paperwork, we followed the city patrol car to the downtown station. After a brief exchange with the transporting officers, we tagged each item found on the illegal suspect, placed them in a bag, and carried it to a storage room. Next, we fingerprinted, photographed, and placed our prisoner behind bars. An officer handed Henry the booking forms.

Looking around the crowded jail, we found a small desk in front of several holding cells, each filled with men. Henry took a seat while I positioned myself behind him. But no sooner had Henry begun filling out the form than one of the inmates behind us began cursing wildly, his spit flying out between the bars. I glared at him but Henry seemed unruffled, remaining focused on the report.

After several minutes, I saw three Seattle police officers enter the room. They casually strolled our way when the inmate again let loose with a string of obscenities. Stopping directly in front of our desk, one of the officers commented,

"I suppose he's another one of those crazy Vietnam vets."

Henry's head snapped up, his hand tightened around the pen, his jaw clenched tightly. I realized Henry thought the officer was talking about him.

"Yeah, too bad the VC didn't keep him over there."

Henry's face flushed with anger as he slowly began to rise from the chair. I stifled my laughter as I watched the misunderstanding heading toward an all too familiar scene.

"Just what we need around here, another crazy vet."

The officers shook their heads, not knowing how close they were coming to a brawl. Henry's legs were ready to launch across the desk when I leaned forward and laid a heavy hand on his shoulder.

"They're talking about the guy in the cell behind us. So calm down you crazy, Vietnam vet."

Henry's expression went from rage, to relief, to gratitude. An unspoken understanding passed between us, the kind only soldiers who have been in battle, shared. We resumed our positions, Henry filling out papers, me watching his back.

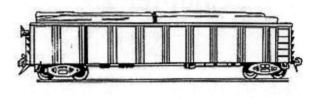

Gondola

Courtesy of Sedalia Heritage Foundation * 600 E. 3rd St., Sedalia, MO 65301*
www.sedaliakatydepot.com

Chapter 25

On the day after Thanksgiving, the lucrative side of Christmas officially began and Seattle businesses wanted to make sure no one missed out. Holiday music blared from store speakers loud enough to be heard by shoppers strolling beneath streetlights yoked with giant wreaths. Rustic mangers on church lawns sheltering statues of the Holy Family competed with velvet-suited Santa's on ornate golden thrones for the true meaning of Christmas. Nodding Salvation Army bell ringers graciously smiled at all who dropped money for the needy into their hanging red kettles. And everywhere, in offices, homes and stores, conversations inevitably drifted to gifts, parties, and family dinners.

During the first half of December, Cassie and I had been hiding presents for each other around the house and garage. Only one thing remained to make our preparation complete. Stopping at a roadside lot one evening, we entered a miniature forest of trees nailed to pieces of wood whose needles glistened from the recent rain. Pulling my jacket's hood up for warmth, I breathed deeply of the pine smells while Cassie ran through the neat rows, shaking branches and giggling when hundreds of drops sprayed her. When I heard her squeal, I knew she'd found the perfect one.

Once home, we dragged the fragrant evergreen through the front door and bolted it into a stand, its top bough bent at a right angle where it met the ceiling. To the familiar melodies of Christmas songs from our cassette tape player, Cassie danced with the dogs, sang and hung ornaments.

"Come on, Dean, try and guess what I got you this year."

"Uh, is it fiberglass, made by Chevy and bright red?"

"No, guess again… should I hang this one here or there?"

"Hmm, either's fine…okay, is it 45 feet long, has tall masts and floats?"

She put her hand on her hip and pouted. "You're not even trying…so now it's my turn to guess. Is it made of fabric or steel?"

I sat on the ladder, pretending to be too absorbed with untangling strings of lights to give her any clues. Fortunately, she soon gave up and wandered into the kitchen to look at recipes for Christmas cookies – I didn't know how much longer I could have resisted her pleading.

The next morning, I sleepily opened my eyes to the familiar sight of Snoopy's face peering intently into mine. It was the signal he'd been waiting for—he wildly licked my cheeks and chin, officially starting our day. Bounding back and forth over the pillows and under the covers, Snoop did a thorough job of bringing me from half asleep to fully awake. My laughter, and Snoopy's yips, soon attracted the other two, who joined in the wrestling. When I retreated under the bedspread, Snoopy wriggled under, leading the way for his cohorts.

"Okay, okay, I give up!" I threw off the covers and held up my hands. "I surrender. You guys win."

Reluctantly crawling out of our warm bed, I called out for Cassie but she didn't answer. Hmmm, where could she be? I padded around the house, checking closets, garage and kitchen—no Cassie. It was time to call in a professional tracker.

Squatting down beside Snoopy, I scratched his ears. "Hey, little buddy, do you know where Cassie is? Where's Cassie? Go get her, Snoop!"

He bounded down the hall to the bathroom and looked back at me, wagging his tail. "Good boy, you found her."

I softly knocked on the door, hearing faint splashing sounds. "Hey, you in there. What's going on?"

Cautiously, I pushed the door open, watching for any signs of an ambush. But to my surprise, sliced fruit, toast and two glasses of juice were arranged on a shiny silver tray. Surrounding it were numerous flickering candles, a delicious mix of floral and spice scents wafting past my nose. And from the bathtub, a bubble-bearded face peered back at me. "Ho, Ho, Ho. Have you been a good boy this year?"

"I'm counting on it."

Closing the door behind me, my throat tightened as I realized for the millionth time how fortunate I was to have her as my wife. Kneeling by the tub, I caressed her cheek. "With you, every day is a gift."

She leaned over to kiss me but ended up covering me with bubbles instead. With a splash in my direction, she giggled. "Why don't you join me and I'll tell you just how good you've been."

Undressing, I sank into the warm water and we spent a blissful morning in each other's arms, not wanting it to end. But too soon, Cassie had to leave for work.

Running her fingers through my wet hair, she kissed me. "If I don't leave now, I'll be late and have to explain why to the boss."

I reluctantly let her go. "Let's start more days like today, just you and I together. We've been too busy lately."

She began to dress and gave me a wink. "We can start tonight. Don't work too hard and I'll have another bath waiting for you."

"You're on. I'll let Henry do all the fighting."

After a final lingering kiss, she left the house. I stood at the window and waved goodbye as she backed out of our driveway in her latest re-built VW. Missing her already, and looking forward to our reunion, I wrapped a few of her gifts and placed them under the tree. By early afternoon, it was time to head to work.

Henry greeted me from the office recliner, looking like the proverbial cat that swallowed the canary.

"Okay, I know that look -- what's going on?"

"You know the transient camp we've been dismantling for the last three nights?"

"Yeah – did you figure out how to keep the bums from re-building it?"

Dragging his feet off the desk and leaning forward in the chair, Henry's grin confirmed my guess. "Yup - we leave it alone and do nothing."

"Uh, that's your plan?"

"I got a call from a Mr. Levine. He's some kind of Hollywood director and he told me someone keeps tearing down their *set*."

I laughed. "You're kidding! The camp was really a movie set?"

"You got it. And I assured him we'd *personally* make sure this malicious crime would be stopped."

"Ha! Maybe he'll give us a part in his movie. Now let's get to work."

Since our offices shared a building with Amtrak, we walked outside to survey the depot's Jackson Street entrance. Whenever passengers disembarked from trains, they were often distracted with luggage and looking for loved ones, making them perfect victims for having wallets and purses stolen. With only thirty minutes until the next train arrived, we wanted to find the pickpockets before they committed a crime.

Scanning the passing crowd, a grating sound like nails on a chalkboard rose from somewhere close, above the traffic noise and sidewalk conversations. We followed our ears to a grizzled man in a long, black coat, leaning against one of the depot's window ledges. His weathered, lined face wore a thatch of gray stubble beneath a ball cap that had seen better years.

With eyes closed and head tilted back, he croaked out melodies in heartfelt but horribly flat notes. When each ended, he'd smile and nod as if acknowledging an applauding audience calling out requests.

With an exuberant wave, he bellowed, "I'd be appy to shing that shong."

He coughed from deep down in his throat, spit out a glob of phlegm onto the sidewalk and croaked, "Hark n' herald were shepherds…..way up high….in da shky….. wit Shanta drivin' da sleigh." He kept tempo with a swinging wine bottle held precariously in one hand.

We covered our ears and winced. "He's so bad, it hurts."

I approached him and lightly kicked his foot. "Hey, Mister, you picked the wrong place for a concert. You're scaring everyone."

He stopped. "I ain't shcarin' nobody, they want me to shing. Hey, lady, tell dese guys you love my shingin'."

The woman he pointed to looked disgusted and hurried off.

"Concert's over, pal, now move on." Henry tapped the guy's arm.

The once happy minstrel became agitated. "I ain't goin' no place an' you cain't make me." He swung his bottle in a wide arc, narrowly missing me each time. Annoyed, I stuck out my steel flashlight, shattering the bottom half of the bottle. I immediately realized my mistake and grabbed his wrist.

Henry shook his head. "I think providing the homeless with weapons is carrying the season of giving too far, Dean."

"Are you going to criticize me or help?"

Henry grabbed the man's other arm and with my free hand, I carefully removed the knifelike glass from the man's fist. "Hey! Gimme my wine back!"

"Santa would take us off his list if we did. Now wish Henry and I a merry Christmas and start walking."

He leaned precariously from side to side, trying to find his balance. Finally, with a limp wave, he placed one foot in front of the other in a diagonal direction. Once he got his momentum, he resumed his unique holiday medley. "Shilent night.....baby shleep.....wit da sheep.....but one had a shiny nose"

I found a piece of cardboard from a trash can to clean up the broken glass and then said to Henry. "Let's get back inside and catch some pick-pockets before we all start singing off key."

Taking the escalator down to the main floor, Henry and I split up and took positions at opposite ends of the terminal, within sight of each other. A train had just entered the station and people now streamed into the depot. Watching the moving crowd, I noticed a man in an oversized coat but before I could follow, my portable radio crackled. "Stacy Street Yardmaster, calling Special Agent, Dean O'Shea."

Reaching for my radio, I wondered why dispatch used my name. Looking across the terminal where Henry held his radio to his ear, I shrugged my shoulders.

"This is Special Agent O'Shea. What can I do for you?"

A long pause. "I'm sorry to tell you but your wife's been in an accident and we need your location. Seattle Police will take you to the hospital."

A strange, tingling sensation began at my head and ran down to my feet. Had I heard correctly? "Uh, what…please repeat."

"Dean, your wife's been seriously hurt and city PD will take you to Harborview Hospital. That's all I know…I'm sorry."

I felt like I'd been sucked into a vortex, an invisible wall rising up to separate me from the crowd—my world had stopped, theirs continued. I caught Henry's eyes across the terminal and for the first time in all our years of patrolling together, I saw fear.

Pressing the respond button, I forced the words through my closing throat. "A serious accident? What, how did…where is she?"

"The police will take you. Where are you?"

I walked on shaky legs to the front doors. "I'm uh, I'm at the depot, King Street entrance."

Handing my radio to Henry, I felt closer to him than ever before. He lightly touched my shoulder. "I'll take care of everything here."

Moving through the doors with the sea of holiday passengers, I felt like a piece of driftwood—awkward and out of sync. A blue and white police car pulled to the curb. I numbly got into the front seat, relieved I knew the officer. He merged into traffic, keeping his gaze straight ahead.

Trying to control the panic threatening to overtake me, I asked softly, "Do you know what happened, Burt?"

"I wish I did, Dean. My orders were to pick you up at the depot and take you to Harborview E.R. I wish I knew more, but I don't."

Watching the blurred lights through the window, my mind refused to accept the news. It had to be a mistake. Cassie was home, safe, waiting for me. She told me she'd be waiting for me. We were going Christmas shopping in the morning.

Moving my lips, I sent a whispered prayer into the night sky. "Dear God, please be with Cassie and don't let her be hurt."

Trying to avoid the image of my precious Cassie lying on a hospital bed, in pain, I wiped my eyes as we drove to the emergency entrance. Getting out of the car, I mumbled thanks to Burt.

He squeezed my hand. "I'm praying for both of you, Dean."

The sliding doors automatically parted and I entered a place as foreign to me as Mars. Approaching the nearest desk, I stood mutely watching a woman at a computer screen. She looked up and raised her eyebrows, expecting me to have something to say.

Fighting back tears, I stammered out fragments of a sentence. "I'm Dean O'Shea. My wife...Cassie ...I, uh, need to see her."

Her fingernails clicked on the keyboard. She scanned the monitor and then shook her head. "Hmmm, no one by that name has checked in."

My body slumped forward with relief. I could go home and Cassie would be there, just like she'd promised. "I was told she was in an accident but if she's not here, it's a mistake--right?"

"Let me see if she's en route." She picked up the phone and pushed a few buttons. I heard her say Cassie's name and then she hung up and looked straight at me. "An ambulance is bringing her in right now. They'll be coming through those doors."

My last thread of hope had unraveled. I crossed the room and stepped outside, forcing myself to breathe as I watched the flashing red lights approach. In those moments, when my heart threatened to stop beating unless it knew Cassie would be all right, I'd never felt more alone.

The vehicle stopped, the rear doors burst open and uniformed EMT's pulled out a stretcher; on it lay the woman I loved. I looked into her face for reassurance, but her eyes were closed. Except for an oxygen mask over her nose and mouth, there were no signs of trauma; no blood or bruises, not even a rip in her clothes.

I gently touched her arm and spoke into her ear. "I'm right here Cassie, and I won't leave until you can come home." Tears sprang to my eyes. "Oh, God, please be with her!"

Attendants pushed the gurney into the hospital. I trotted behind on shaky legs, willing her to wake up. We needed to go home to our dogs and finish wrapping Christmas presents and signing cards. A nurse stopped me. "Are you the husband?"

Looking past her, I watched them push Cassie through another set of doors. Reluctantly, I met the nurse's all-business expression. Did she have any idea how terrified I felt at this moment? "Yes, I'm her hus... can you *please* tell me what happened? Is she...going to be...alright?" The faltering, choking words sounded like someone else's voice.

"The doctors are examining her now and someone will be out shortly to answer your questions."

"I'll be here, waiting...however long..."

She looked into my eyes and a flicker of compassion crossed her face. "I'll come back as soon as I know something, okay?"

She turned abruptly and strode through the same doors Cassie had been taken. As they swung open, I saw people in blue scrubs frantically working over the still form on the gurney. Helplessness washed over me like giant waves -- I wanted to burst through those doors and take my beautiful wife away from all this confusion.

I don't know how long I stood there -- minutes and hours felt the same when you're in shock -- but the nurse did return. With a soft voice, she asked, "Would you please follow me?"

I took hold of her arm, as if grabbing a life preserver. Feeling desperate for any information, I pleaded. "Please tell me...how..."

"I'm sorry, I can't. But one of her doctors can answer your questions. We have a private waiting room for you."

Forcing my feet to move, I followed her into a tiny room with some chairs and four sterile white walls. "It should only be a few minutes."

The door closed and my chest heaved uncontrollably as I sobbed into my hands. Leaning against the colorless walls, I let my raw emotions run riot. My world had changed from light and love to intolerable pain and darkness -- in a moment. After what seemed like eternity, I collapsed into a chair, spent, drained and sickened. An image of Cassie's child-like trust in God came to mind. I knelt on the cold linoleum floor, shut my swollen eyes and with shaking hands, forced out the words. "Oh God, please touch Cassie with your healing hands, please don't let her feel any pain. I know you love her more than I do but please don't take her from me, not now."

Unable to say more, I slumped in a chair, emotionally exhausted. The door opened tentatively and a middle-aged man wearing glasses, scrubs and a weary expression, entered. A surgical mask hung around his neck. "Mr. O'Shea?"

Nodding, I searched his eyes for any sign of reassurance. "Yes...that's me."

I willed him to say, "Your wife's just fine" but his sagging shoulders and downcast face told me otherwise.

"I'm afraid your wife isn't doing well."

I wanted to argue with him -- she's only 24, full of life and mischief and potential -- and what about her future with me? How could she *not* be doing well?

He continued in a low tone. "Your wife has been shot."

His words hit me like a blow to my stomach, knocking the wind out of me.

"*Shot*!? How could she......what do you mean?"

The doctor sat in the chair next to mine, staring at the floor while I tried in vain to absorb the news. "She couldn't have been shot....this has to be a mistake. Just tell me when we can go home."

"We don't know how it happened," the doctor spoke carefully, "but your wife has a bullet wound to the chest and it's damaged two of the arteries to her heart."

My senses reeled from the image of Cassie, hurt and bleeding from a wound to her heart...her *heart*!"

"She's lost a lot of blood and it doesn't look very good right now. We're doing everything we can for her."

He kept his eyes averted--this had to be the worst part of his job. He rose from the chair as if he'd aged a hundred years.

Taking hold of his arm, I hoarsely whispered, "Are you telling me she...she could die?" I could barely say the words, let alone believe them.

"Yes, your wife could die." He paused. "Do you have family you can call?"

His words about the unthinkable were screaming in my head.

"I think you should call them....right away."

I still held his arm. "Doctor, please don't let her die." This stranger had become my hope -- my only hope. He left the room without looking back.

The shock caused spasms to well up from my chest and into my throat. I cried out to God. "Shot! She can't be shot. If anyone had to be shot, it should've been me, it should've been me..." I slumped against the walls, sobs racking my body. "Please God, don't take her from me, don't take her from me...oh dear God."

Somehow, I managed to call family members, remaining coherent enough to say the strange words, "Cassie's been in an accident," before breaking down and crying.

During the night, doctors worked to repair the damaged arteries in order to stabilize her enough for admission to the Intensive Care Unit. She remained in a coma with a tube down her throat, connecting her to a respirator.

Over the next several days, family members arrived, spoke in hushed tones, stood in waiting rooms and called home for updates. I felt as though I'd slipped into a nightmare, one that trapped me in its madness, preventing me from waking and discovering that everything had been a dream, after all. When sleep would finally overtake me, I'd collapse into a chair by Cassie's bed. What food I managed to keep down came from vending machines or the cafeteria.

Time, instead of flowing, became compartmentalized by progress or setbacks. The call about Cassie's accident, telling family, arrival of my parents and sister, daily talks with doctors, seeing her worsen, crying, praying, crying alone and on the shoulders of family.

Miraculously, Cassie did manage to hold on in the ICU. My co-workers donated blood and received permission from our supervisor to include the hospital in their daily patrols. Every day a Special Agent stopped by to see me, put his hand on my shoulder and share words of encouragement. Their support meant more than I could ever say.

As the vigil continued, doctors urged me to go home and get some routine in my life. It wouldn't do Cassie any good if I fell apart. So I began spending a few hours each night in our bed, my arm touching the place where she should've been, where she'd always been. Before the sun came up, I'd arrive at the hospital and jog to her room -- would this be the day she'd be taken off the respirator? Would her beautiful eyes open so I could look into them just one more time? Would this be the day I'd prayed for, the day she'd return to me?

But the sight of her limp body beneath a white sheet, tubes and wires connecting her to humming machines, would seize my heart yet again.

One morning, I became nauseated and ducked into a bathroom to splash water on my face. Catching my reflection in the mirror, I was shocked to see dark circles beneath my bloodshot eyes. My once blonde mustache now shone silvery white.

Christmas came and went without us that year and so did New Year's Day. Cassie remained in a coma while my entire life revolved around dressing changes, sponge baths, and surgeries.

One day, another patient was moved into Cassie's room and placed in a bed behind a thin curtain. From visiting family, I learned the young man had tried to kill himself. After firing a gun point-blank into his abdomen, he'd driven his car off a road and down a steep ravine. Against all odds, he'd been found and now lay hooked up to his own tubes and machines.

And then, one glorious morning, I found Cassie sitting up in bed, smiling weakly, but smiling nonetheless. Her beautiful eyes were open and looking into mine. Euphoria filled my entire being, making me giddy with joy. She was going to make it after all—God had answered our prayers!

She held out trembling arms and I fell into them, kissing her neck and face as our tears mingled. She explained how the nurses had propped her up so she could surprise me. I assured her it was the most wonderful surprise of my life. My hands couldn't stop touching her face, her hair, her lips. She'd come back to life—*our life!*

She told me what happened that fateful night. She'd arrived home from work around 6:00 p.m., took her handgun out of the glove compartment and put it in her pocket. She opened the front door and our dogs gave their usual enthusiastic greeting but when she bent over to pet them, the gun fell out of her pocket. It hit the floor and discharged into her chest. Somehow, she managed to call 9-1-1 before passing out.

I filled her in on everything that had happened in the three weeks since she'd arrived at the hospital. We expressed our love for each other, as if at any moment, this connection might end. I told Cassie I'd been praying for God to heal her and He had!

She listened quietly and smiled. "I trust Him, Dean."

I left the room to let family members know she'd come out of the coma and they could talk with her. One of her doctors met me in the hall. When I told him the news, I expected him to share my joy. But his face remained stoic as he explained cases such as Cassie's typically had dramatic improvements and then marked worsening. He warned me not to get my hopes up, that she had something called "acute respiratory distress syndrome" and that her lungs were getting worse, not better.

His words fell on deaf ears. "You'll see, doctor, she's going to be healed."

Cassie and I had two wonderful days of reconnecting. I held her hand every moment, afraid I'd lose her if I let go. At night, I sat in a chair by her bed and watched her sleep. But on the third morning, her eyes remained closed – she'd slipped back into a coma and I, to my nightmare. The tubes were reinserted.

Several times that day, I whispered into her ear, "I'm not going to let you die, Cassie. There's so much more for you to do, so much more I want to show you. I love you too much to let you go." I believed as long as I didn't give up, neither would she. Together, we would cheat death.

A few days later, nurses moved the suicidal young man to another floor. He no longer needed intensive care and was expected to make a full recovery. The irony that someone who didn't want to live had been given a second chance left a bitter taste in me for which I felt ashamed.

Four weeks after the accident, I sensed a change in both of us. I held Cassie's hand that morning, as I did every morning, while I read to her. When done, I gently kissed its softness and placed it near her side. I left the hospital, crossed the parking lot and ran until I found a private place surrounded by trees. There, I turned to the One in whom Cassie trusted, reaching into the deepest part of my soul to say the words I never thought I could. "Father, thank you for bringing this beautiful woman into my life. I know you didn't cause her to be shot but I have to trust you for what happens next."

Placing my precious wife into His hands confirmed my acceptance of His will for our future, even if it meant losing her.

I retraced my steps to the hospital room with its familiar sounds and smells. Standing by her bed, I studied her face for a long time, trying to memorize each feature. I intertwined our fingers, gently kissed her forehead and whispered, "I love you, Cassie, and having you as my wife made me the most blessed of men. I had so many plans for us, but it's time to place you in God's hands and trust Him the way…you always…did."

A shadow seemed to lift from her face, replaced with an expression of peace. Nurses came in on rubber-soled shoes and pulled the tubes out of her lungs. The respirator was taken to a new patient whose own crisis had just begun, while ours came to an end.

Our families gathered around us in a circle of shared grief. Sniffles and muffled cries and the cardiac monitor's beeps made me acutely aware this would be the last time all of these hearts -- ours breaking, hers dying – would beat together.

I wrapped myself around the love of my life, pressing tear-soaked cheeks against her soft face. Stroking her hair and kissing her over and over, I held on tightly until the inevitable changes in her breathing and heart freed her spirit to slip away from me -- *from us* -- and into the waiting arms of God.

Flat Car

Chapter 26

I sat in a small room adjacent to the main chapel, staring at Cassie's flower-covered coffin. My parents and in-laws hovered over me while the sounds of feet walking on thick carpet and murmuring voices let me know others had arrived. Every few minutes, someone would squeeze my arm and mumble condolences but I didn't have the energy to respond, let alone look up.

I'd placed a large, framed photograph of Cassie's beautiful face on the closed white casket. I wanted to commit each detail to memory, afraid I might forget, yet inconceivable that I could. This ceremony would be the last scene of our life together, the last time she would rest near me before being lowered into a cold, dark hole. Visualizing that moment sickened me.

The funeral officially began with taped choir music. Our pastor stepped up to the podium and welcomed everyone in that subdued voice reserved for funerals. Then he read a letter I'd written, describing the Cassie I'd love forever. I wanted everyone to know the magnitude of her heart when it came to caring for others and how greatly she'd be missed. Burying my face in my hands, my soul reached upward. "I don't think I can get through this...dear God, help me."

I squeezed my eyes shut, trying to block out the grief and despair threatening to suffocate me.

When the service ended, and only close family remained, Cassie's dad approached me. His red-rimmed eyes and quivering lips revealed his own private agony. Without speaking, we walked down the hall away from everyone. After standing motionless for a minute, he took hold of my arm.

"What can I do to see my little girl again?" His voice strained with each word.

Putting my arm around his shaking shoulders, we wept together. When I regained my ability to speak, I explained what Cassie and I believed.

"I learned a lot from your little girl, Fred. And the most important thing is that we have a God who loves us so much, He gave His Son to die our death so we could live His life. He asks only that we allow His love to change us from the inside out. And one day, He'll come back for us. Think about it, Fred, you and I will see Cassie again and that celebration will last forever."

My mind lingered on the image of holding her again and for a moment, I felt the tiniest twinge of joy.

"I've never had anything to do with God...what do I do?"

"Just tell Him you're ready to know Him...He already knows you."

Holding onto each other, we sank to our knees. Fred's words of pleading and anguish touched me deeply as Cassie's dad prayed for the very first time.

The days that followed were a blur of sleepless nights and crushing pain. Family members returned to their homes and lives while I faced an existence without either.

From our bedroom closet, I removed Cassie's clothes, one by one, from their hangers. I'd hold each to my face, inhaling deeply of her essence that still clung to the fabric, triggering sweet memories.

The silk burgundy dress evoked an image of Cassie twirling in our living room, giggling with delight. It became her favorite dress for church. A dark blue knit sweater was a late night stroll along the river, holding hands and laughing at our dogs' antics. For our engagement photo's, she'd worn the white blouse and light brown pleated pants.

Hours passed unnoticed. I ran my fingers over a brush that still held strands of her hair. Picking up her perfume bottle, I sprayed it onto my palms. Immediately, I felt her in my arms, this fragrance on her neck.

When finished, Cassie's clothes lay folded in small cardboard boxes that I somehow managed to take to Goodwill. It proved the most difficult part of letting her go. Returning to the house -- a house that now lacked any tangible evidence of her -- I sank into blackness.

Within two weeks, I returned to work, desperate to be around people and distractions. But at the end of each shift, depression would smother me like a heavy blanket as I drove back to a house I once called home.

One cold rainy afternoon in March, I sat slumped on the couch, my mind in its usual fog. A soft whimper caught my ear. On the floor at my feet sat three dogs, each looking at me with cocked faces and wagging tails. Snoopy leaned forward and put his paws on my lap, his large dark eyes searching mine. Gazing back at him, I realized he sensed my grief, as only dogs can.

My little buddy picked up his rubber ball and dropped it at my feet. Bobby and Poo-Poo's ears perked up. But I didn't respond. Snoopy pushed the ball with his nose, against my leg, making a playful rumble in his throat. When this failed to engage me, he once more pushed the ball against me and let out a sharp bark. The other two dogs positioned themselves next to him, shoulder to shoulder. My eyes focused on the little band of trusting faces.

"You're right, Snoop. I need to live again, don't I?" My voice sounded tired and flat.

Snoopy bent down, chest to the floor, rear in the air and tail wagging. He remained in this position, mouth slightly open, until I picked up the ball and threw it across the room. The result was a flurry of curly hair and racing feet. When they returned the ball, I threw it again. After several minutes, we went outside for more play and ended our day with a walk along the river. Taking deep breaths of cool, clean air, I felt the first glimmer of hope the shadows might lift some day.

That night, as I lay in bed surrounded by three sleeping bodies, I reflected on the kindness of coworkers, calls and cards from family and friends, and a little dog's determination to get me off the couch. I believed God's tender presence had been in each one.

The weeks passed and my grief began to channel itself in taking risks; the more dangerous, the better. One evening, late into our shift, Henry and I received a call about a gang fight under the Fourth Street Bridge. We sped to the scene, turning off Fourth Avenue and onto the dirt road that ran the length of the bridge, between its two sets of concrete pillars. To our left, several sets of tracks paralleled the road.

"See anything?" Henry peered into the darkness.

"Not yet, but let's keep going."

Since this road was rarely used and the only people around could be presumed lawbreakers, Henry turned off the headlights and proceeded. Straining my eyes for movement, I relished this distraction from my grieving.

About fifty yards ahead of us, the glow from the nearby depot's lights illuminated a vacant lot beneath the bridge.

"I see silhouettes moving around up there." I pointed straight ahead.

"Yeah, I see them too. Looks like about twenty guys."

We rolled to a stop, surprised our arrival hadn't been noticed. Young black men, dressed in black pants and sleeveless shirts, and wearing identical bandanas around their heads, were fighting one on one, with fists and legs.

I unfastened my seat belt, tightened my grip on my steel flashlight and made sure my firearm lay within easy reach. Taking hold of his gear, Henry looked at me with a grin. "Well, ol' buddy, let's see what kind of trouble we can get into."

He flicked on the car's high beams and we bailed out of the car, positioning ourselves on opposite sides. We hoped the lights would confuse the trespassers.

"Police, break it up--now!"

"You heard the man," Henry bellowed. "Break it up!"

The men stood frozen in their positions, an eerie silence filling the damp night air. And then, as if on cue, the fighters came together in straight lines and moved toward us like a well-trained squad of soldiers. Without a word, they split in half, one side facing Henry, the other facing me. Their clenched jaws and fists made me uneasy. Perhaps we should've called for backup.

"Everyone just stay where you are." I rested my hand on my pistol.

But it didn't slow their advancement. Over the pounding of my heart, I heard the steady shuffle of feet marching closer…and closer. Realizing this might be my last fight released a wave of euphoria -- if I died tonight, I'd be with Cassie. But the chance Henry could go down with me snapped me out of my death wish. I decided to stick it out.

"Back off now before you do something you'll regret."

I braced for the rush of bodies slamming into me. But the line of men stopped abruptly, breaths steaming from their mouths, just yards away.

From the other side, I heard Henry call out, "Stand still and keep your hands in plain view."

Suspecting a ploy to catch us off guard, I watched their expressions for any clues of intent but their faces remained grim masks.

Henry and I walked back toward each other when one of the fighters broke rank and approached us. Standing well over six feet tall and 250 pounds of solid muscle, bold confidence showed in his glistening, ebony face.

"You in charge of this group?" I asked, feeling like an elf questioning a giant.

His eyes bore into mine. I stared back without blinking. Maybe I'd be joining Cassie tonight, after all. "You going to answer me or just stand there?"

He held himself proudly, like a commanding general. Tilting his head slightly, he stated, "Gentlemen, there's no problem here. We're improving our street fighting techniques and needed a place to practice."

"You're telling us you're teaching these guys how to street fight?" Henry's voice dripped with sarcasm and suspicion.

"No, we already know how to fight. We want to improve our technique."

Looking down at us, he smiled slightly. "There's something else you should know. We're on the same side. It's our goal to take care of the crime you cannot stop."

We found his implication we weren't doing our jobs, annoying but given his army of young muscular men, we decided not to argue.

"If we're on the same side, why did you and your buddies act like you were going to fight us when we first got here?" I asked.

"We wanted to see what you were made of."

Henry swore under his breath. "So now you know. Take your guys and move on."

"We're not bothering anyone here."

"You're bothering us," I snapped. "This is private property, not your personal training ground."

His jaw tightened as he glared at me for several seconds. Abruptly, he spun on his heels and shouted to his men, "Move out. Seems these cops don't appreciate what we do for them." His order unleashed hostile looks in our direction as they left in silence.

Returning to the patrol car, we noticed four Amtrak employees standing on a loading platform on the other side of the tracks. Henry nudged me. "Let's see if they can fill us in on what these guys were doing before we arrived."

We approached three men and a woman wearing the company's uniform.

"Good evening. Did any of you happen to see that gang under the bridge?" Henry asked.

"We sure did," the woman spoke, flicking her cigarette's ashes onto the concrete dock. "We all came out here for a smoke and when we saw those guys fightin', we called you. But then only two of you showed up so we figured you were gonna get your butts kicked and we didn't wanna miss the show."

The three men laughed as if we were talking about a casual sports event. Stunned to think these coworkers would find entertainment in watching us get beaten, or even killed, I muttered, "Sorry to disappoint you!" and stormed off. The dull ache in my chest pounded with renewed pain as I tried to comprehend how anyone could view life so carelessly.

Back in the car, I wiped sweaty palms on my pants and took several deep breaths. Conflicting emotions were at war within me. Forcing an interest I didn't feel, I asked,

"Where we eating tonight?"

Henry didn't answer as he directed the vehicle back to Fourth Street. But before we'd reached the last set of pillars, a figure loomed in our headlights. Henry tapped the brakes. "Looks like dinner will have to wait until we get this clown out of here."

The man stood tall and wide, legs far apart, arms crossed over a grossly protruding belly that stuck out from beneath a tight T-shirt. A worn belt held up a pair of ripped pants that ended several inches above his scuffed leather boots. Tangled strands of hair framed a flushed, puffy face from which an oversized, bulbous nose jutted out like a glob of purplish-blue play-doh.

Leaving the headlights on, we got out of the car and cautiously approached him from either side. Directly behind his feet, I could see a carpet remnant stretched across the dirt road with a pile of blankets mounded in the middle. That would be his bedroom. A large plastic bag bulging with clothes would be his closet and the duffel bag containing food and utensils - his kitchen.

"Hey buddy, you picked a bad place to set up camp." I forced a friendly tone into my voice.

"I camp wherever I wanna." His foul body odor kept us from standing too close to him.

"We're with the railroad police," stated Henry. "And this campground is closed."

"You bulls can go ta hell!"

"Looks like we've got an attitude problem before we even get to know each other." I could feel my pain intensifying the anger in my words.

He came at me with an awkward tilted gait from the excess weight he carried, both fists drawn back behind his head. With adrenaline still surging from the recent gang encounter, I shoved the end of my steel flashlight hard into his stomach. He exhaled putrid air into my face in a half belch, half yell. Pushing my light again and again into his soft abdomen, I didn't stop until he stumbled on his thick legs.

"Don't you *ever* come at me like that. Understand?"

With a final shove, he toppled over backwards. "Change your attitude or you're going to jail. Now what are you doing here?"

" None 'a yur bizness."

"Oh, it's our business, alright," Henry snarled. "In the first place, you're camped on a road and if someone runs you over, *we'll* have to clean up the mess. Second, you're on private property, which is called criminal trespassing. And third, I don't like you."

The man let loose with curses as he rolled over onto his stomach to get his legs beneath him. But his enormous, turgid belly left him flailing his limbs like a high-centered turtle. We watched in amusement until a gaseous explosion erupted from the man's pants. Jumping back in unison, we gagged from the stench.

"They *really* don't pay us enough, Henry!"

Holding our breath, we stood on either side of the man to steady him so he could get back up. He sullenly showed his ID to Henry who copied it onto an information card.

"OK, get your stuff and head back to the streets or to the mission – your choice."

"I'm gonna leave my stuff an' come back for 'em."

I'd run out of patience. "You leave your stuff and I'll burn it."

The man waved his hands in the air and snorted, "You can't burn my propaty an' I know it."

He trudged off toward Holgate Street. As soon as his steps faded into the night, I took a fuse out of the car's trunk. Dumping the contents of his bags onto the carpet, I tossed the flaming stick into the heap.

At first, only wisps of smoke emerged from between clothes and magazines like ghostly snakes, but soon tiny orange flames licked the pile's edges. Henry jabbed my arm. "Let's check the depot and then come back to make sure this hasn't spread, but this dirt and concrete should keep it contained."

"What about dinner?"

"Right after we check the fire." We headed to King Street.

But something began to nag at me. I reasoned it couldn't be that I'd burned the man's belongings because our local missions had clean bedding and clothes, as well as mental health counseling, for anyone who showed up sober. I decided to dismiss it.

Once we cleared the depot of pickpockets and transients, we returned to the dirt road beneath the bridge, finding a bright glowing orange mound. And close to the encroaching flames lay a human-shaped outline.

"Like bugs to a light," Henry muttered, slamming the car into gear. In an instant, we were beside a small-framed youth whose snores were louder than the popping, hissing fire behind him. Henry kicked the sleeper with his foot, but no response. He tapped his shoulder, and still no response. With an exasperated sigh, Henry lifted the thin boy by his shirt, shook him and tried to stand him up, only to have him collapse onto the ground.

A low moan escaped the boy's mud-caked lips. His eyes fluttered open.

"Hey, you need to wake up before you get burned," I said.

He continued staring blankly at the flames as rolls of smoke engulfed him but oddly, he didn't cough or close his eyes. Exchanging glances, Henry and I each grabbed a skinny arm and swung him away from the fire. We supported him until he found his balance but judging by his unfocused expression, he didn't seem aware of our presence or touch.

Waving my hand in front of his face, I asked, "Anyone in there?" We're railroad police."

"Must be high on something," Henry muttered.

I tried again, cupping my hands around my mouth. "Can-you-hear-me?"

His entire body jerked as if electrocuted and he said in disgust, "Yeah, I can hear you."

"What's your name?"

He raised his chin and looked at us with defiance. "Little Satan."

Henry laughed, finding humor in the irony. "Well, if we hadn't come along, you'd have felt the fires of hell--literally."

With a shrug, he smirked. "That's my domain."

Then, without warning, his body sagged and he toppled to the ground in a heap at our feet. Henry pulled him back to a sitting position but his face had returned to its original doll-like stare, his jaw hanging open and loose. I felt a chill as I headed to the car to call for transportation to a hospital.

When I heard the wailing siren, it took me back to that darkest of nights when I'd waited in the hospital parking lot for Cassie's ambulance. After she passed away, I'd become obsessed with joining her by taking risks I hoped would end my life. I'd seen my death wish as somehow noble and this boy's as wrong and pathetic.

Watching the EMTs strap his limp body onto a gurney, I realized neither of us valued the gift of life – we were both pathetic.

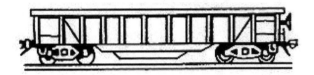

Hopper

Chapter 27

"Snoopy, Bobby, Poo-Poo, let's go." I held the car door open as the curly-haired trio jumped into the back seat. Even though spring had begun to stir all around us, it still felt like winter in my heart. So to help ease the emptiness, the dogs and I made daily pilgrimages to Cassie's burial site so I could do something tangible for my beloved wife.

The cemetery's road wound through acres of headstones, each a tribute to someone who lived in the memories of those who loved them. Parking my car, I opened the door and with Snoopy in the lead, all three dogs trotted straight to Cassie's grave. After sniffing around for a few minutes, Snoop curled up on the mound, the poodles on either side -- seeing this always brought tears to my eyes.

They watched me place a fresh bouquet on each side of her headstone before joining them on the damp grass. For the next hour or so, I'd lay on my back so I could look up at the sky and relive scenes from our life together.

Bobby's wet nose on my cheek brought me out of my reverie. Time to go home.

"People will see these flowers and know she was loved a whole lot, won't they?" I petted their heads.

Gazing up past the billowing clouds, I whispered, "Father, I miss her so much." For the first time, I began to wonder if my healing would require moving far away from the memories.

Ⓘ───────────────────────────

At the start of our swing shift, Henry asked offhandedly, "You doing alright, Dean?"

Staring straight ahead, I answered in a flat tone. "Yeah, I'm doing okay." But I knew neither of us believed it. To change the subject, I asked, "So, where we eating tonight?"

"How about you pick this time." But before I could respond, a call came through from the Stacy Street Yardmaster.

"Special Agent, we just got a report of a man crawling into the second unit (what we sometimes called engines) of a line of engines as they passed the depot on their way to tie up at Stacy Yard."

""We'll take care of it, Yardmaster."

I pointed at six train engines entering the west end of the yard, paralleling our location under the Alaska Way Viaduct. "Good timing."

I spoke into the radio mike. "Special Agent to engineer on engine 2163."

"This is the engineer on 2163," a raspy voice crackled over the radio.

"You have a rider on one of your units. We need you to stop so we can remove him."

"Special Agent, I'm stopping now."

We pulled up alongside the idling locomotives. "Do you want to take the other side, Henry?"

"See you in the cab." Henry leaped out of the driver's seat.

I ascended the metal steps and opened the heavy steel door, proceeding to where the engineer normally sat. There, on the floor, a well-dressed man lay on his back, moaning loudly.

Henry nudged him with his boot. "Hey, Mister, what are you doing here?"

He looked at us, gasping, "Who…are you?"

"Railroad police. What happened to you?"

With an exasperated sigh, he rolled his head from side to side on the steel floor. "Got into a fight with my ol' lady so headed to Pioneer Square for a drink. When I crossed the bridge and saw trains, I got the idea to use one to get outta town and away from *her*. So I jumped to get down to the tracks and ended up breakin' my ankle so I crawled in here."

"Ouch--that had to hurt." The man's face appeared ashen and his right foot stuck out at an unnatural angle from his leg. Henry used the engineer's radio to call the Yardmaster, letting him know about the trespasser's condition and the need for an ambulance. Replacing the mike, he asked, "Where did you think this train was going?"

Wincing in pain, the man waved his arm. "Kinda' hoped California."

I shook my head. "These engines weren't going anywhere but here."

The man blew air through his pursed lips. "I break my ankle hoppin' a train goin' nowhere after getting' in a fight with my ol' lady over a drink I never had. She's right-- I am a loser."

We stayed with him until the paramedics arrived, trying to keep him comfortable. But thinking about the guy's predicament with his wife brought the slightest hint of laughter and a moment's relief from the acute pain I carried inside me. It felt like I could take a deep breath again.

We headed over to a remote part of Balmer Yard to check for more trespassers. As we passed beneath the tall security lights, a body jumped into a boxcar. Henry rolled the car to a stop and we quietly got out and strode across the ballast rock.

Standing to one side of the boxcar's opening, I looked inside, then drew back. A man stood in the corner, no obvious weapons.

"Railroad Police!" I announced.

"Railroad bum," came the gruff reply.

"Get out here – now!" I noticed the opposite side of the boxcar was open.

"Sure thing, ossafer." I heard his shuffling steps cross the dirty floor until his large form stood framed in the doorway. With a sneer and the finger, he said, "Adios, Bull!" and jumped out the other side.

As soon as his feet hit the ground, there was a "thud!" and a muffled scream. Confident he'd been at the receiving end of a flying tackle by Henry, I clambered over the boxcar's coupling just as the broad shouldered, bearded man rose to his feet. By the obscenities flowing from his mouth, he clearly hadn't heard about Henry's intolerance for rude transients.

"You stupid pig, I'm gonna kick your..."

Henry's knuckles made direct contact with the man's face and the vagrant sank to his knees, clutching a nose that now bent to one side.

"Now that I've got your attention," Henry snarled, "change your attitude and do what you're told."

The man tried in vain to stem the blood streaming down his lips and chin. He looked genuinely shocked at Henry. "You bloke my nodes!"

"Remember that the next time you talk to an officer of the law."

Dark circles began to form under his eyes but he refused our offers to get him medical attention. We filled out the routine information card and escorted him out of the train yard. I gave him a final warning, "Next time, you're going to jail."

Despite his folded hands on either side of his crooked nose, I could see the rage in his eyes. "Ah'll be lookin' ulright, but it won't be fer a twain." He stumbled off.

Henry, I think he just threatened me." We walked back to the car. "But why me? I didn't punch him."

He rubbed his knuckles. "Guess I have the winning personality on this team."

Grabbing Henry's arm, I pointed at several dark forms running into the yard close to where we stood. "This sure is a popular place tonight."

We watched them cross two sets of tracks and hop into a boxcar with only one open door. I quickly ran and took a position on one side, Henry ducked under the platform and readied himself on the other side.

Seeing no one from my angle, I looked at Henry. He nodded and held up six fingers. We drew our pistols and pointed them into the car's shadowy interior. "Railroad police --come out of there now!"

Henry stared for a few seconds and then swore. "El Policia. Put your el handos in the airo and get your el buttos over here-o."

Fortunately for the Mexicans, they understood enough of Henry's tone to comply. One at a time, six dark-eyed men jumped out of the car and lined up in front of us. By the way they glanced at the first man, I guessed him to be their leader. His black shiny hair lay slicked back against his head and a tight white T-shirt and black jeans accentuated his stocky build.

Holstering my pistol, I directed the group away from the tracks. Standing them shoulder to shoulder, I frisked their clothing, around their ankles and inside their pockets while Henry stood behind them.

When I got to the leader, he looked at me with fire in his eyes. "Turn around." I pushed his chin with my finger and patted him down.

We didn't find any weapons or drugs, so we completed an information card on each man. A few years prior, Border Patrol would have picked them up but due to a lack of funding, we no longer had that option.

The leader never took his eyes off of me. Between clenched teeth, he murmured Spanish words, his hatred clear in any language.

"Do you speak English?"

"Good 'nough, Senor."

I leaned in close. "You'd like to hurt me right now, wouldn't you?"

His lips curled ever so slightly, but he refused to answer.

"Well, tonight's your lucky night." I removed my gun and handcuffs, giving them to a puzzled Henry. "And Henry here won't step in to help, isn't that right, Henry?"

Excitement coursed through me, as I motioned with both hands. "Come on, you know you want to….your amigos can help you…I'll take you all on."

I danced on my toes like a prizefighter, leaning in close and then jumping back from one suspect to the next. I reveled in their nervous glances and demeanor, as they shuffled their feet and averted their eyes.

"Come on, take a swing at me," I taunted. But when I looked over their shoulders at Henry, I was surprised to find him pacing like a caged tiger, anger flashing in his eyes. I lowered my fists and stood nose to nose with the leader. "Looks like you're not so tough after all...now get out of here."

He spoke sharply in Spanish to the others and they trotted away but then he stopped and pointed back at me. "Next I see you, Senor, I keel you."

He turned and disappeared into the brush. I elbowed Henry jokingly. "They always say that but they never follow…"

Henry took hold of my shirt, fury in his face. "Don't you *ever* do that again. If they'd have taken you up on your offer, what would I have done?"

He pushed me away and stormed off to the car while I stood awash in shame. I realized I'd treated our friendship carelessly, absorbed only in my grief. I decided right then and there to never let Henry down again -- even if it meant leaving Seattle.

After a tense dinner, we drove through the suburb of Magnolia, a combination of homes and industrial buildings set close to the train yard. Henry pointed straight ahead.

"We've got a trespasser in the weeds just above the tracks up there."

Getting out of our car, we walked through the four-foot high brush, sweeping back the branches until our lights revealed a familiar face — the Mexican leader but this time, without his followers. "I take train you no stop me."

Henry and I backed out of the weeds. "Let's talk about this."

He reluctantly came out of his hiding place and stood sullenly, hands in his back pockets. When I put my light away to frisk him, he lunged past me, knocking me off balance with his shoulder. He sprinted across the street toward a cluster of houses.

Henry shrugged. "He's too fast for me."

"And I want to keep dinner in my stomach."

When he saw we weren't going to pursue, the Mexican stopped running and began to curse us in a combination of Spanish and English. A fist-sized rock flew in our direction, narrowly missing us. When another, larger stone hurled by my head, rage welled up inside, sending long-checked emotions seething through a crack in the boundaries of propriety. "Henry, give me the keys. We're done playing his game."

Raising his eyebrows, Henry tossed them and we jogged to the car. As soon as Henry shut his door, I turned on the ignition. There, in our headlights, stood the suspect, a board in his hands, defiance on his face.

"Hang on, Henry." I slammed the accelerator to the floor.

The Mexican stood wielding the plank like a baseball bat at the oncoming ton of steel on wheels. When we were close enough to see the sweat on his face, he looked at his weapon and our car, drawing the obvious conclusion. At the last possible moment, he dove out of our way.

To make sure he got the message, I aimed the car for him again. This time, a mixture of surprise and terror were in his eyes as he spun on his heels and took off down the street, an easy target to follow. He maneuvered from one side to the other, looking fearfully over his shoulder. And each time, Henry waved.

When a sidewalk appeared, the Mexican jumped the curb and landed on the concrete, obviously believing the chase had ended. Boy, was he wrong. I drove over the curb and came down hard on the wheels. "Remind me to have the shocks checked," I called out to Henry who hung onto the dashboard with both hands.

The tiring Mexican made a ninety-degree turn down an alley leading to the industrial section of Magnolia.

"Nice try, amigo," I murmured, tightening my grip on the steering wheel as we swerved between structures. I could tell his strides were growing weaker but I didn't care. He finally lucked out when he found an access road too narrow for our car. With a backward, gasping glance, he disappeared into the shadows.

I slid to a stop. For a few minutes, we sat in silence, reveling in the adrenaline rush. "Well, that one got away."

Henry sat back in his seat. "Then there's no need for a report, is there?"

After the shift ended and I'd crawled into bed, an inner something rose to the surface again, pushing hard against my conscience like accusing fingers. I stared at the ceiling, replaying the scene earlier tonight when I'd actually toyed with running a man down. Had I finally reached a point where I couldn't trust my own reactions? Or worse, not control them? Perhaps, instead of helping my recovery, these confrontations were actually keeping my nerves raw and reason distorted.

I covered my face with my hands and shouted, "Stop it! You're just tired, you'll be fine in the morning."

Rolling over to bury my head in my pillow, I kept my eyes tightly closed until I fell into a fitful sleep.

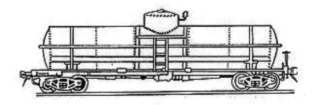

Tank Car

Chapter 28

To get through my first Christmas without Cassie, I worked both Christmas Eve and Christmas day. I also decided to throw out the holiday decorations we'd purchased during our too few years together.

When the New Year dawned, I pulled a dust covered box from the top shelf of the closet with the letters "CHRISTMAS" printed on the side. Lifting the lid, I found carefully wrapped ornaments, each holding memories of a union that no longer existed. Slamming it shut, I carried it out to the garage for a trip to Goodwill.

Looking out my living room window at the cold January morning, the rare sunlight gave me an idea. Standing over the line of dogs bent over food bowls, I announced,

"You've all got two minutes to finish your meals and then we're going kayaking." Their tails wagged in agreement.

A few months earlier, I'd purchased a one-man, thirteen-foot sea kayak with open storage areas for my canine crew. We'd taken a few trial excursions close to shore so each of us could find our sea legs. And now we had a perfect day for our maiden open-water voyage.

I strapped the long but light vessel onto the car amidst the dogs excited chorus and drove to Redondo, parking a short distance from where I'd picked up Cassie for our first date. Ignoring the lump in my throat, I stood on the sandy beach, knowing she'd want me to continue enjoying the water we both loved.

"Okay, gang, let's go."

I held the kayak steady while each dog stepped in; First Mate Snoop stood proudly in the bow, Bobby and Poo-Poo snuggled close in the stern.

Pushing off from shore, I wriggled into the seat and placed my portable radio in a cup holder between my legs. The air actually felt warm enough to remove my life jacket, so I placed it behind my back for an even softer ride. With Snoop's nose pointing the way, we set out on our adventure.

Breathing deeply of the salt tinged air, I felt my spirits lift as the kayak's closeness to the water created an intimacy with the sea. Closing my eyes and humming along to a Beach Boys' song, I imagined we were paddling to a tropical island ringed with palm trees.

"Grrrrrrrrrrrrr."

My eyes flew open. The First Mate had given the alarm, confirmed by the tiny second and third mates behind me. Shushing them, I listened and looked. Orcas were often seen in the Sound but to my relief, no black dorsal fins rippled through the water's surface.

"Hey, little buddies, I think you're hearing..."

Three whiskered heads popped up in quick succession on either side of us, snorting mist-soaked air through round nostrils. Surprised at their enormous size and proximity, I nearly dropped my paddle. The dogs leaned out over the water for a better smell but fortunately, the sea lions seemed unperturbed, their dark, bulging eyes showing only a mild interest in us.

"Snoopy, Poo-Poo, Bobby, stay put."

For several magical minutes, the beautiful creatures paralleled our path, their dark sleek bodies effortlessly rolling and diving beneath us. Eventually their curiosity abated and the sea lions dove beneath the waves, leaving us alone once more.

Checking my position, I made a forty-five degree turn and headed for Maury Island a few miles away. We glided over gentle swells as my shipmates stretched out on their beds, quivering noses tuned to the air like tiny beacons. Like balm for my soul, the cries of gulls overhead, the rhythmic slap of waves on the hull, and the constant whooshing of the ocean's breath blowing past my ears gave me the sweet sensation of being enveloped in a creation that reflected its Creator.

By the time Maury Island lay just a few strokes away, the steady breeze had turned into a gusty wind. Looking back at my launch point, I saw a bank of dark clouds piling up over the mainland.

"Uh, oh, a winter storm. Better head home."

Turning the kayak around with my paddle, I pointed the bow toward Redondo, scolding myself for not paying closer attention to the weather. Ignoring the waves that now broke over our bow, I focused on keeping us plowing through the whitecaps. I took a quick inventory of the crew. Snoopy stood drenched but confident in my ability, leaning and bending his legs with each rise and fall of the kayak. Bobby and Poo-Poo, however, were miserable. Huddled together, soaking wet and shivering, they pressed their noses against the back of my seat, mournful eyes asking, "Do you *have* to take us everywhere you go?"

I didn't dare try to put on my life jacket or stow the radio -- one gust could knock us into the frigid Puget Sound. Every ten strokes, I'd lift my head to make sure we were headed for the right beach, otherwise, I never stopped.

At the halfway mark, my shoulder and neck muscles burned from the tension of striving against the wind and waves. Large cold drops splattered on my head and soon, a gray curtain of heavy rain made it difficult to see.

Shouting above the storm, I tried to reassure the dogs, as well as myself. "It's okay guys, we'll be home--ouch!"

My words were cut off by a strange sensation between my legs. It happened again, causing me to jump. Looking down, I realized seawater and rain were shorting my portable radio, sending electric shocks into my groin.

"Aaaahhh!"

Another shock, another reactive flexing. Fearing a shifting of my weight might tip the kayak, a maneuver I'd never practiced, I became even more determined to keep going. Gritting my teeth, I paddled like a mad man.

The wind howled across the curled tips of the rollers, tossing us up and down like a twig. But the distance to shore had lessened and after several more frightening minutes, I heard the wonderful sound of sand scraping the bottom of the bow as we slid onto shore. I dropped my head onto my heaving chest, feeling the cold rain run down my cheeks and neck in rivulets but I didn't care--we were safe.

Pulling the kayak behind me, I leaned down to pet the dogs, expecting them to be paralyzed with fright. Instead, three blurs ran past me, straight to the car where they waited with mutiny in their eyes. Clearly, their days of kayaking were over.

Once the dogs were towel-dried, fed and snuggled in their own beds at home, I left for work. But before meeting Henry, I went to the boss' office and found Jerry at his desk, surrounded by the usual piles of paper.

"Hi, Jerry. Just wanted to let you know if you hear of any job openings outside Seattle, I think…I think I'm ready for a change."

Jerry studied my face before speaking. "Actually, Dean, we just got something about an opening in Spokane. You sure about this?"

"Yeah, it's time…and can we keep this between us?"

He smiled. "Sure thing, Dean."

I found Henry waiting in the car. "Sorry I'm late. Let's check the Amtrak Depot and see what kind of trouble's brewing there."

He started to turn the key but stopped. "Aren't you going to ask where we're eating?"

"Oh yeah. Where we eating tonight?"

"Let's check the Amtrak Depot first."

Driving north on King Street, we saw an ambulance in the depot's parking lot.

"Never a dull moment," I muttered, as we quickly parked the car.

Entering the main terminal, we spotted a cluster of people in the lobby, murmuring and craning their heads at something. Squeezing through, we found a pudgy young boy sprawled on the marble floor, his dimpled arms folded across a plump belly. A paramedic shone a small light into his eyes.

Squatting down beside him, I noticed fresh blood on his swollen upper lip, with lines of tears and dirt around his eyes and cheeks.

"We're with the police department. What happened here?"

"I'd say this young man was mugged," the medic answered while the boy solemnly nodded.

Resting my hand on his shoulder, I gently asked, "Can you tell us what happened?"

"These two men came up an' punched me in the stomach an' hit me in the face. Then they stole my stuff an' then I crawled here an' a lady called 9-1-1."

He dragged his sleeve across a trickle of blood from his nose, leaving a smear of red across one cheek.

"Where did all this happen?"

He gulped a few times. "I was takin' a shortcut 'cross the tracks, behind here."

"Did they take anything?"

"My tape player, head phones an' some cigarettes I found."

"What did these men look like?" Despite his being shaken, I was impressed with how well he was holding up.

"They were old an' dressed in camouflage pants."

"When you say 'old,' what do you mean?"

"Ya' know—*old*...like you."

I heard Henry's muffled laugh behind me. Shaking my head, I looked at my partner. "Now I'm *old*?"

"He sure wasn't lookin' at me."

Assuring the boy we'd do what we could to catch those geezers, we left the depot. Settling into the car, I couldn't get over the image of my being old to anyone. And the more I obsessed about it, the older I felt.

After thoroughly checking the area without finding anyone, Henry interrupted my vision of being fed through tubes in a nursing home.

"Maybe they went through the tunnel. Let's check it out."

"Yeah, fine, I just hope I can push my walker over the tracks."

We parked in the nearest public parking lot and strode in silence to the west end of the tunnel, straining our eyes and ears for anything out of the ordinary. Incoherent murmuring floated out from its depths.

"Sounds like we've got customers," Henry whispered.

"I hope they're over 60 so I have a chance of catching them."

Henry muttered something and un-holstered his gun. I followed suit and we stepped into the cold, damp darkness, each knowing the plan from years of working together.

About thirty feet inside, I could make out human forms pressed close together. Pointing my gun and flashlight, I shouted, "Police! Stop what you're doing and turn around with your hands in the air!"

Three wide-eyed Hispanic faces blinked into my light, and from one's fist, I could see the end of a syringe. We'd obviously interrupted a drug shoot-up, most likely heroin. They remained frozen except for the one holding the needle – he casually flicked it onto the tracks.

Sensing movement to my right, I knew Henry would be getting into position. And none too soon, because the suspects were getting ready to bolt. When Henry's disembodied voice spoke from behind them, "Hands up, amigos, " they resignedly raised their arms.

I retrieved the discarded evidence and we walked the three men out to the parking lot. Putting on leather gloves, we prepared to search each trespasser.

"Okay, gentlemen, face the...."

They turned in unison, spread their legs and put their hands on their heads. They'd obviously had practice being arrested.

From their pockets, we recovered a second syringe, plastic bags holding a brown substance, surgical tubing, a spoon and matches. We called dispatch to transport the prisoners and sat them on the ground to wait for their ride.

Henry looked past me. "See that guy sneaking around over there?"

I followed his glance. An older man with gray hair and glasses peered at us from behind a sports car. He then sprinted to a truck, ducked behind it and cautiously raised his head to where he could see us over the hood.

"Yeah, I see him."

"Maybe he's their getaway driver," Henry mused. "I'll go talk to him while you watch these three."

I squatted in front of our cuffed captives and pointed to the man in the lot. "Your amigo, si?" They glanced at the man and shrugged.

"Oh, that's right, you guys wouldn't hang out with a mucho *old* guy like him. So what about me—am I too old for you too? Huh, am I?"

The Mexicans tilted their heads and frowned, clearly confused.

I could hear muffled conversation from behind the truck, no doubt questions from Henry, but when I placed the last of the evidence into plastic bags, shouting erupted. I could see the old man jabbing a finger in my partner's face.

"Uh, oh, I hope he's not telling him where to go or..."

Henry grabbed the man by the back of his collar and belt and swung him, arms and legs flailing, toward a green hatchback. Henry said something to the man who yelled something back. The man's head slammed onto the hood of the car. Again, Henry said something, the man yelled back an answer, a second shove of his head against the metal hood, followed by more yelling.

By now, the man's nose bled freely. Henry cuffed his hands and walked him to where we waited. I could hear a steady torrent of accusations punctuated with "my lawyer!"

"Is he with these guys?" I asked Henry.

Before Henry could respond, the man broke in with his own explanation.

"Just mindin' my own ___ ___ business when this___ ___ jumped me for no ___ ____ good reason, an' next thing I know, I'm a_____ hood ornament!!!"

Henry looked at his watch, waiting for the man to finish his tirade. "I asked you three times to leave. An arrest was taking place and you refused to go."

"What're you gonna charge me with?"

Henry stared up at the sky, chin in hand. He snapped his fingers. "Got it -- vandalism to an auto."

"Whaaattt!!!"

The outraged man jumped up and down, kicking the curb and screaming like a maniac. The Mexicans began laughing so hard at his antics, one of them fell over onto his side. This was probably the most fun they'd had in awhile.

A city police car pulled up. When the driver recognized Henry and I, he lowered his window and smiled. "Should've known it was you two. What have we got?"

"Hi Sarge. Afraid it's been a slow night. All we have are these three shooting up and this guy with a lousy attitude, big mouth and a sore ear."

After giving him details about the vandalism charges, the sergeant laughed. "I think we better drop him off a few blocks from here and give him the choice of going to jail or forgetting the whole thing."

"Sounds good, just don't drop him off next to the tracks," I added.

I pushed the gray haired man into the back seat of the city patrol car. "You'd think an old guy like you would know better."

"I ain't old!" he snapped. "Just 'cause you're young, don't make me old."

I grabbed his shoulder. "You're absolutely right -- I'm *not* old!"

"What're you talkin' ..."

But I never heard him. Slamming the door in his face, my years as a young man once more stretched far into the future.

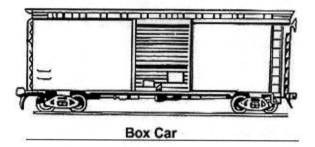

Box Car

Chapter 29

I awoke with a start to a strange noise coming from somewhere in the house. Reaching for the dogs, I felt the two poodles cuddled up against me but Snoopy was missing. Quietly slipping out of bed, I tiptoed down the hall and turned on the light, alarmed at seeing Snoopy wandering aimlessly around the living room, bumping into walls as if in a daze. "Hey little buddy. What's going on?"

He showed no recognition of my voice or me. A splattering of vomit lay on the carpet. Kneeling beside my friend of many years, I pulled him to me and gently stroked his soft, curly fur. "Are you sick, Snoop?"

When his legs continued to move in a walking motion, fear gripped my heart. Something must be terribly wrong. I dialed the animal clinic's after-hours number and spoke to a sleepy sounding vet who I'd obviously awakened. When I described Snoopy's symptoms, he told me to bring him in immediately. I cringed at the tone in his voice.

Assuring the two poodles we'd be back because I wanted to believe it, I held Snoop on my lap during the drive to the hospital. When we pulled into the empty parking lot next to the one-story brick building, a man in a lab coat waited at the front door for us.

Carrying Snoop, I followed the vet into a room that smelled like antiseptic, and gently lay him down on a cold metal table. I watched as he examined Snoop's listless eyes, listened to his heart and palpated his stomach.

"Dean, I'm going to have you wait here while I take Snoopy to another room for some tests. It shouldn't take long."

The minutes ticked by as the hands on the clock advanced forty minutes. The door finally opened and the vet returned without Snoopy.

"He's a very sick dog." The young doctor seemed genuinely sorry. "Snoopy's kidneys have failed and at his age, there's nothing we can do to fix them."

My legs shook as the room spun around me. A memory came into sharp focus. I was leaning over a litter of lively pups, trying to tell which tail went with which head, when I noticed one of the furry bundles instigating the rest. I bent over for a closer look. The pup noticed me, let out a puppy yip and clambered over the others on uncoordinated puppy legs to attack my shoe. From that moment, we'd been inseparable--until now. My chest constricted; where had the years gone?

The vet broke into my thoughts. "Dean, he's pretty miserable right now. You need to make a decision."

Closing my eyes I prayed for strength to do the right thing. Tears streamed down my cheeks but I managed to force out the words. "He doesn't deserve...to be in pain." I couldn't say any more.

The vet retrieved a quivering Snoopy and placed him in my arms. Then picking up a syringe, he placed the tip of the needle into a vein in Snoop's front leg. Quickly pressing my cheek against his soft ear, I inhaled sharply, not believing it was time to say goodbye to this dear pet who'd been a faithful companion on our many adventures. How I'd miss waking up to those wonderfully happy eyes and cute overbite. "You've been a...true friend," I whispered.

The syringe's solution made its way to his heart, and seized it. He took a deep breath and then sagged limply against my heaving chest, the light of life fading from his eyes until they were glazed and empty.

Somehow I managed to stay on the road back home despite bouts of gut wrenching sobs. Once there, I threw away Snoop's bowl and toys, listlessly played with Bobby and Poo-Poo, and cried some more.

That afternoon, when I slid into the patrol car next to Henry, I managed to keep my emotions in check long enough to tell him what had happened. After a long silence, Henry spoke. "I'm really sorry, Dean. I know Snoopy meant a lot to you."

Taking a deep breath, I drew on a strength I didn't feel. "Thanks, Henry...let's head to the waterfront."

He nodded with the understanding that close friends share, the kind that needs no explanation. He simply knew.

We parked at the west end of Stacy Street Yard, just under the Alaska Way Viaduct. Close to the tracks and traffic on East Marginal Way, the bridge had always been a favorite place for troublemakers to hide out. And sure enough, someone loitered beneath the stained concrete pillars -- someone I recognized.

The portly gray haired man with trimmed mustache and beard claimed to be a retired sea captain. And since claims about prestigious careers were typical from the transients we arrested -- the most common being Navy Seals – I'd taken his with a grain of salt.

Approaching him from behind, I distractedly asked, "How's it going, Captain?" I'd spoken to him earlier in the week about trespassing and he'd been his usual pleasant self. But when the neatly dressed man in navy blue pants and jacket turned to face us, his appearance shocked me. Puffy, bloodshot eyes peered out from a face seething with intense rage and hatred. The smell of liquor was strong.

"Hey, remember me? We talked a few days ago about trespass...."

The blow came out of nowhere, hitting me on the left side of my jaw and snapping my head back. Flashes of light went off before my eyes and a ringing filled my ears. My knees buckled and I dropped to the ground. Disoriented, I shook my head and feebly tried to regain my balance only to topple over sideways.

As if in a dream, I saw my partner tackle the captain, smashing him to the ground, face first. By the time the dizziness passed and I could stand again, Henry had his knee in the captain's back and the old man's words were muffled by the dirt in his mouth.

Quickly slapping cuffs on him, Henry rolled the spitting, cursing captain onto his back. We each grabbed an arm and pulled him up to a sitting position. A butcher knife lay on the ground.

Henry and I exchanged glances. "Looks like our friend was going to do more than give you a fist sandwich."

Realizing how close I'd come to being killed hit me hard. I'd used poor judgment when questioning this man by not keeping my focus and watching for signs of threat or danger. Squatting down at eye level with the Captain, I said between clenched teeth, "You just bought yourself jail time for assaulting a police officer, and I'm throwing in criminal trespassing as a bonus."

Looking at Henry with more appreciation than I could express, I clasped his shoulder. "Thanks, buddy. I owe you."

He picked up the knife. "You'd have done the same for me."

We called Seattle police and soon the captain was on his way to a badly needed de-tox.

We continued our patrol and for the first time in all my years with Henry, I felt uneasy. With Snoopy's death fresh on my heart and memories of Cassie everywhere I went, the time had come for a change. But I dreaded telling Henry. I knew what he'd think of my decision. My chest tightened as I forced a casual tone to my voice.

"Did you see that job promotion in Spokane?"

"Yeah...what about it?" He turned to study my face.

"Just wondering who might get it."

A long pause. "What if they offered it to you?"

I looked straight ahead, wishing I could say something that wouldn't hurt this closest of friends. "Wherever I go, I think about her... and now Snoop's gone... I just need a change."

"I'm sorry to hear that, Dean." Strong emotion cracked his voice.

"Henry, patrolling with you has been the one thing that's kept me going. I've hoped and prayed life would get easier but... it hasn't."

We drove in awkward silence, the radio's chatter filling the empty space. Henry cleared his throat and slapped the steering wheel hard. "Aw, hell! Now I'll have to break in another partner. And he better not have a tapeworm *or* religion."

With relief washing over me, I knew Henry and I would be okay. I pointed to the clock. "Hallelujah! It's dinnertime. Where we eating tonight?"

Henry punched me softly in the arm and we continued our patrol down Elliott Avenue. As we passed a supply lot on the bay side of the street, a face popped out from behind a pile of stacked, oil-stained railroad ties, looked directly at me, and then disappeared.

"We've got someone in there, Henry."

He pulled into the lot where the ties were stacked. The face again peeked out, gaped at us with open mouth and wide eyes, and then retreated like the fish I'd seen hiding in rocky crevices while diving.

We approached the man in plain sight but he showed no awareness of us. He wore a long heavy yellow coat tightly buttoned around his thin frame and a thick orange stocking cap. His feet were encased in high black rubber boots more befitting an Alaskan fisherman.

We stepped closer, hands resting on our firearms. I cleared my throat. "Hey, Mister. What's going on?"

He spun around so quickly, he stumbled over his feet, and then regained his balance. Squinting suspiciously at Henry and I, he stood in a hunched position, as if expecting an attack.

"We're with the police," Henry informed him. "What are you doing here?"

He stretched his stocking cap over his face, holding the edges to his shoulders and shrieked, "They're after me! They're after me! They're after me!"

Our suspicion was confirmed--we had a crazy. And when it came to maniacal hysteria, Henry had sensitive ears. "If he doesn't shut up in five seconds, I'm going to be after him."

Henry counted to five out loud. Swearing under his breath, he climbed over the ties, slammed the palm of his hand into the man's shoulder and bellowed, "Stop screaming or I'll give you something to scream about."

Henry pulled the man's hands from his cap and yanked it off his head. The ranting abruptly stopped and he resumed a hunched position, eyes darting in every direction.

"Who's after you?" I asked.

"They, they, they are!" He pointed to an office building across the road.

"Why would anyone in there be after you?"

He turned his jiggle-eyed gaze from me to Henry and stumbled backwards, his boots knocking against each other. "You, you, you could be one." He pointed at Henry and then his trembling finger made an arc until it aimed at me. "And you, you, you could be one."

We checked his ID. Where a photo should've been, he'd drawn a stick figure with "ME" scrawled beneath it. We called the local hospitals and clinics to see if any were missing a patient. They weren't. Since we had no reason to detain him, we had to release him.

"We're letting you go but you have to stay off railroad property." I pointed to the sidewalk bordering the street. "There's the boundary— don't cross it." The man put his cap back on and clomped noisily away. But before Henry and I reached our car, the sounds of screeching brakes and horns erupted behind us.

"What now!?"

In the middle of Elliot Boulevard's four lanes stood our crazy, resembling a screaming survivor from the Bering Sea. As he dodged between cars, slapping and kicking their sides with his flailing limbs, some vehicles maneuvered wildly around him while others braked dangerously in heavy traffic.

"They're after me! They're after me!"

I grabbed the radio mike and called dispatch, asking them to contact city police. We now had a reason to arrest him.

We crossed the street but when the crazy saw us, he jogged back to the sidewalk despite his loose, heavy boots. I quickly closed the gap between us. But as soon as he came into view of the allegedly evil office building, he slapped his hands against his head and screamed, "They're after me! They're after me!"

I cuffed his hands behind his back "Calm down, Mister. We'll protect you."

The man stared into my eyes for the longest time. At least he'd stopped screaming. "Protect me from who?"

Henry stepped between us and whispered to the man, "From *him* 'cause he's one of *them*." The man squinted at me over Henry's shoulder, nodding slowly, as if he'd suspected all along. He looked closely at Henry. "Then….who are you?"

City police arrived and the man quietly slid into the back of their car. After giving the officers the charges, we returned to our patrol but instead of feeling satisfied about the arrest, I felt a sharp pang of sadness.

Henry broke in. "Still want to get something to eat?"

With a weak smile, I nodded. "Sure, why not."

A dark cloud settled over me throughout dinner and the rest of the shift. When we were checking out at the office, the next shift's patrolman greeted us. "Dean, the boss called. Wants to talk to you 'bout something. You're to call him at home ASAP."

Henry flashed a look in my direction. "I better get home. Talk to you later, Dean."

After everyone left, I sat by the office phone for several minutes. I knew why the boss wanted me to call. I wearily picked up the headset and pushed the buttons. The phone rang twice before he picked up.

"Hi Jerry, this is Dean. What have you got for me?"

When we were done, I replaced the phone in the cradle and slumped back in the chair. I'd accepted the promotion in Spokane but instead of relief, I felt anxiety surging through me as memories paraded past my mind's eye. I buried my face in my hands. Moving on would be harder than I thought.

Chapter 30

Nothing is familiar. I'm standing alone on an empty street, facing a row of houses huddled close together. Curiously, there are no people in or around any of the homes.

"Woof, woof, woof!"

Immediately recognizing the bark, I eagerly search for the source. Could Snoopy really be here? And then I see him, jumping wildly on a porch. Clearly, he wants to run to me but he seems held back by an invisible barrier. The house looks inviting so I decide to go to him. But when I try to take a step, my foot won't move, as if glued in place. I struggle to lift it but a voice stops my efforts.

"It's not time for you to live on this street."

I accept the words as true and call out to my buddy. "Hey Snoop, you're looking good, still handsome as ever."

He whimpers and dances on his feet, tail wagging furiously. Swallowing hard, I continue. "I sure do miss you but we can't play right now."

He listens intently, head cocked to one side. An understanding seems to pass between us. His tail lowers and he lies down, resting his curly head on his paws. The steadfast look in his deep brown eyes tells me he'll wait.

I'm compelled to leave the neighborhood and my feet carry me to a wide expanse of silvery blue, a bay whose golden beach extends to where I stand. On the other side is a high embankment crowned with homes. A slight breeze riffles the shining water and when I look up, the clear sky is arched over me like a rainbow. I innately know this place holds some purpose for me but when I try to ask, my mouth doesn't open. Sky, water and homes melt together in a dizzying swirl, and I wake up.

I lay in bed for some time, staring at the ceiling and pondering the dream's meaning. What could the empty neighborhood and water represent? Will I recognize the area when I see it or were these symbols of something else?

Dragging myself through my morning routine, I dreaded my last day of work. Seattle's skyline, waterways and people had been a part of my life for several years. And during those years, my professional partner had become the closest of friends. We'd fought with and for each other under extreme circumstances, creating a bond so strong, I knew I could trust him with my life.

I halfheartedly ate breakfast and played with the dogs, carefully maneuvering around stacks of boxes in each room. The moving van would be arriving the next morning.

With Bobby and Poo-Poo, I drove to the cemetery to deliver two bouquets to Cassie's grave -- and tell her goodbye. The dogs took their usual position by her headstone while I carefully arranged the flowers in their holders. When done, I knelt on the damp grass.

"We're here to say goodbye, Cass," I whispered to the memory of the woman who'd changed me forever. "I love you and no matter where I go, I'll carry you in a special place in my heart. But I can't live there with you anymore…I have to start planning a future…without you."

I choked back a sob as the painful reality hit me for the millionth time. Leaning forward, I gently kissed her engraved name. "Goodbye, my love."

Hours later, I reported to work emotionally spent. Walking through the depot's lobby for the final time, I stopped to shake hands and speak with several employees who wished me well. When I'd first stepped into the building with the clock tower, I'd wondered if the people inside would accept someone from a small-town in Nebraska. And they had, with the same open attitude with which they embraced their northwest lifestyle. I slid into the patrol car beside Henry and waited for him to start the engine before tuning the radio to a Christian music station.

"And friends are friends for eternity..."

Henry's head snapped up, his intense glare challenging me. But then his expression softened. "Aw, hell, a little heaven won't hurt me— but only for a few minutes."

"Because in heaven then we'll see..."

He adjusted the rearview mirror. I found the song's words both meaningful and difficult to listen to. "Hey, Henry, where we eating tonight?"

Without looking at me, he responded. "Anywhere you want, ol' buddy."

Unfortunately, our last patrol had few calls, forcing us to drive around and talk about general, mundane things, carefully avoiding the feelings simmering beneath the surface. An uncomfortable silence settled over us.

When our headlights illuminated an object beneath the Dravas Street Bridge, we scrambled out of the car in record time. My flashlight shone across the black, ripped fabric of a backpack that had seen better days. "Hmmm, it's not like a bum to leave his stuff."

Rocks and dirt tumbled from the slope behind us. We stepped out from under the bridge, our lights exposing a fat, dark-skinned man sprawled at the base of the hill, holding his hands over his face. "Peek-boo, hoossh dere?"

Henry approached the man and helped him sit up, his movement causing multiple bottles sticking out from his jacket pockets to clank together.

"We're with the Washington State Litter Patrol." Henry flashed his badge open and shut. "Do you know there's a fine for each and every one of these bottles?"

"Huh? Whash you talkin' 'bout?"

"You heard me. It's a government program to clean up the tracks. And whoever we find with the bottles, pays the fine."

I began counting, "100, 104..."

Henry struck a thoughtful pose and then pointed at the man. "But tonight, just for you, we're offering a special deal. If you climb this hill and avoid all bottles from now on, we won't take you to the dump."

"Dese bottles ain't mine. I jessh shittin' here..."

Henry interrupted. "Just because your Momma called you sonny doesn't mean you're bright. Now get up and get moving."

Squinting into the light, the man rocked back and forth, trying in vain to stand up. But after only a few tries, he gave up with a loud sigh. "Thish hill's too sshteep fer me."

With exasperated groans, Henry and I turned off our lights, took a position on either side of him and lifted him to a shaky standing position.

"I'll grab your backpack so don't fall over." I leaned over to pick it up, my left arm and leg straining to keep him upright.

"I ain't got no packback."

"Guess it's not his," Henry shrugged.

I let the pack drop to the ground. Transients typically carried unwashed utensils, porn, and filthy clothes in these – none of which I cared to touch.

We directed the man to the path that would take him to the sidewalk and street forty feet above us. But when he looked upward, his head tilted too far back and his body began to tip over. We steadied him again and waited. As soon as he managed to place one foot more or less in front of the other, we let him go. And down he went, landing clumsily on his hands and knees.

Henry slapped my back. "You're elected, buddy, since you're the one with the muscles."

"Hey, wait a minute..."

"AAAAUUUUUGGGGHHHH!" A scream pierced the blackness below us.

"EEEEEEEEE! Get outta here!"

"Henry, looks like we've got another customer."

"Then you better get this drunk out of here."

Placing both hands on the man's rear end, I dug my toes into the slope and pushed with all my might. "Come on, Mister, you're getting up this hill."

When he felt the pressure on his backside, the man jerked his butt high into the air and began climbing like a sloth, making wide arcing steps with his hands and feet. Henry's cackles told me he was enjoying this spectacle far too much, while I fervently hoped the man's pants didn't have any holes.

"EEEEAAAAUUUGGGGHHHH! Get out, get out!"

The deranged voice had grown closer. With renewed energy, I pushed my shoulder against the man's enormous jelly bottom, grunting and yelling, "Move it, move it, move it, we're almost there!"

We reached the top just as my legs felt on fire. The drunk toppled onto a grassy strip near the sidewalk, breathing heavily. "I did it."

"Yes, you did. Now move on and stay out of the yards." I slid back down the hill, eager to tackle a crazy with Henry.

Once I'd reached the bottom of the slope, we faced the approaching footsteps, still unable to see their source. Henry positioned himself behind and to the right of me. I turned on my flashlight.

"EEEEEEEEEEEEEEEAAAAAUUUUGGGGHHHH!"

From the darkness, a well-muscled man with long tangled red hair stepped into my beam. His unblinking, dilated pupils looked like black holes burned into his skull. Streams of drool ran from each corner of his slack jawed mouth. In one hand, he brandished a large hunting knife above his head, its metal flashing reflections of my light. His screams escalated with each step.

Dropping to one knee, I pulled out my revolver, rested it on my left hand that held the flashlight, and took aim. "Police! Stop where you are or I'll shoot!"

The man kept coming. I began applying pressure to the trigger. "Stop or I'll shoot!"

For a moment, I wondered if he couldn't hear me above his screams. A calm came over me as the hammer moved back with an audible "click." The man came to an abrupt halt, proving he could hear quite well. He lowered his hand to his side without letting go of the knife, and snarled, "Get outta here!"

Taking my finger off the trigger, I quickly closed the distance between us and rammed my light beneath his sternum. It had the desired effect. Dropping the knife, he gagged and clutched his gut, trying to regain his breath. Knowing Henry would be covering me, I holstered my pistol, dropped my light, and grabbed him by one shoulder. With my left leg, I swept his feet from under him, causing him to hit the ground hard.

I cuffed him and lifted him by his belt. "Take it easy and you'll get your breath back."

Sure enough, he recovered his ability to inhale and renew his verbal assault. I decided to use Henry's method to snap him out of it. "Shut up!" It worked.

Henry picked up the weapon while I tried to reason with the suspect. "Do you have *any* idea how close you came to being shot? One more step and your guts would've been splattered all around us." I shuddered at the image.

The man spit out his words. "You were messin' wit my pack."

"That's *your* pack beneath the bridge? And you were going to kill us for it?"

"Cuz it's *mine*."

Henry held the long blade in front of the man's face. "It's obvious you were ready to use this on a police officer. If someone else had come along who didn't have a gun to protect themselves, would you have stabbed them?"

"Like I said, it's *my* pack."

"Well, it can keep you company in jail. You're being arrested for criminal trespassing and assault on an officer with a deadly weapon."

Henry radioed the Yardmaster with instructions to call Seattle Police about our prisoner. We'd meet them on the sidewalk, above the Dravas Street Bridge.

Pushing the suspect ahead of me, I looked up the steep hill. "I'm sure getting my exercise tonight."

Henry shined his light on a second trail, about twenty feet past the one I'd used earlier to push the drunk up. It looked wider and with less of an incline. "Why don't we take the easier way?"

I narrowed my eyes. "Did you know that was there all along?"

Henry held up both hands. "Hey, who am *I* to tell *you* what to do?"

"Yeah, yeah. Let's get this guy up there."

Two patrol cars were already waiting at the street and the officers recognized us as soon as we appeared. "What have you got for us tonight?"

"This guy attacked me with the knife Henry's holding, but lucky for him he changed his mind before it was too late."

"They're messin' wit my pack."

One of the officers turned the man around and replaced my cuffs with his pair.

"Sounds like a good reason to kill someone. By the way, do you two know anything about the big guy sitting over there on the sidewalk?"

The drunk still sat where I'd left him, his enormous bulk forcing officers walking back and forth from their vehicles to step around him. With each passing, he lifted his hands to be cuffed and cheerfully said, "Hi, ossifer, ready ta go now."

With a sigh, I explained, "Yes, he's one of ours."

With the information collected and another crazy on his way to jail, I joined the inebriated man on the sidewalk, seeing a chance to pay back Henry. "See my partner over there? He likes you."

The drunk blinked several times and waved both arms at Henry, almost falling over in the process. Henry scowled and turned his back.

"I think you need to tell Henry you like him too."

"Enry, come home wiff me."

Henry's mouth dropped open and his hand automatically rested on his pistol. I knew an explosion wasn't far behind. "Whatever he told you is a damn lie!" With that, Henry disappeared down the hill.

Helping the man to his feet, I noticed he was a bit more stable. "Do you live close by?"

"Got partment down thet way...or mebbe thet way."

"Well, I think it's time you go home, don't you?"

"Yeah, I'ssssleepy."

I waited until he could amble at a fair pace on the sidewalk and then scurried after Henry, sliding down through the brush.

We ate our last meal at Andy's, teasing each other like old times about the night's arrests. But with the dawn came the end of our last shift, and the end of our professional partnership as railroad special agents. We stood in the parking lot, each ready to head home but hesitating, as if something more needed to be said.

I extended my hand. "Take care of yourself, partner."

He grasped my hand tightly, looking into my eyes with his usual intensity. "It's been great working with you, Dean."

In those few seconds of silence, a hundred unspoken words passed between us. We released our hold and I quickly walked away.

"Hey, Dean."

"Yeah, Henry?" I didn't turn around.

"Where am I eating tomorrow night?"

A sharp pain pierced my heart. Despite my blurring vision, I made it to my car, relieved when I could shut the door behind me. I drove past Henry who still stood where we'd said goodbye. He raised his hand in a half salute, which I returned. Once out of sight, the tears fell.

The light gray clouds stretched like a puffy down comforter across the sky on my last morning in Seattle. I locked the front door to where my best and worst memories had been played out, knowing I'd never return.

The dogs and I settled into the car for the five-hour trip to Spokane. As soon as our neighborhood faded in the rearview mirror, I impulsively turned the wheel and headed for a familiar beach in Redondo. I had to look at the ocean one last time.

When I reached the street where Cassie had lived with her mom, I parked and let Bobby and Poo-Poo run and smell the latest canine news. I followed behind, my shoes sinking into the soft sand until I reached the water's edge.

Closing my eyes, I listened to the surf touch the land with a hush. My years in Seattle seemed like a dream—had I really been in love and married? Had I once explored underwater reefs and sailed to islands with a beautiful woman who wanted to spend her life with me?

I tried to remember what she looked like when we walked this very beach. Fixing my eyes on one spot, I imagined her tall, slender form, barefoot and laughing. Her long hair danced across her face and shoulders with the sea's breeze. Snoopy jumped beside her, black curly hair shining in the sun. I held the vision for as long as I could and then blinked-- the beach and my heart were empty once more.

Something scratched my leg. I looked down at Bobby's petite face, his front legs stretched out, rear-end in the air and tail wagging furiously. He was ready to move on.

"It's time we got to Spokane, isn't it, boy?"

Taking a deep breath, I reluctantly turned my back on my first loves – the sea and Seattle -- and returned to the car. But from Highway 99, I headed north instead of east, to one last place I needed to say farewell; Stacy Street Yard, where I'd learned the most about friendship.

I turned onto a dirt road paralleling the tracks and parked next to an abandoned tin-roofed shed. Patting the dogs' heads, I assured them, "I won't be long."

Opening the door, my feet touched on rocky ballast that had spilled out from the tracks, making the usual scraping sound beneath my shoes. I hesitated, unsure how to approach a place that now belonged to my past.

I committed to memory the yard's oil and diesel smells, vagrant hiding places, trains and switch engines, lines of containers waiting to be loaded and the people who worked here around the clock – from yard and trainmasters to brakemen and crew callers. The goods off-loaded from enormous ships docked in Elliott Bay depended on this ingenious railway system for transportation and distribution across America.

My reminiscing was cut short when I saw a stranger wearing the typical ragged, dirty clothes of a transient staring at me from across the tracks. I started to speak, to tell him he's not welcome or allowed here, but something about his demeanor stopped me. Instead of the expected defiance, I could now see weariness and fear – or had those always been there, invisible to me until arising from my own baptism of loss?

I studied him closer. The same dark circles beneath haunted eyes, the same palpable pain emanating from his soul afforded me a glimpse into a hazy image coming sharply into focus – until I recognized myself.

Rails of steel separated us like a barrier that couldn't be crossed, a reminder that we stood on opposite sides of society and the law. But were we on opposite sides when it came to God's love? I felt a sudden conviction about the value of souls, and therefore a connection to this human being.

A quote came to mind -- "Adversity introduces a man to himself." I realized two possible results of adversity stood here, facing one another. If life took its usual path for people like us, I would once again experience joy and love and he would die alone and unmissed, for this man had suffered the greatest loss of all – a loss of self. Had we responded differently to the trials and tests that mold our lives, I could be standing in his shoes and he in mine.

He lifted his hand slightly and nodded his head, more tentative than friendly. I returned the nod, a seed of compassion taking root amongst the sharp rocks of prejudice and disdain within me.

We turned and walked in opposite directions, to whatever future awaited us.

I secretly wished him well.

Afterword

So glad our first impression of each other was wrong. Working nights in the yards to keep Seattle's criminal element on the run was never boring with you as a partner. But the best was knowing each other so well, we didn't have to make a plan or talk about it - just count on each other. We had some great times and now you managed to stay awake long enough to write a book about them.

So here's to second impressions, retirement and fishing adventures - I'll bring extra sandwiches